MERRY CHRISTMAS SUSAN!

THERE ARE QUITE A FEW INTERESTING
TID BITS IN THIS BOOK. HOPE
WE GET TO SHARE A FEW OF
THESE LITTLE KNOWN PLACES TOGETHER

MERRY CHRISTMAS AND
HAPPY 2023!!

LOVE
KEVIN
XOXOXO

New England's

HIDDEN PAST

360 OVERLOOKED,
UNDERAPPRECIATED,
AND MISUNDERSTOOD
LANDMARKS

DAN LANDRIGAN AND
LESLIE LANDRIGAN

Down East Books
Camden, Maine

Down East Books

Published by Down East Books
An imprint of Globe Pequot
Trade division of The Rowman & Littlefield Publishing Group, Inc.
4501 Forbes Blvd., Ste. 200
Lanham, MD 20706
www.rowman.com
www.downeastbooks.com

Distributed by NATIONAL BOOK NETWORK

British Library Cataloguing in Publication Information available

Library of Congress Cataloging-in-Publication Data

Names: Landrigan, Dan, author. | Landrigan, Leslie, author.
Title: New England's hidden past : 360 overlooked, underappreciated and misunderstood
   landmarks / Dan and Leslie Landrigan.
Description: Camden, Maine : Down East Books, [2020] | Includes bibliographical references. |
   Summary: "New England is so compact that even casual visitors can sample its diverse history
   in just a short time. But travelers and residents alike can also pass right by historic buildings,
   landscapes, and iconic objects without noticing them. New England's Hidden Past presents the
   region's history in an engaging new way: through 58 lists of historic places and things usually
   hidden in plain sight in all six New England states" —Provided by publisher.
Identifiers: LCCN 2020005414 (print) | LCCN 2020005415 (ebook) | ISBN 9781608939862
   (cloth) | ISBN 9781608939879 (ebook)
Subjects: LCSH: Historic sites—New England—Guidebooks. | Historic buildings—New
   England—Guidebooks. | New England—Guidebooks.
Classification: LCC F5 .L36 2020 (print) | LCC F5 (ebook) | DDC 917.404—dc23
LC record available at https://lccn.loc.gov/2020005414
LC ebook record available at https://lccn.loc.gov/2020005415

Contents

CONTENTS

INTRODUCTION

ENOUGH WITH THE MONUMENTS TO GENERALS, the statues of presidents, and the rich people's houses. There are plenty of landmarks all around you, whether you realize it or not. A lot of it is pretty interesting, even if you think you don't like history.

If you just know where to go, you can stand on the exact spot where something big happened. Like the place where twenty-six pirates were hanged all at once. Or the place where striking mill workers were massacred.

You can park where men in pea coats and Halloween masks robbed the Brink's Armored Car depot. You can stay in a hotel listed in the *Negro Motorists Green Book*. You might even take a road to work without knowing it was once filled with thousands of French soldiers marching to Yorktown.

There's so much history all around us, it's hard to know where to begin. So we started with lists, sixty in fact. And if you're into *New England* history, it only makes sense to draw up lists of six—one item for each New England state.

That can get tricky sometimes, but it also takes you to unexpected places. For example, a list of revolutionary forts takes you to the top of Mount Independence in Orwell, Vermont, for one of the largest, least disturbed revolutionary sites in America. Who knew? A list of mysterious stone structures takes you to the Hirundo Wildlife Refuge in Alton, Maine, site of a fishing village the Red Paint People once inhabited.

Lists can also tell you something else: Why and how things change. Every New England state, for example, had at least one Little Italy. But after urban renewal took off in the 1950s, Portsmouth, New Hampshire, and Burlington, Vermont, lost their Italian neighborhoods. New Haven fought against urban renewal and now most people would call lively Wooster Square an asset to the city.

All of the items on the lists in this book are physical artifacts or places, and in most cases you can visit them. You can even have a drink in five of the six former speakeasies listed, and a meal in every old stagecoach stop. Some you'll just have to look at from afar, like a couple of private residences listed in the *Negro Motorist Green Book.*

We didn't completely leave off wars and presidents. You can't do lists of New England history without the American Revolution or the French and Indian wars. And it's tough to resist a list that includes John Adams having a spa day in Connecticut or Calvin Coolidge wearing overalls on his farm in Vermont.

We also included *some* house museums, not because of the houses so much as the things that happened in or near them. The Governor William Sprague Mansion, for example, was the home of a murdered textile baron. We called it an Irish landmark because an Irishman was hanged for the crime—which he didn't commit.

We hope you enjoy these lists, and that they inspire you to start your own.

WHY IS IT CALLED THAT?

THE ENGLISH WEREN'T THE ONLY ONES WHO NAMED New England, but history, after all, is written by the winners. The truth is, French, Italians, and Native Americans all had a hand in creating New England's state names. And, of course, someone had to name the region itself.

When Captain John Smith of Jamestown fame sailed up the coast and first laid eyes on New England, there was no doubt what he would call it. The land virtually spoke to him. Nothing else would do. It shall be called: North Virginia.

If the colony of Virginia could be named for Queen Elizabeth, the virgin queen, why not the rest of the colonies? Wait, strike that. King James thought a better idea was "New England." And, as you might imagine, everyone responded that, of course the king was right. Brilliant! New England it must be! Stupid to think anything else . . .

HOW THE STATES
GOT THEIR NAMES

AND SO THE REGION GOT ITS NAME. Today we take for granted the New England state names. Around four hundred years ago, however, colonists, would-be colonists, kings, and queens scratched their heads trying to figure out what to call these lands they intended to settle.

The responsibility for coming up with an appropriate name was taken seriously. Then the name had to pass muster with the king or queen sponsoring the voyage that brought the discoverer to the land. And, finally, it had to stick with the people who would use it.

Through this roundabout manner, the six New England state names we use today came into place.

1. NEW HAMPSHIRE

New Hampshire has one of the most straight-ahead names in New England. The English explorer and colonizer John Mason sought and received a grant of land, roughly half the area between the Merrimack and Kennebec rivers. And the grant called the property New Hampshire, after the county of Hampshire in old England. Mason, though, was born in Norfolk, so go figure.

Mason actually knew Newfoundland better than New Hampshire. He explored the island and drew up the first known English map of it.

Though he may have named New Hampshire, Mason never actually set foot on it. He died in 1635 while preparing to make his first trip to his new colony. Eventually Massachusetts took control of the territory for a while. But the name was a keeper.

2. MAINE

The naming of Maine is less straightforward and its origins less certain than the other New England state names. While Mason received the southern part of the land between the Kennebec and Merrimack rivers, the northern portion was granted to Sir Ferdinando Gorges, another early colonizer.

But how did Gorges settle on Maine? It's not completely clear. The original charter splitting the territory from New Hampshire named it Laconia. Derived from the name of the region in Greece, it also gives us the root for the word "laconic," appropriate for Maine. However, it never took as the official name.

Gorges himself is on record proposing the area be called New Somerset, after his home in England. King Charles, however, hated that name. He declared the land would be known as the province or county of Mayne. Which seems official enough, but throughout the next decades the name was still discussed and debated.

How did Maine finally win out? One suggestion is that the name clearly distinguished between the islands off shore and the mainland, and for many years the region's farmers and fishermen had called it simply "the maine." Whatever the final reason, Maine it was and Maine it is.

Gorges was another colonizer who never saw his colony, though he paid to help found Maine's Popham Colony. He was destitute upon his death and his son sold all the land covered by the charter to Massachusetts in 1677. It would take the state nearly 150 years to get its independence back.

3. MASSACHUSETTS

When the Pilgrims arrived in Massachusetts, they found the Algonquins already had a name for the place. They called it Massachusêuck, which meant "about the great hill." It was a reference to Blue Hill and the Native American tribe that populated that area. William Bradford and company kept right on using it.

Now why did Bradford not assign Massachusetts a name of English choosing? Sensitivity to the rights of Native Americans? Political correctness? Unlikely. He probably simply adopted what the locals called it to better communicate.

Plus, since the Native Americans probably saved the Pilgrims from starvation that first year, perhaps it seemed only right not to go about changing the names of things even if you did intend to appropriate the land.

4. CONNECTICUT

Connecticut is another of the New England state names derived from a Native American word, Quinnehtukqut (roughly translated "the long tidal river"). This was the name the Pequot Indians gave to the Connecticut River, as early trader and Dutch explorer Adriaen Block learned.

Block stayed with the name of the river already in use. Perhaps he was trying to communicate with the Native Americans he traded with, or perhaps he wanted to avoid confusion. Over time it got anglicized into Connecticut.

5. RHODE ISLAND

In Rhode Island, Block named Block Island for himself. Florentine explorer Giovanni da Verrazzano had earlier dubbed it "Claudia" for the queen consort of France. But Block preferred to simply give it his own name, and Block it was.

Verrazono rarely had any luck giving anything a name that stuck. Rhode Island and the Providence Plantations (its official name) proved the exception, though an inadvertent one. When exploring the island he called Claudia and Block called Block, he noted its striking resemblance to the Isle of Rhodes. While not necessarily what he intended, map makers branded the whole area Rhode Island. It was one of the few names he created that endured, at least partially.

Years later, Roger Williams was run out of Massachusetts as a heretic, and he settled in Rhode Island. He was so pleased divine providence had allowed him to escape a trial for heresy. And so he called his new home the Providence Plantations.

Today, the two are melded together in one simple phrase that trips off the tongue so easily that most people have shortened it for ease of use. Score the win for Verrazano.

6. VERMONT

Finally, we come to Vermont, perhaps the most obviously named of the New England state names. While all the New England colonies debated their destiny as the push for independence took hold, Vermont had a free-for-all argument.

Should the state join up with France and become a part of New France? Or should it remain English? Should it join with the other colonies in breaking away from England? Or maybe it should be its own country?

Each of these points of view had its own strong supporters over the years, so much so, perhaps, that no one ever managed to dislodge the informal, original name applied to it by explorer Samuel de Champlain.

When Champlain noted Vermont on his 1647 map, he made a simple notation: Verd Mont (Green Mountains).

If it was good enough for Champlain, it was good enough for the people of the state and so, with a little anglicization, the Green Mountain state is today Vermont.

TOWNS WITH
UNIQUE NAMES

DRIVE AROUND NEW ENGLAND AND YOU'LL NOTICE the oldest towns have very English-sounding names. Like Hingham and Harwich, Yarmouth and Newbury. You'll also notice a lot of duplication. New England has six Warrens, five Bristols, five Manchesters, four Newports, and three Coventrys. Plus there are dozens of twosomes, like Portsmouth, Brooklin, Salem, and Arlington.

Of course that's no coincidence. Many of the early English settlers named their settlements after their hometowns and shires.

The Puritans even named groups of towns in New England after groups of towns in England: Boston and Lynn, for example, lie next to each other in East Anglia as they do in Massachusetts. So do Worcester and Leominster, and Amesbury, Salisbury, Newbury, and Andover.

The Scots-Irish also named their towns after home. New Hampshire has a Derry, Dublin, and Antrim; Massachusetts a Colrain and a Charlemont; Maine a Belfast, a Limerick, and a Newry. Both Vermont and New Hampshire have a Londonderry, and Connecticut has a Waterford.

If a town has an Irish name, you can bet it was once on New England's frontier. The Puritans found it useful to send the fighting Irish to the outskirts of their colonies as buffers against unfriendly French and Indians.

Settlers rarely named places after actual people until after the American Revolution. Before the war, New England colonists had an aversion to naming towns for heroes or statesmen. They got over that, though, and started naming towns after John Adams (Maine and Massachusetts) and John Hancock (Massachusetts and New Hampshire). And every state but Rhode Island has a Washington.

1. ST. JOHNSBURY, VERMONT

St. Johnsbury was organized in Vermont's Northeast Kingdom in 1790, a time when the un-English custom of naming towns after individuals began to take hold.

Michel Guillaume St. Jean de Crevecoeur, also known as J. Hector St. John, gave St. Johnsbury its name. A French writer living in New York, he praised American agriculture in his 1782 book, *Letters from an American Farmer.*

St. John was a friend of George Washington and Benjamin Franklin. He also corresponded with Ethan Allen, who wanted to name the town St. John after him. The writer suggested St. Johnsbury, realizing that several places were already named St. John.

St. Johnsbury became a minor manufacturing center, and today it is a quintessential Victorian industrial town with a large historic district.

2. HENNIKER, NEW HAMPSHIRE

New Hampshire's flamboyant colonial governor, Benning Wentworth, had no problem naming towns after people. He had an ulterior motive for doing it.

Wentworth wanted to expand his colony westward. So starting in 1749, he claimed land in western New Hampshire and what is now Vermont. To win support for his land grab, he named towns after friends in high places.

And that is how a bucolic New Hampshire town came to its signature boast.

Henniker prides itself on being "the only Henniker on earth." People called it Todd's Town or New Marlborough until 1768, when Wentworth gave it a charter and named it for his friend, Sir John Henniker, a wealthy British merchant.

3. MIANUS, CONNECTICUT

One way to have a unique name in New England is to take it from the Indians. In the seventeenth century, English settlers named a river "Mianus" after the chief of the Siwanoy tribe. The land along it became part of Greenwich, but it didn't really become a village until after World War II. Then, the Veterans Administration and the Town of Greenwich built forty starter homes for returning servicemen and their families.

The name is pronounced "maɪˈænəs," but mispronunciations have made it the butt of jokes involving weiners, er, frankfurters.

4. KENNEBUNK, MAINE

A large sign in town once proclaimed, "Kennebunk, the only village in the world so named."

"Kennebunk" was an Abenaki Indian word meaning "the long cut bank," which refers to the bank behind Kennebunk Beach. The town's presence on the Kennebunk and Mousam rivers made it an early center of shipping, shipbuilding, and, later, manufacturing.

Today Kennebunk is a bedroom community and a destination for upscale tourists attracted by its beaches and shopping. The town was overshadowed by its neighbor, Kennebunkport, also with a unique name. Kennebunkport often made the world's news when President George H.W. Bush summered there at his family compound.

Kennebunk is home to the Rachel Carson National Wildlife Refuge, historic buildings, the 1799 Inn, Tom's of Maine, and the Brick Store Museum.

5. DRACUT, MASSACHUSETTS

Dracut, Massachusetts, started out as Augumtoocooke, a Pennacook word. Passaconaway, the sachem who brokered peace in the Merrimack River Valley, spent most of his life there.

The name changed when Passaconaway's daughter Bess sold the land in 1665 to Captain John Evered. Evered had been in charge of the execution of Mary Dyer, the Quaker who refused to stay banished from Massachusetts. Her statue now stands in front of the Massachusetts Statehouse.

Evered's family was associated with Draycot Cerne in northern England. John Evered made the name unique in the world by shortening and corrupting it.

Dracut belonged to Chelmsford until 1701, when it formally separated. Part of Dracut was set aside as a Praying Town for Christianized Indians. Then the paper and textile mills came, attracting French Canadian and Irish immigrants. Modern real estate development swallowed much of it, and the City of Lowell annexed large parts of the town.

6. BURRILLVILLE, RHODE ISLAND

By the time Burrillville, Rhode Island, broke off from Glocester in 1806, it wasn't unusual to name a town after a national hero or, in this case, a favorite son. James Burrill, Jr., was only thirty-four years old in 1806, but he had established himself as a leader in Rhode Island. He had become Rhode Island's attorney general and elected a U.S. senator. Shortly before he died in 1820, he delivered an eloquent speech opposing the Missouri Compromise. The clause that banned free blacks and people of mixed race in Missouri "was entirely repugnant to the Constitution of the United States," Burrill said.

Burrillville originally comprised sixty square miles, but lost land to Massachusetts over a border dispute. Many mills, now gone or shuttered, were built in Burrillville, which today belongs to the Blackstone River Valley National Heritage Corridor.

PLACES THAT ONCE BELONGED TO A DIFFERENT STATE

Early New Englanders were a grabby lot, always coveting the land next to them. Connecticut tried to grab most of Rhode Island, but failed. Massachusetts also failed to get hold of New Hampshire, but New Hampshire managed to snatch Vermont from New York. Then the Republic of Vermont got its independence. Maine, however, wasn't so lucky. Massachusetts took the entire state, but sold it back in 1820.

Minor skirmishes over borders continued into the twenty-first century. Here are six of them, which all resulted in a town or a village getting a new postal code.

1. WOODSTOCK AND SUFFIELD, CONNECTICUT

Two surveyors who may have had too many cocktails caused a 162-year dispute over Connecticut's northern border.

Enfield and Suffield began their colonial history as part of Massachusetts. In 1642, Connecticut sought a charter from the English King Charles, and Massachusetts thought it wise to survey its southern border. The colony hired two English surveyors—Solomon Saffery and Nathaniel Woodward.

They made a mistake, though, and drew a line seven miles below the spot where the Massachusetts border was supposed to end.

Some historians said the pair were drunks, others just called them unqualified. More charitable historians suggested that surveyors back then had to use unreliable instruments. Further, Saffery and Woodward took a shortcut, extrapolating from mathematical calculations rather than walking the land. They had to because the Indians considered the land to be theirs.

Regardless, Massachusetts had the upper hand in the debate at first because Connecticut didn't have a charter. But Massachusetts had one little problem: It was clearly wrong. Every time the colonies investigated, surveyors concluded the Saffrey-Woodward line missed by more than a mile.

In 1713, the two colonies made a deal. They both agreed to accept the erroneous 1642 line with regard to the towns of Suffield, Enfield, and the newer town of Woodstock. The towns would stay in Massachusetts. In return Connecticut would receive unsettled land in Massachusetts.

The 1713 compromise satisfied everyone but the people who lived in the disputed towns. They still wanted to belong to Connecticut—probably because Connecticut had lower taxes and a more liberal government. So in 1749, the disputed towns declared themselves part of Connecticut. This later prompted residents of Southwick, now bounded on three sides by Connecticut, to petition to join Connecticut, too.

Massachusetts officials couldn't accept the loss of those towns. But the little matter of a revolution got in the way. Finally, in 1804 they got together and agreed Southwick and Enfield would stay in Massachusetts. The others would stay in Connecticut.

The result was a small, square cutout in the border known to this day as the Southwick Jog.

2. CHARLESTOWN, NEW HAMPSHIRE

In the 1600s, governors of both New York and New Hampshire were merrily giving away sections of Vermont to their friends. James I, King of England, intervened in 1624. He established the New Hampshire border as the western edge of the Connecticut River.

In 1778, the middle of the American Revolution, sixteen New Hampshire towns from Chester to Haverhill proclaimed themselves part of the brand-new Republic of Vermont. Ethan Allen, commander of the Green

Mountain Boys, didn't want trouble. He used his political clout to send the towns back to New Hampshire.

In 1781, the towns again seceded from New Hampshire and joined Vermont. This time they meant business, and they had Ethan Allen's support. The Vermont General Assembly even met in what is now Charlestown, New Hampshire.

New Hampshire took the news badly. It threatened to withdraw support for the American Revolution and to send a thousand troops into Vermont to restore its borders. Even George Washington got involved in whipping the towns back into line.

The Continental Congress put more pressure on Vermont, saying it couldn't join the Union if it didn't give the towns back to New Hampshire.

Vermont caved, acknowledging the western bank of the Connecticut River as the border, and withdrew its claim to the towns.

3. VERNON, VERMONT

Vernon, Vermont, started out as Northfield, Massachusetts, in 1672. The settlement bordered New Hampshire, which was just too tempting for New Hampshire's sticky-fingered Governor Benning Wentworth. He claimed Vernon, Massachusetts, as part of another town he chartered, Hinsdale.

What followed was a century of squabbling and bad surveying. By 1779, four states had claimed Hinsdale: New York, Massachusetts, New Hampshire, and Vermont.

When in 1782 Vermont agreed to the western bank of the Connecticut River as its border, that split Hinsdale into two towns, one in Vermont and one in New Hampshire.

The Vermonters wanted their own identity, so in 1802 they changed the name of Hinsdale to Vernon.

4. FALL RIVER, MASSACHUSETTS

Fall River used to be two towns. One part of Fall River belonged to Freetown, part of Plymouth Colony. Then when Plymouth joined the Massachusetts Bay Colony, so did Freetown.

In 1803, a section separated from Freetown and called itself Fallriver, Massachusetts, for a year. Then it changed its name to Troy. Thirty years later, the town decided to change its name back to Fall River. And it's been that way ever since.

The other town that became Fall River has a more complicated history. It started out as farmland that belonged to Plymouth. By the time it incorporated in 1694 as the Town of Tiverton, Plymouth had been absorbed into the Massachusetts Bay Colony. So Tiverton started out officially as a Massachusetts town.

But there was a problem. In 1663, King Charles II had given Rhode Island a charter that extended the colony's boundaries three miles into Plymouth Colony. So Rhode Island thought Tiverton belonged to Rhode Island, thanks to the generosity of Charles II. But Plymouth, and then Massachusetts, had no interest in giving up Tiverton.

Little Rhode Island appealed to a new king, George II, and in 1746 he gave Tiverton back to Rhode Island. Rhode Island happily ordered surveyors to draw a new boundary line. But the surveyors ended up grabbing too much Massachusetts land for Rhode Island.

Massachusetts was not pleased.

As the two states quarreled over the boundary, Tiverton began to change. Textile and fish oil mills developed in the town's northern section, right next to the generous (to Rhode Island) border.

Tiverton decided to lose the noisy mills and stinky fish oil factories, and so it spun them off into a new town called Fall River, Rhode Island.

The two states continued bickering, finally bringing their border dispute to the U.S. Supreme Court. The court settled the matter by giving Fall River, Rhode Island, to Massachusetts in 1861. And so the two Fall Rivers became one.

5. PAWTUCKET, RHODE ISLAND

So when the U.S. Supreme Court gave Fall River to Massachusetts, it kept Barrington, Bristol, Cumberland, Little Compton, and Warren in Rhode Island.

But of course it wasn't all that simple. A Massachusetts border town called Pawtucket had once (of course) belonged to another town—Rehoboth, in Plymouth Colony. Massachusetts carved out part of Rehoboth and called it Seekonk. Then in 1828 the commonwealth carved out part of Seekonk and called it Pawtucket.

But across the river a town named Pawtucket, Rhode Island, had grown up around the first water-powered textile mill in the United States. The Rhode Island Pawtucketians were not happy about their Massachusetts imitator.

So in 1861 the Supreme Court justices had to decide what to do with four densely populated towns—two named Fall River and two named Pawtucket. Since the court gave a Fall River to Massachusetts, it was only fair to give a Pawtucket to Rhode Island as a consolation prize.

And as a bonus, Pawtucket got the industrial section of Providence.

6. SEAVEY'S ISLAND, MAINE

The Portsmouth Naval Shipyard, created in 1800, lies in the middle of the Piscataqua River, which separates Portsmouth, New Hampshire, and Kittery, Maine. The yard was cobbled together over the years from five islands, now called Seavey's Island.

The federal government owns the island, and for decades the U.S. Navy viewed it as part of New Hampshire.

Shipyard workers have come from New Hampshire, which doesn't have an income tax, and from Maine, which does. New Hampshire shipyard workers had to pay Maine income tax because Maine claimed Seavey's Island.

So in 2001, New Hampshire tried to make its shipyard workers happy. Lawyers went to the U.S. Supreme Court and asked for Seavey's Island back.

New Hampshire claimed it owned the Piscataqua River to the Maine shoreline. Unfortunately, the state had agreed in a 1977 lawsuit over fishing rights that the border ran down the middle of the river.

Maine got Seavey's Island.

TOWNS RENAMED OUT OF SPITE

When the European settlers arrived, they usually changed Indian names to those from their home country. And then they changed them again.

The Puritans, for example, first called Boston Trimontaine, after the three hills on the peninsula. John Winthrop soon renamed the town Boston after the hometown of several prominent colonists. It was just as well, since Bostonians eventually cut down their three hills.

Townspeople, though, sometimes renamed themselves because they didn't like what the old name represented. Sometimes they didn't have a choice, as when a new authority arrived and tried to assert his power over a town.

1. GORGEANA, MAINE

When King James I in 1620 gave Sir Fernando Gorges a patent to colonize the New World, Gorges thought that included Massachusetts. After all, the king had specified he was to "plant, rule, order and govern" all the land between New France (Canada) and Virginia.

Gorges, an Anglican and a Royalist, began by financing the settlement of Maine. He hoped to turn it into a series of feudal plantations, and he named one settlement after himself—Gorgeana.

Maine's neighbor, Puritan Massachusetts, grew in population, wealth and power. Anglican Maine did not. So by 1658, the Puritans from Massachusetts went town by town to persuade what is now Maine to join Massachusetts.

Names carried great importance to the early New England Puritans. And so when Gorgeana agreed to join Massachusetts, the Puritans decided to rename it York. The name York carried a special sting because it was the name of a Royalist city in England that fell to the Puritan Parliament during the English Civil War.

2. HAVERSHAM, RHODE ISLAND

In 1684, British authorities sought to assert their control over their colonies in New England. They annulled the colonial charters and combined the colonies into the Dominion of New England. Then in 1686 they appointed Joseph Dudley, a native of Roxbury, Massachusetts, as president of the Council of New England, which included Massachusetts, New Hampshire, Maine, and the Narragansett Country in Rhode Island.

Dudley had a tough time of it. Magistrates and military officers refused to serve and Puritan leaders ignored him. He traveled to Narragansett to establish his authority there, and he spitefully renamed Westerly "Haversham." Kingstown became "Rochester," and Greenwich "Dedford."

Sir Edmund Andros took over from Dudley with the added territory of Connecticut and Rhode Island. He didn't last long, only until 1689, when Bostonians sent him packing. In England, a new king took the throne and restored the colonial governments. Haversham went back to its old name of Westerly.

3. NEW GLASGOW, MASSACHUSETTS

Scots-Irish families first came to Blandford in 1735 and called their settlement "New Glasgow." Their reason: The people of Glasgow, Scotland, promised them a church bell if they named their town after them.

The Massachusetts Bay colonists only tolerated the Scots-Irish because they provided a useful buffer against hostile Indians on the frontier. In 1741, the settlers petitioned royal Governor William Shirley for incorporation as the Town of New Glasgow. Shirley instead renamed the town Blandford, supposedly for the ship that had just carried him to Boston.

But in reality, Shirley probably wasn't keen to recognize the Scottish city. After all, enraged Glaswegians had recently rioted against a malt tax, driven out the British military, and destroyed the home of their parliamentary representative.

Blandford didn't get its bell.

4. POCHAUG, CONNECTICUT

Westbrook, Connecticut, originally belonged to Saybrook, which came under attack by Indians during the Pequot War. When the Pequot threat ended, about forty families moved to West Saybrook to an area known by the Indian name of Pochaug. The word meant "place where the river divides," and refers to the Patchogue and the Menunketesuck rivers.

But the townspeople didn't like the name, probably because they didn't like Indians. In 1810, the town petitioned the General Assembly to rename it Westbrook. The petition noted that very few, if any, could spell or pronounce the name correctly. It was said to be "inconvenient to the said inhabitants and to the public."

Connecticut is full of towns with portmanteau names, and "Westbrook" could have derived from "West Saybrook." However, it's worth noting that Colonel Thomas Westbrook had fought Indians during the French and Indian wars.

5. ADAMS, NEW HAMPSHIRE

Nestled in the White Mountains near Maine's border, Jackson, New Hampshire, was originally named New Madbury after the Seacoast town from which its first settlers came. The town renamed itself Adams in 1800 to honor John Adams, just elected president of the United States as a Federalist.

Back then, partisan feelings ran high. The Federalists hated the Democratic-Republicans, and the Democratic-Republicans despised the Federalists.

John Adams served only one term, and the Federalists began to fade as their rivals rose to power. Benjamin Pierce, father of the unfortunate Franklin Pierce, was a rising Democratic-Republican who won election as New Hampshire governor in 1827. Then in 1829, Andrew Jackson—another Democratic-Republican—won election as U.S. president.

That year Adams petitioned New Hampshire's General Court for incorporation as a town. Governor Pierce decided to score a political point. He let Adams become a town, but only if it changed its name to Jackson.

Adams was renamed Jackson.

6. SODOM, VERMONT

Back in the day, quarrying often attracted rough men who enjoyed women and liquor when they weren't blasting rock. Sodom, an unincorporated village in the central Vermont town of Calais, was apparently one such place. Sodom had several active quarries, but no church. A curtain was drawn across the bar at Barney's Hall for Sunday services.

According to lore, a local preacher pounded his fist on the pulpit and said, "I am adamant that we change the name of this town!" Citizens in 1905 petitioned the Legislature to change the name from Sodom to Adamant.

There's another story, though. A local farmer named Albert Bliss refused to receive mail with the distasteful Sodom postmark. He petitioned the U.S. postal service to change the name. The postal service granted permission, but only if the new name was unlike any other in the state. Adamant was chosen to reflect the hardness of the granite.

PLACES WITH
FRENCH NAMES

New England cities and towns rarely have French names, despite the region's significant Franco-American presence. If the French had won the French and Indian wars, perhaps things might be different.

The French names that do appear on New England maps generally got there as a result of a great historic event. Perhaps the residents wanted to honor the French for their help in winning the American Revolution. Perhaps they wanted to show their support for the French Revolution. Or perhaps they wanted to express their joy at a new French king, as the people of Orange, Connecticut, did.

1. ORANGE, CONNECTICUT

Edmund Andros probably shouldn't have tried to seize Connecticut's charter.

King James II wanted Andros to tighten control of Connecticut, newly consolidated into the Dominion of New England. But Connecticut's Puritans didn't think much of Andros, who brought with him a strong whiff of papistry.

Andros went to Hartford to demand Connecticut's charter, thinking that would demonstrate the charter was no longer valid.

There are several legends about what happened next. Most say the charter was hidden in a big oak tree, known ever after as the Charter Oak. Today, any number of Connecticut institutions, landmarks, and thoroughfares bear the name.

Charter Oak isn't French. But Orange is.

A French prince named William of Orange deposed Edmund Andros's boss, King James II. Soon Andros packed up and left for England, much to the joy and relief of the people of the town of Milford, Connecticut.

William of Orange became William III, and a village in Milford became Orange. Then in 1821, Orange broke off from Milford and became its own town.

2. BARRE, VERMONT

Barre in 1776 took its name from an Irishman of French Huguenot ancestry who gave the Sons of Liberty their name.

Isaac Barre, the son of Dublin's high sheriff, served the British Army with distinction before representing Chipping Wycombe in Parliament. He had a long, colorful parliamentary career, during which he vigorously opposed the taxation of the American colonies. While addressing Parliament, he coined the phrase "Sons of Liberty."

Until 1788, roving bands of Indians were the only inhabitants of the area described as "primeval forests, granite hills and green valleys." The first settlers named it Wildersborough, but the residents didn't like it and the name didn't stick.

According to one story, the settlement's selectmen decided the person who contributed the most to a meeting house could rename the town. For sixty-two pounds, Ezekiel Wheeler got to name the town Barre.

According to another story, two men from Massachusetts put forward their preferred names at a Town Meeting. Both Captain Joseph Thompson of Holden and Jonathon Sherman of Barre (also named after Isaac) wanted to name it after their former towns. They decided to fight it out in a barn, and Sherman won.

3. ORLEANS, MASSACHUSETTS

Orleans, on Cape Cod's elbow, was captured twice by the British during the American Revolution.

The town had been part of Eastham until it split off in 1797, when memories of the British occupation still stung.

Americans who supported the American Revolution supported the French who supported the French Revolution.

Isaac Snow, a descendant of Mayflower Pilgrim Stephen Hopkins, supposedly suggested the French place name for the new town. The British had captured Snow during the American Revolution and confined him aboard a prison ship in England. Snow then escaped to France, where he more than likely learned about the popular Louis Philippe Joseph, Duke of Orleans, a supporter of the French Revolution.

Isaac Snow's family opened its first store in Orleans in 1887. The Snow family still runs Snow's, where you can probably find whatever you need.

4. CALAIS, MAINE

Acadians first settled the region on both sides of the St. John River, so it's natural that Calais, Maine, and St. Stephen, New Brunswick, should have a close friendship.

The British had no idea just how friendly they were. During the War of 1812, the British military gave St. Stephen gunpowder to defend itself against Americans. St. Stephen instead gave the gunpowder to Calais for its July 4th celebration.

The townspeople named Calais for the French city in 1809 to honor France's help to the American colonies during the Revolutionary War.

5. LAFAYETTE VILLAGE, RHODE ISLAND

When the Marquis de Lafayette made his triumphal tour of the United States in 1824, enthusiastic Rhode Islanders renamed a village in North Kingstown after him. Previously, people had given it a less glamorous name: the North Kingstown Cotton Factory.

Lafayette, though, remained little more than a French place name for a cotton mill, a smattering of houses, and an unusually wide road. The road had been ordered by the Rhode Island colony in 1703 so farmers could bring their goods to the port of Wickford.

Today, the National Register of Historic Places lists Lafayette Village as a monument to Robert Rodman, a paternalistic textile manufacturer. He incorporated as the Rodman Manufacturing Co. in 1883 and employed five hundred workers by 1900. The company lasted into the 1940s.

6. FREMONT, NEW HAMPSHIRE

Fremont took its French place name from the illegitimate son of a French Canadian schoolteacher. John C. Fremont also happened to be a military hero and the Republican Party's first candidate for president of the United States.

Fremont's mother was the daughter of a wealthy Virginia planter. At seventeen she married a well-to-do army major in his sixties. The major hired a Canadian immigrant, Charles Fremon, to tutor his young wife. They fell in love and ran away to Georgia, where John Fremon was born out of wedlock. The major refused to divorce John's mother, so she could not marry his father.

Charles Fremon died, and John Fremon and his mother lived in poverty and disgrace. He compensated with pride and ambition.

During his lifetime he fought in the Mexican War, rose to the rank of major general, explored the West, gained and lost a fortune, served in the U.S. Senate from California, and ran for president in 1856. He also met and married Jessie Benton.

Jessie's father, U.S. Senator Thomas Benton, earned immense popularity for his support of western expansion. In 1840, the town of Coventry, New Hampshire, decided to change its name to Benton in honor of the senator. Fourteen years later, a New Hampshire town called Poplin—about a hundred miles to the south—changed its name to Fremont after the senator's son-in-law.

TOWNS NAMED WARREN

NEW ENGLAND HAS SIX TOWNS CALLED WARREN, ONE IN EACH STATE, but the reason for those place names is more complicated than you might think. There were two Warrens—Peter and Joseph—and they were two different heroes of distinctly different eras.

1. RHODE ISLAND

In 1623, the Wampanoag sachem Massasoit became seriously ill in a village called Sowams, and Pilgrim Edward Winslow traveled from Plymouth to restore him to health. They stayed friends, and Massasoit sold Sowams to the colonists. Sowams became Swansea, and then Massachusetts gave Swansea to Rhode Island to settle a border dispute.

The town finally became Warren in 1746, one year after Vice-Admiral Sir Peter Warren became a military hero during the third French and Indian War. He was an Irish officer in the British Royal Navy who, along with American troops, captured the fort at Louisbourg in Nova Scotia—a very big deal at the time.

The capture of the fort led to the British victory in the French and Indian War, which in turn stimulated trade between New England and Canada. The capture of the fort not only made Warren very wealthy, it made him an early New England celebrity.

2. NEW HAMPSHIRE

Peter Warren's luster hadn't dimmed by 1770, when Warren, New Hampshire, incorporated as a town. It had only been settled three years earlier by a man named Joseph Patch on a grant from Governor Benning Wentworth.

The tiny town continues its military theme with a Redstone missile that towers over the flagpole on the common.

3. MAINE

The other Warrens trace their name to a more well-known figure in U.S. history: Dr. Joseph Warren.

If that Warren hadn't died at the Battle of Bunker Hill, we might never have heard of George Washington. He was the one who told Paul Revere to take his midnight ride, and he led the fight for independence in many other ways.

Warren could have fought as a general in the Battle of Bunker Hill, but he chose to serve as a private. Nevertheless, a British officer recognized him and shot him in the head, killing him instantly. The British army buried him in disgrace, in a mass grave without any identification.

To Americans, however, Joseph Warren died a martyr to the cause of freedom. A gloom, it was said, settled over the colonies. For decades afterward the name Warren was affixed to schools, monuments, and towns throughout America.

In the District of Maine, Scots-Irish from Londonderry, New Hampshire, had settled a tract of land called the Waldo Patent in 1736. But the French and Indian wars prevented the settlers from doing very much with it for about forty years. Finally, in 1776, the settlers got their charter and named their town after Joseph Warren.

4. CONNECTICUT

A small farming community in Kent, Connecticut, broke off in 1786 and incorporated itself as Warren, after Joseph. The town emerged from obscurity in 2006 when a local businessman tried to sell much of its commercial district for five million dollars on eBay.

5. VERMONT

Warren, Vermont, got its name eight years before anyone actually settled there. It received a charter in 1789, fourteen years after Joseph Warren died at Bunker Hill. Not until 1797 did anyone settle the town. Better known for the Sugarbush Ski Resort, it's a tiny town on the Mad River.

6. MASSACHUSETTS

The last of the towns named Warren was once named Western—in central Massachusetts. Well, it used to be western when the settlers arrived in 1664. It was still pretty far west when it was incorporated in 1741. But another town west of Boston had been calling itself Weston. Because so much mail got misdelivered, Western decided in 1834 to rename itself Warren. After Joseph.

ROADS AND ROUTES

WHEN COLONISTS ARRIVED IN NEW ENGLAND, they inherited (well, appropriated) a network of Indian trails that covered every state and extended as far west as the Rocky Mountains.

White-tailed deer had actually arrived before the Indians, about ten thousand years ago at the end of the Ice Age. Thousands of deer populated the region, traveling single file to find water and tasty vegetation to graze.

The Indians followed the network of deer paths, wearing them down even more. They used them to migrate from their summer to winter homes, to make war, and to hunt deer.

INDIAN TRAILS
THAT ARE NOW
SCENIC BYWAYS

SOME INDIAN TRAILS WERE THE EQUIVALENT OF INTERSTATE HIGHWAYS, if the Indians had had states. The Mohawk Trail and Kennebec Trail were two of the longest and best-traveled of the old paths.

During the American Revolution, Benedict Arnold found those old Indian trails useful before he turned traitor. He led his soldiers along the Mohawk Trail from Cambridge, Massachusetts, to capture Fort Ticonderoga in New York. That turned out so well for him he decided to lead a larger group along the Kennebec Trail in Maine. He intended to capture Quebec, but he didn't come close to succeeding. The expedition ended disastrously. He lost hundreds of men to smallpox, starvation, the enemy, or capture.

Today, many of those old Indian trails have been paved over. New England's splendor can now be enjoyed without the inconvenience of smallpox or armed combatants, though slow-moving leaf peeping motorists may pose a problem.

1. OLD KING'S HIGHWAY

Cape Cod's Old King's Highway may well be the most beautiful drive in America. Native people used it for centuries as a trade route, and the early European colonists widened it with carts and horses. Today, it's officially known as Route 6A, and runs from Sandwich through Barnstable, Yarmouth, Dennis, and Brewster. Think "quintessential New England towns" and that's what you'll get. Plus beaches, salt marshes, taverns, and those odd little houses known as "half Capes."

A long stretch through Barnstable is even listed on the National Register of Historic Places. About five hundred historic buildings, some dating to the seventeenth century, line the Old King's Highway Historic District.

2. OLD CONNECTICUT PATH

The Old Connecticut Path was one of the most important Indian trails, stretching (roughly) from Boston to Hartford. Nipmuck Indians used the path to take furs and surplus corn from the Connecticut River to coastal settlements. There they traded with other tribes and Europeans for manufactured cloth, metal tools, weapons, and alcoholic beverages.

John Oldham, whose death started the Pequot War, followed the Old Connecticut Path to explore the continent's interior in 1633. Three years later, the Rev. Thomas Hooker spent two weeks on the Old Connecticut Path with his followers, moving from Cambridge, Massachusetts, to Hartford. John Adams followed the Path from Tolland to Windsor in 1771. "Today I rode through paradise," he wrote.

Generally, the Old Connecticut Path headed west along the Charles River from Boston, curved south in Wayland through Framingham, to Webster and to Lake Chaubunagungamaug. In Connecticut it continued to Hartford, Wethersfield, and Windsor.

In 1944, a group of Boy Scouts followed roads that approximated the Old Connecticut Path from Boston to Hartford. They wanted to commemorate the journey taken by Connecticut's early pioneers.

Today, people are trying to restore parts of the Old Connecticut Path as an off-road heritage trail. Their goal is to connect the state's open spaces with trails and quiet roads. For example, a proposed path in Vernon joins the Hop River Rail trail in Valley Falls Park. Then it goes west downhill to Dobson Road and on to the Talcott Ravine trail. In Manchester it would join the Hockanum River Greenway Trails.

The Old Connecticut Path even has a Facebook page.

3. WALDOBORO MAST TRAIL

Maine's Indians paddled their canoes along waterways connected by trails from the coast to the interior. Indians carried their canoes or cargo over narrow strips of land from one body of water to the next. These carrying trails, or portages, let Maine tribes to get anywhere—even theah from heah.

One path from inland Maine to the coast is known as the Waldoboro Mast Trail. It now follows Route 220 from Montville to Waldoboro. It was the most direct route from Lake St. George to the shellfish beds of the seacoast.

Wawenoc Indian families migrated along that path from the seasonal hunting camp to the seasonal fishing camp. They hunted for moose and beaver in the winter and brought their fur as trade goods to the coast.

English settlers found the trail a convenient route to carry the giant trees they cut down for the King's masts. Shipyards in Waldoboro made hundreds of vessels for the British Royal Navy.

Today Route 220 winds through rural Maine from Montville to Waldoboro, known by travelers for Moody's Diner.

4. WINNICOEK TRAIL

The Winnicoek Trail today is better known as coastal Route 1A between, roughly, Hampton and Portsmouth in New Hampshire. The trail connected the Merrimack River in Massachusetts through Winnicoek, now Hampton, to the Piscataqua River in Portsmouth.

The Pennacook and Abenaki Indians migrated along the path in the summer to Odiorne Point, now a wooded park in the Town of Rye. The park has sweeping views of the Atlantic Ocean and the Town of New Castle. (It also has abandoned concrete bunkers from World War II.)

When the English colonists arrived in 1635, they used the Winnicoek Trail as a bridle path. Today it's a scenic drive also known as Ocean Boulevard, running along New Hampshire's eighteen-mile shoreline. It features beaches, marshes, and nineteenth-century summer cottages in the Little Boar's Head Historic District.

5. PEQUOT PATH

For hundreds of years, Narragansett and Pequot Indians traveled along the Pequot Path. It ran about seventy miles near the mainland shore from Providence, Rhode Island, to New London, Connecticut.

In 1636, Roger Williams took the Pequot path through Apponaug, now Warwick, on a journey to the trading post at Cocumscussoc near present-day Wickford.

"It is admirable to see what paths their naked hardened feet have made in the wilderness in the most stony and rockie places," Williams wrote. He probably saw a dozen Narragansett villages along twenty miles of the path.

English settlers began using the Pequot Path until it evolved into the lower part of the Boston Post Road. Today, parts of scenic Route 1A (not to be confused with US Route 1A) follow the old Pequot path along the South Coast.

Scenic Route 1A follows the shore from Wickford to Narragansett Pier, passing large, exclusive homes and views of the bay.

6. ROUTE 22A

Route 22A through the Lake Champlain Valley in Vermont was once part of a network of well-worn Indian trails linking villages and other overland trail networks.

The St. Francis Indians came down from Canada along the trail by Lake Champlain to find warmer fishing grounds. The trail finally stretched to the Bronx, New York, where it became known as "the road to Bedford and Vermont." Today Vermont Route 22A continues New York Route 22A; it's a scenic drive in foliage season.

CANALS THAT
CHANGED
NEW ENGLAND

In 1803, one of the first New England canals made Boston the undisputed commercial center of New England.

Called "the Incredible Ditch," the Middlesex Canal allowed a barge to haul thirty tons of goods back and forth between Chelmsford, now Lowell, and Charlestown, now part of Boston. A horse and wagon could haul one-tenth that amount—perhaps three tons—over the rough roads of the era.

Canal fever really broke out in New England with the opening of the Erie Canal, finished in 1825. It gave New York City an unbeatable advantage over other port cities. As a result, New England and the Mid-Atlantic states went into a frenzy of canal building.

New England states built dozens of canals, first to transport goods to seaports and then to power mills and factories. But the rise of the railroads made canals obsolete, and the Canal Era ended around 1855.

Today the canals are mostly gone, filled in, paved over, or maybe declared Superfund sites. One notable exception is the Cape Cod Canal, heavily used by recreational and commercial vessels.

1. AMOSKEAG CANALS

In 1807, Manchester, New Hampshire, was a tiny town called Derryfield when industrialist Samuel Blodget declared his canal would turn it into "a manufacturing town, the Manchester of America!"

Blodget had already broken ground on the canal, which ran parallel to the Merrimack River. It took ten years to build and wasn't finished until 1808. But it made travel possible along the river by bypassing the fifty-four-foot drop at the Amoskeag Falls. A series of locks allowed barges and boats to get past the waterfalls.

In 1810, the first textile mills were built along Blodget's canal, then renamed the Amoskeag Canal. Manufacturing floundered until the Amoskeag Manufacturing Company bought the land and water rights along the canal in 1831. It then built the enormous brick Millyard, a manufacturing powerhouse until the 1920s.

Then a second canal was built one block east of the Amoskeag Canal. The two canals powered the mills until steam took over in the 1880s.

The canals were paved over in the 1970s. One became Commercial Street, the other a railroad track. Today, the remains of two small canals can be seen at the top of Manchester's Millyard near PSNH's Energy Park.

2. FARMINGTON CANAL

The Connecticut Legislature granted six canal charters to private companies, but only two—the Enfield and Farmington—were actually built.

Beginning in 1825, Irish immigrants and farmers dug the Farmington canal, four feet deep and twenty feet wide, using handmade shovels, wheelbarrows, and wagons. It took ten years to dig the canal, which began at New Haven, snaked through Granby and ended at the Connecticut River in Northampton, Massachusetts. The laborers also built sixty stone locks along the eighty-mile waterway.

The opening of the New Haven-to-Farmington leg of the canal in 1828 was a very big deal. Four African American boys rode gray horses that pulled a boat carrying two hundred dignitaries sipping refreshments.

For a while the towns along the canal prospered, as farm produce and wood flowed south to New Haven, and imports like coffee and molasses headed north.

But heavy rains damaged the canal, and toll revenue covered only 20 percent of expenses. Operations were slowly phased out, and the canal was eventually sold to a railroad company that built the New York, New Haven, and Hartford Railroad.

The railroad became a rail trail in the 1990s, and today the Farmington Canal Trail runs from downtown New Haven to Northampton, Massachusetts.

3. CUMBERLAND AND OXFORD CANAL

Unlike Connecticut, Maine lawmakers decided the state should support a new canal from inland lakes to the Portland seaport. A state lottery raised $50,000 and a bank was chartered to provide the funds for the $206,000 project.

The Cumberland and Oxford Canal opened in 1832 and connected the large lakes of southern Maine with Portland along the Presumpscot River. It passed through the towns of Standish, Windham, Gorham, and Westbrook. The thirty-eight-mile canal required twenty-seven locks to reach Sebago Lake. Passengers paid a half cent to go through each lock.

Barges carried lumber, firewood, masts, barrel hoops, and apples from Maine's forests and farms to the sea. From Windham, the Oriental Powder Company mills sent down the canal a quarter of the gunpowder used in the Civil War.

The canal started its decline when the railroad that became the Maine Central opened a station in Sebago Lake. A steamboat company continued to carry tourists between Portland and the Lake Region until the last steamboat, *Goodrich*, burned at its dock in 1932.

One of the canal's locks, Songo Lock, is still in service for pleasure boats.

4. LOWELL POWER CANALS

Lowell, Massachusetts, contains the world's largest system of canals that generate hydroelectric power. They began, though, as a modest transportation waterway in 1796.

The little Pawtucket Canal was built so New Hampshire logs could be hauled around the Pawtucket Falls in East Chelmsford, Massachusetts, then down the Merrimack River to Newburyport, Massachusetts.

By 1806, the bigger, better Middlesex Canal made the Pawtucket Canal irrelevant.

But then in the early 1820s, business associates of Francis Cabot Lowell realized the Pawtucket Canal could be used to power textile mills. They had the Pawtucket Canal widened and deepened, and the subsequent canals that fed off it created the City of Lowell.

First the Merrimack Canal powered the Merrimack Manufacturing Co. Then waterpower from the Hamilton Canal was sold to other companies. Then the Northern Canal and the Moody Street Feeder increased the waterpower to the system. The canal owners finally built the Pawtucket Gatehouse to control flow from the Pawtucket Dam into the Northern Canal.

Lowell's six-mile canals are still there and working. They are part of the Lowell National Historical Park, established in 1978.

5. THE BLACKSTONE CANAL

During the canal mania of the 1820s, merchants in Providence, Rhode Island, wanted to profit from trade with the farming communities near Worcester County and the Blackstone Valley. Until then, farmers sent their products by wagon to Boston.

In 1823, shortly before the Erie Canal opened, Massachusetts gave a charter to the Blackstone Canal Co. Rhode Island soon followed. Irish immigrants dug a ditch next to the Blackstone River that became the canal. In Providence, the Moshassuck River became the lower part of the canal.

The forty-five-mile canal opened on October 7, 1828, when the canal boat *Lady Carrington* arrived in Worcester. For the next twenty years, the canal brought prosperity to farmers, sparked the construction of textile mills along its banks, and sustained the growth of Providence and Worcester.

But then the Providence and Worcester Railroad opened in 1847, putting the Blackstone Canal out of business the next year.

Today, sections of the canal belong to the Blackstone River and Canal Heritage State Park in Massachusetts and the Blackstone River State Park in Rhode Island.

Every summer in Providence, the Moshassuck and Providence rivers attract tourists to the WaterFire Festival. Eighty-six fires are lit in braziers anchored just above the waterline as musicians play world music.

6. PINE STREET BARGE CANAL

In the 1860s, Burlington, Vermont, was one of the busiest lumber ports in the United States, and the Lake Champlain waterfront near Battery Street was out of room. City planners dreamed up the Pine Street Canal to expand the waterfront and allow boats to be loaded and unloaded. A breakwater was also built near the shore of Lake Champlain.

The plan worked. Commerce flourished and factories sprang up along the Pine Street Barge Canal. Unfortunately, the factories also dumped toxic waste into the water.

The Pine Street Canal is now a thirty-eight-acre polluted swamp designated a Superfund site—perhaps the only one with four shipwrecks in it. Surveyors found three construction barges from the mid-twentieth century and the mid-nineteenth century schooner *Excelsior*.

The brick factories that grew up around the Pine Street Barge Canal are now restaurants, an antiques mall, and yoga studios.

STAGECOACH STOPS
YOU CAN STILL VISIT

HISTORIAN ALICE MORSE EARL CREDITS THE FIRST STAGECOACH TRIP to Jonathan Wardwell. On May 13, 1718, Wardwell took a stagecoach from his Boston tavern to Providence, Rhode Island. The stagecoach had many names over the next decades—like stage-chaise, stage wagon, stage chariot, flying machine, and flying waggon.

The heyday of the stagecoaches in the 1800s caused the post roads to develop. They grew from the first Upper Post Road into a maze of roads that wound their way into every corner of New England.

Stagecoaches needed to stop every twelve to twenty miles or so. Drivers announced their arrival at stagecoach stops by blowing on a trumpet—a happy sound, as they brought money and jobs. The stagecoaches supported innkeepers, drivers, ticket agents, coach makers, blacksmiths, stable hands, and farmers.

Today, the vestiges of the stagecoach era remain with us.

1. LONGFELLOW'S WAYSIDE INN, SUDBURY, MASSACHUSETTS

The Wayside Inn in Sudbury, Massachusetts, boasts of accommodating travelers since 1716, longer than any other inn in the United States. It began life as How's Tavern just a few miles down the Boston Post Road from Concord, well within earshot of the shot heard round the world. David How ran the tavern out of his own home, typical at the time.

David handed the property to his son Ezekial—a militiaman during the American Revolution. The How—later Howe—family ran the inn until 1861, serving traffic between Worcester and Boston.

Then in 1861, the new owners converted it into something more like a boarding house and dance hall.

But in 1862, Henry Wadsworth Longfellow sealed the Wayside Inn's place in history. After a visit, Longfellow published his famous *Tales of the Wayside Inn* in 1863. From then on, tourists and literary pilgrims came to the inn to experience the inspiration for Longfellow's book.

In 1923, the inn took another important step into immortality when automobile magnate Henry Ford bought the property. Ford then restored and expanded it, creating its current configuration.

2. OLD RIVERTON INN, RIVERTON, CONNECTICUT

Several years before the American Revolution, stagecoaches and stagecoach stops appeared on the Upper Post Road from New York to Boston, and from Hartford to Norwich and Providence. When the Revolution ended, stagecoach service expanded quickly on the new turnpike roads and postal routes.

Levi Pease began a stage service between New York and Boston on the Upper Post Road, which ran through Springfield, Hartford, and New Haven. He got the mail contract for all of New England from the U.S. Congress in 1789. Then he expanded his business into Northern New England and to Albany.

During the early part of the nineteenth century, Connecticut developed the most complex network of toll roads in the country. The state had few centers of wealth like Providence or Boston, and market towns competed fiercely for the trade of the back country. Between 1792 and 1839, Connecticut created sixteen hundred miles of turnpike road. The Talcott Mountain Turnpike was key to the route from Hartford to Albany.

Jess Ives opened the Ives Tavern or Ives Hotel in 1796 along the Hartford-to-Albany Route in Riverton, Connecticut. Today it's known as the Old Riverton Inn and overlooks a wild and scenic section of the Farmington River.

3. THE COACH STOP INN, BAR HARBOR MAINE

Stagecoach lines began regular service between Maine towns after the Revolutionary War. The first stages ran between Portland and Portsmouth, New Hampshire, a journey that took three days in 1787.

The Coach Stop Inn in Bar Harbor was built in 1804 for newcomers who came to build homes, farms, and ships on Mount Desert Island. Known as the Halfway Tavern, it often hosted sailors in the early days. Patrons arrived by sea and took a stagecoach from the tavern into Maine's interior towns.

Wealthy patrons charmed by fresh air, beautiful scenery, and hiking trails made Bar Harbor a fashionable summer resort during the Gilded Age. In 1947, a fire that burned much of Maine also destroyed some of Bar Harbor's hotels and mansions. The oldest hotel to survive the fire is now the Coach Stop Inn, a bed and breakfast on State Highway 3 in Bar Harbor.

4. COACH STOP RESTAURANT & TAVERN, LONDONDERRY, NEW HAMPSHIRE

In 1791 the New Hampshire legislature expanded the system of post roads to reach four sections of the state. Though the earlier post roads moved mail and people between Portsmouth and points west and north, only later did the routes reach deep into the western New Hampshire towns.

One such line ran from Portsmouth across the state's southern tier over to Amherst and back, creating the need for stagecoach stops.

Londonderry's Coach Stop Restaurant & Tavern began life in 1810 as the town doctor's home. But it was conveniently located at the junction of post roads, one heading east to west, the other north to south, and it became Plummer's Tavern.

Today the restaurant and inn on Mammoth Road maintains much of its historical charm as a coach stop.

5. STAGECOACH INN, WATERBURY, VERMONT

At the start of the nineteenth century, ancient footpaths connected Burlington and Montpelier in Vermont. In 1805, the thirty-six-mile Winooski Turnpike along the Winooski River was chartered to connect the state's two major towns.

It turned into U.S. Route 2, the main highway connecting the White Mountains to the Adirondacks. It cuts through Waterbury, where Ben and Jerry make their ice cream.

In 1826, someone (it isn't clear who) built a structure on the corner of the Winooski Turnpike and what is now Route 100 in Waterbury. It became an inn servicing stagecoach travelers. Though a railroad put the east-west stagecoach line out of business, people continued to ride by stagecoach heading north and south until 1898.

By the mid-1800s, a well-to-do farming family named the Henrys owned the inn. Their tobacco-chewing daughter Nettie married an Ohio rubber manufacturer, who gave her the means to transform the farmhouse into a Queen Anne-style showplace.

Nettie died in 1947, and the home grew shabby. A young couple from Boston bought the house in 1985 and rebuilt it. Today it's the Old Stagecoach Inn on Main Street in Waterbury.

6. STAGECOACH HOUSE INN, RICHMOND, RHODE ISLAND

Sometime around 1800, an inn was built at a strategic crossroads in Wyoming, a historic village in Richmond, Rhode Island.

Textile mills sprang up in the area, and in 1815 the New London Turnpike opened right past the inn. By 1835, the New London Turnpike—now Route 3—connected Providence and New London. The village thrived, and for many years an inn once known as Dawley Tavern continued as a stagecoach stop.

By the twentieth century, industry began to founder along the Wood River. That, however, allowed Hopkinton and Wyoming to retain much of their historic nineteenth-century character. Today the Dawley Tavern is called the Stagecoach House Inn.

STOPS ON THE UNDERGROUND RAILROAD

THE UNDERGROUND RAILROAD WAS A NETWORK OF PEOPLE WHO HID fugitives from slavery in their homes during the day and moved them north by night to free states, Canada or England. Escaped slaves often traveled north on coastal vessels, where they could blend in with the many black sailors. Or they could take a real railroad with forged papers or in disguise or both.

People who helped African Americans escape used railroad terminology as a code to describe their activities in case someone overheard their conversation. Those who moved the refugees were called conductors. The buildings that sheltered them were stations, and the people who fed and clothed them until they could move on were stationmasters.

But conductors on the Underground Railroad risked a thousand dollar fine and six months in jail if they got caught helping anyone escaping slavery. So they operated in strict secrecy.

The Underground Railroad helped one hundred thousand people escape slavery between 1810 and 1860, according to one estimate.

1. 20 HIGH STREET, ASHAWAY, RHODE ISLAND

Rhode Island had both a sizable number of Quakers who supported abolition as well the densest African American population in New England. As a result, the tiny state had a busy Underground Railroad in the years before the Civil War. Free blacks and wealthy industrialists both conducted fugitives north to safety.

Jacob Babcock's house in the village of Ashaway served as the first Rhode Island stop on the Underground Railroad. Babcock, a prosperous mill owner, believed strongly in temperance and in abolition. He hid fugitive slaves in tunnels under his house, then brought them to a Mr. Foster farther north.

Babcock enlisted his sixteen-year-old nephew, Isaac Cundall, to take the escapees in a wagon to Mr. Foster. Six decades later, Cundall recounted to the *Providence Journal* about one close call.

In March 1858, Uncle Jacob told him he had to transport a woman fugitive in broad daylight. The sheriff and the slave owner were looking for her in the neighborhood, and Jacob knew the sheriff would get a warrant to search his house. So Isaac asked his cousin Sarah Babcock to take a ride with him. She put on a big hat, a veil, and a heavy shawl, and they took off in a wagon.

Sure enough, they ran into the sheriff. They made sure to chat with him, making it clear he was talking to Miss Babcock. Then they rode on for a mile and turned around. They saw the sheriff and told him it was so cold they were headed back to get warmer clothes.

Back at Uncle Jacob's house the fugitive woman put on Sarah's clothes plus another wrap, and they easily passed by the sheriff. Isaac took her to a minister's house, and she safely made it to the next station.

Jacob Babcock's house still stands, though it is privately owned.

2. NATHAN AND MARY JOHNSON PROPERTIES, NEW BEDFORD, MASSACHUSETTS

Quakers Nathan and Mary Johnson harbored an escaped slave named Frederick Bailey in 1838 at their home on Seventh Street. Bailey changed his name to Douglass and became a world-famous abolitionist. But he wasn't the only one the Johnsons helped. According to Douglass, helping fugitives was routine for them.

Nathan and Mary Johnson were successful free blacks who owned several businesses and became civic leaders. Nathan, a pharmacist, was elected president of the 1847 National Convention of Colored People.

As many as seven hundred fugitives from slavery lived in New Bedford at any one time before the Civil War. African Americans came to New Bedford because they could get jobs in the city's whaling and maritime industries. By 1853, New Bedford had the highest population of African Americans in the Northeast.

The Johnson properties, which include a residence and a Quaker meeting house, are owned by the New Bedford Historical Society.

3. AUSTIN F. WILLIAMS HOUSE, FARMINGTON, CONNECTICUT

Austin F. Williams played a central role in a major drama before the Civil War: The *Amistad* Affair.

In the *Amistad* case, a group of slaves on board the sailing vessel *Amistad* freed themselves and killed the ship's captain in 1839.

They were subsequently brought to America and arrested. Their case resulted in acquittal on the ground that they acted in self-defense, an important victory for abolitionists.

Following the trial, Williams, a conductor on the Underground Railroad, built a house on his Farmington property. The freed Africans stayed there before returning to Sierra Leone in 1842. Today the Austin F. Williams House and Carriage House on Main Street is a private residence.

4. ROKEBY, FERRISBURGH, VERMONT

Rokeby was the home of Rowland T. Robinson, a stationmaster on the Underground Railroad. Robinson wrote extensively about how the Railroad worked, and historians view his correspondence as an important archive.

Rowland inherited the big old farmhouse from his parents, who raised Merino sheep. A devout Quaker, he made abolition the cause of his life. Not only did he shelter fugitives, he negotiated freedom papers with slave-holders and found jobs for freedmen.

Today Rokeby is a historic farm property and museum that includes a 1780s farmstead, eight agricultural outbuildings, and hiking trails. It's located on Route 7 in Ferrisburgh.

5. THE JAMES WOOD FARM, LEBANON, NEW HAMPSHIRE

Like Rowland Robinson, James Wood was a prosperous farmer and a Quaker abolitioinist who lived in northern New England. His eight-hundred-acre farm served as a stop on the Underground Railroad.

Not much was known about Wood's work as a conductor for the Underground Railroad. But then his journal was discovered in a New Hampshire antique shop, and it contained a line about helping a slave.

On June 1, 1862, Wood noted: "A fugitive slave? come here abt 10 o'clock this eve to stay all night. I fixed him a bed in wool room."

There is little additional information about the fugitives helped by Wood. Historians say the slight mention suggests that Wood did not consider the event to be particularly unusual, and he probably helped others passing through.

The Wood farm, on the Croydon Turnpike just before the East Plainfield town line, is not open to the public.

6. ABYSSINIAN MEETING HOUSE, PORTLAND, MAINE

Portland became a northern hub of the Underground Railroad because it was so easy to get to by rail and sea. The city's six hundred or so free blacks clustered in the Munjoy Hill neighborhood, and they mostly worked as mariners, on the waterfront, or on the railroads.

In the 1820s, Portland's African Americans got fed up with shabby treatment by the Second Congregational Church. They formed their own church, the Abyssinian Religious Society, in 1828. Then they started building the Abyssinian Congregational Church, a wood-frame building on a high brick foundation on Newbury Street.

The meeting house hosted a school for black children, church suppers, concerts, and, of course, religious services. Abolitionists Frederick Douglass and William Lloyd Garrison both spoke from the Abyssinian's pulpit.

After the Fugitive Slave Act passed in 1850, the church's members organized escape routes for fugitives to England and Canada. They found safe houses for escaped slaves, fed them, and transported them. Reuben Ruby, a church founder and hack driver, conducted slaves to freedom in his coach.

Portland's Underground Railroad operated in complete secrecy, and the only written record of a successful escape appeared in the memoirs of a stationmaster's descendant. The Abyssinian's Rev. Amos Noé Freeman hid a fugitive from slavery in the meeting house.

The 1866 Portland fire destroyed the neighborhood, but church members saved the meeting house by putting wet blankets on the roof. The Abyssinian Meeting House fell into disuse, though, and a landlord converted it to a tenement house. The city of Portland seized it for back taxes and then in 1998 sold it to the Committee to Restore the Abyssinian for a small fee.

The committee is still trying to restore the Abyssinian, which stands at 75 Newbury Street.

HISTORIC
TRAIN RIDES

THE NICE THING ABOUT TAKING A HISTORIC TRAIN RIDE in New England is that there's no danger of running off the road while taking in Mother Nature's handiwork.

New England has more than two dozen so-called heritage railways, museums on wheels that re-create the experience of train travel during the golden age of passenger rail.

Sometimes heritage railways are run as profitable tourist attractions, but more often they're maintained by enthusiastic volunteers. Lovers of historic railroads restore and maintain vintage steam and diesel locomotives, passenger coaches, track, stations, and other infrastructure.

1. ESSEX STEAM TRAIN AND RIVERBOAT RIDE

Back in the day, travelers often journeyed by train to a steamboat landing, then continued on their way by water. Alas, only one steam-train-and-steamboat trip remains in the United States: in Essex, Connecticut.

The Essex Steam Train & Riverboat ride is part of the Valley Railroad. For a while it operated as a branch line of the New Haven Railroad. By 1961 the New Haven Line declared bankruptcy and all service finally stopped in 1968. The New Haven Railroad became the Penn Central (later Amtrak), and Penn Central gave the Valley track to the state of Connecticut, which leased it to a group of volunteers.

The Essex Steam Train & Riverboat ride runs from May through October. It begins at the Essex Station, then runs for a twelve-mile round trip through the quintessential New England towns and unspoiled parts of the Connecticut River Valley. Then comes an hour-long riverboat ride along the scenic Connecticut River on the *Becky Thatcher*.

2. CAPE COD CENTRAL RAILROAD

The Cape Cod Central Railroad offers a historic train ride along twenty-seven miles of track from Hyannis to Buzzards Bay.

It's a remnant of the Cape's first train, built in the mid-nineteenth century. The railroad ran from Wareham, Massachusetts, to Sandwich, home of Cape Cod's famous glassmaker, the Boston and Sandwich Glass Co. The train carried freight between the glass company and Boston.

Eventually the railroad extended to carry passengers between southeastern Massachusetts and fourteen of the Cape's fifteen towns.

When the Cape Cod Canal opened in 1914, it turned the peninsula into an island. Trains had to cross the waterway over drawbridges. But the canal's swift current made it dangerous for boats to wait for the drawbridges to open and close. Canal traffic dwindled and the privately owned canal company failed. The government took over the Cape Cod Canal, and in 1935, the drawbridge problem was solved with the Buzzards Bay vertical train lift.

After a series of mergers, the New York, New Haven, and Hartford Railroad bought the Cape trains in 1893. For the next sixty-six years, passenger service between the mainland and Cape Cod continued under such names as the Night Cape Codder, the Neptune, the Islander, and the Flying Dude. Since 1959, various owners have offered sporadic passenger rail service to the Cape during the summer.

Today the MBTA runs passenger trains to Cape Cod on summer weekends, and the Cape Cod Central Railroad runs heritage rides during the spring, summer, and fall—and sometimes on holidays.

The Shoreland Excursion takes passengers on a two-hour historic train ride past salt marshes, sand dunes, and cranberry bogs, then along the canal. In Bourne, the Gray Gables Station, built in 1892 for Grover Cleveland's personal use, now serves as a rail museum.

3. GREEN MOUNTAIN FLYER

During five weeks of New England's glorious foliage season, the Green Mountain Flyer runs five days a week in Vermont from Burlington and Chester.

The Green Mountain Railroad, one of New England's oldest heritage railroads, formed in early 1964 by a steam-locomotive enthusiast, F. Nelson Blount. He obtained fifty-two miles of track between Bellows Falls and Rutland from the State of Vermont. Blount also ran a museum of steam locomotives, called Steamtown, USA, in North Walpole, New Hampshire.

Blount died in an airplane crash in 1967, but his dream lived on. Today, the Green Mountain Railroad is part of the 350-mile Vermont Rail System. The Green Mountain Flyer, named after the fastest train on the Rutland Railroad, runs for thirteen miles between Bellows Falls and Chester. In the fall, a foliage excursion takes passengers another fourteen miles to Ludlow.

4. NEWPORT AND NARRAGANSETT BAY RAILROAD

The Newport and Narragansett Bay Railroad runs historic train rides on Aquidneck Island, offering gorgeous views of the bay, colonial homes, and the decommissioned USS *Saratoga* in the Newport Naval Station.

The railroad once belonged to the Old Colony Railroad, a major system running from Boston to southeastern Massachusetts, Rhode Island, Lowell, and Cape Cod. In 1976, then-owner Conrail sold the railroad to the state, which then leased it to the volunteers who run the Old Colony and Newport Scenic Railway.

The new railway formed in 2014 when the for-profit Newport Dinner Train and the nonprofit Old Colony and Newport Scenic Railway merged. It runs between the Melville Marina section of Portsmouth and downtown Newport.

Today, Rhode Island's only heritage railroad also offers dining and themed excursions.

5. DOWNEAST SCENIC RAILROAD

Antique rail cars take passengers on a ninety-minute trip through thirteen miles of Maine wetlands and woods. Passengers may see fox, bald eagles, bear, osprey, and moose. More than a century ago, wealthy rusticators saw those same sights when they took the train to their summer cottages in Bar Harbor.

The Downeast Scenic Railroad started as the Calais Branch line, built in 1884 as the Maine Shore Line Railroad. Later the Maine Central Railroad Co. bought the line, but closed in 1985. It stayed closed for thirty years.

Then five local businessmen formed the Downeast Rail Heritage Trust in 2005. The next year they leased thirty miles of track from the State of Maine. Volunteers restored the rails, an engine, passenger cars, and caboose. Service restarted on July 24, 2010, when invited guests took a historic train ride along five miles of track from Ellsworth.

6. WINNIPESAUKEE SCENIC RAILROAD

The Winnipesaukee Scenic Railroad offers a one- and a two-hour historic train ride in restored coaches along the western shore of New Hampshire's biggest lake. Passengers can board at the station in Meredith, or at the Weirs Beach Station on the historic boardwalk. During the train ride they never lose sight of Lake Winnipesaukee.

The railroad once belonged to the Boston & Maine Railroad and brought tourists to lakeside resorts from the Gilded Age to the 1950s. Today, the Winnipesaukee Scenic Railroad still goes through the front yards of gracious old summer homes. Passengers can also take a forty-mile Fall Foliage Special.

MILITARY ROUTES

WAR HAS LEFT ITS MARK ON NEW ENGLAND, AS IT HAS EVERYWHERE. Indian warriors, European soldiers, and colonial revolutionaries once marched down roads we take now to get to work or pick up groceries.

1. MOHAWK TRAIL

The Mohawk Trail, one of the most famous Indian trails, today is one of the most beautiful drives in Massachusetts. Originally a trade route, it connected the Atlantic Indian tribes with the Iroquois tribes in Upstate New York and Canada.

The trail became a warpath when Mohawk war parties traveled it to destroy Pocumtuck settlements in western Massachusetts. Metacomet, or King Philip, took the Mohawk trail in 1676 to try to enlist the Mohawks in his war against the Europeans (he failed). Benedict Arnold had better luck on the Mohawk Trail, which he took to capture Fort Ticonderoga during the American Revolution.

In 1914, the Massachusetts General Court declared the sixty-three-mile Mohawk Trail a scenic tourist route—the first in the United States.

Today Routes 2 and 2A follow the Mohawk Trail in Massachusetts from Athol to Williamstown. Boosters claim 100 scenic and culture attractions, including the Hail to the Sunrise statue, the Bridge of Flowers, and pre-revolutionary homes in Old Deerfield.

Highway markers designate the trail.

2. CROWN POINT ROAD

Lord Jeffery Amherst had ordered the Crown Point Road built during the French and Indian War after the British captured Fort Ticonderoga.

Amherst was determined to keep control of the southern end of Lake Champlain, so he commanded his troops to build Fort Crown Point at a narrows on the lake. He also ordered a road to be built from Crown Point through Vermont to the Fort at Number 4, now an open air museum in Charlestown, New Hampshire.

Colonel John Stark and his colonial militia began work on the Crown Point Road in 1759. They cut down trees and removed stumps, and they built bridges, causeways, and corduroy sections along swampland.

Colonial troops carried supplies along the Crown Point Road to the British army at Crown Point during the French and Indian War. During the American Revolution, they brought supplies and reinforcements to Fort Ticonderoga.

Between the wars, settlers moved west along the Crown Point military route, but it fell into disuse when better roads were built. Starting in the nineteenth century, the route was commemorated with markers. In New Hampshire, a stone tablet a half-mile north of the Cheshire Bridge over the Connecticut River marks the site of the ferry and block house.

Some sections of the road are marked trails, some are undiscernible forest paths, and a few stretches are used as town roads.

3. THE ROAD FROM KEENE TO THE SIEGE OF BOSTON

Late on the evening of April 19 or early the next day, an anonymous messenger brought word of the Battles of Lexington and Concord to Keene, New Hampshire. His news created an uproar in the town. Keene's militia gathered in front of the meeting house, where they were told to gather their own provisions on the way to Concord.

The next morning at sunrise, twenty-nine men from Keene and a few from the nearby town of Gilsum gathered at Wyman's Tavern. The tavern owner, Captain Isaac Wyman, led them on a march down what is now Baker Street (then the Boston Road). They turned right on Marlborough Street, and then headed toward Marlborough on what is now Route 101.

From Marlborough, they probably followed most of what is now Route 124 to New Ipswich, then took 123A across the border to Lunenberg,

Massachusetts. From there they probably marched down what is now Route 2A to Concord. The action had ended by the time they arrived, so they marched on to Medford, Massachusetts. They took the historic Battle Road, where the patriot militia had just skirmished with the British.

When they arrived in Medford, they fell under the command of General John Stark, and fought weeks later at the Battle of Bunker Hill.

4. KENNEBEC TRAIL

Benedict Arnold, before he decided to switch sides, led a force of eleven hundred Continental Army regulars from Massachusetts to Quebec City in the early days of the American Revolution. He hoped to bottle up the British in Canada and prevent an invasion of New England from the north.

The Arnold Expedition was a disaster. Arnold's men traveled three hundred fifty miles—twice as far as they planned—through poorly charted wilderness in what is now Maine. By the time Arnold reached the French settlements above the St. Lawrence River, he had only six hundred starving men. The siege of Quebec failed.

Arnold's transport ships landed on Swan Island in what was once Perkins Township. They traveled through what are now Dresden and Pittston, where Arnold and his men stayed on property belonging to Major Reuben Colburn. The house now has a street address, 33 Arnold Rd., and is the headquarters of the Arnold Expedition Historical Society. The group has been trying to restore Arnold's trail.

Parts of the route they took today make up US 201 from Augusta to the Canadian border. Two markers in Skowhegan show where they marched: at the picnic area on Rte. 2 heading to Canaan and another on the island in town.

Past the Norridgewock Falls, Arnold's men reached a section of the Dead River they couldn't navigate. They had to portage their bateaux over twelve miles of "The Great Carrying Place," a route the Arnold Historical Society has restored as a hiking trail.

5. ROAD TO THE BATTLE OF RIDGEFIELD

On April 25, 1777, twenty-six ships carrying two thousand British troops landed at Cedar Point in Westport, Connecticut.

Their leader, British commander and New York governor William Tryon, planned to destroy rebel military supplies twenty miles north in Danbury.

What he succeeded at was hardening Connecticut hearts against the British after the army cut a swath of destruction through the countryside.

The British marched north on what is now Route 58, ravaging the land. They set fire to provisions in the streets on their way to the supply depot in Danbury. Along a stretch of South Street just beyond Coal Pit Hill Road they destroyed an enormous cache of supplies, including thousands of shoes, tents, and bushels of grain. Whenever they found barrels of rum, they drank them.

Generals David Wooster and Benedict Arnold responded with seven hundred militiamen and Continental Army soldiers. The British got wind the local militia was coming and retreated south from Danbury along Route 33, burning down houses along the way.

On April 27, Benedict Arnold barricaded the center of Ridgefield. He received reinforcements from Colonel Henry Ludington. Ludington's sixteen-year-old daughter Sybil had raised the militia during a horseback ride twice as long as Paul Revere's. The British drove the patriots off in a running battle down Main Street. Eight Americans and sixteen British were killed during the battle. Near the site of a barricade stands a stone tablet marking their graves.

Wooster was mortally wounded at the intersection of Route 1 and Patriots Bank. A small Masonic stone memorial marks the place where he fell.

The British retreated to Westport and never tried another inland raid again.

6. THE WASHINGTON ROCHAMBEAU NATIONAL HISTORIC TRAIL

In 1780, General Jean-Baptiste Donatien de Vimeur, Comte de Rochambeau, was put in charge of the Expédition Particulière. It was a French land force sent to America to support the Continental Army under Washington.

Rochambeau arrived in Newport, Rhode Island, in July 1780 with an impressive fleet and nearly seven thousand French regulars.

Then he sat in Newport for the next year.

Finally, in May 1781, Rochambeau agreed to meet with Washington in Wethersfield, Connecticut, to map out the plan for the war. Rochambeau and his army finally left Newport on June 19, 1781 for the fateful siege of Yorktown, Virginia.

The French troops marched from their campground in Newport between Broad and Plane streets. They then headed north through Middletown, Portsmouth, Bristol, and Providence, then west through Coventry to Connecticut.

The trail passes the Joy Homestead in Cranston, where on June 18, 1781 Job Joy and his family watched Rochambeau lead his army down the road.

Today, the Washington Rochambeau National Historic Trail runs over 680 miles of land and water from Massachusetts to Washington, D.C. In 2009, it became the newest of the nineteen National Historic Trails in the National Park Service system.

YE OLDE
NEW ENGLAND

NEW ENGLAND'S ANTIQUITY CAN COME AS A SURPRISE to visitors who've never seen floors made with wide boards from the King's masts, or dined in a restaurant that was old when George Washington stopped in for a brew.

Europeans settled New England earlier than you might think. Though schoolbooks lavish attention on the Jamestown colony in Virginia and Plymouth Plantation, those settlers arrived later than fishermen from western European. Basque, French, Portuguese, and English fishermen spent summers along the northern New England coast in the late fifteenth century

French colonists actually tried to settle Maine in 1604 on the Island of St. Croix along the Canadian border. The Popham Colony, also in Maine, celebrated the first Thanksgiving in 1607.

OLDEST CONTINUOUSLY OPERATIONAL RESTAURANTS

THE OLDEST RESTAURANTS IN NEW ENGLAND INCLUDE TAVERNS THAT served hungry travelers on horseback and a diner that fed mill workers after their shifts ended. As is always the case with the word "oldest," the choice of a state's oldest restaurant is open to debate.

"Continuosly operating," seemed like a good criteria for winnowing out pretenders. In Maine, for example, the Palace Diner in Biddeford opened sixty years after the Cliff House in Ogunquit. But the Cliff House stopped serving meals for a long stretch. On the other hand, the White Horse Tavern in Newport, Rhode Island, turned into a boardinghouse for a while; but still it operated as a restaurant for its boarders, so it makes the list.

1. WHITE HORSE TAVERN, NEWPORT, RHODE ISLAND

The White Horse certainly embodies New England tavern-ness. But the name "White Horse Tavern" is relatively new, dating to 1730, nearly eighty years after Francis Brinley built the first building on the site in 1652.

Today the White Horse Tavern is not only a national landmark but the oldest tavern in America—as well as one of the oldest restaurants in New England.

William Mayes bought the property in 1673, added to the building, and opened a tavern. The Rhode Island General Assembly used it as a meeting place, and so did the court and the city government. Mayes's son William, a pirate, ran the tavern into the eighteenth century.

Loyalists and British troops stayed at the White Horse while they occupied Newport. For many years it declined into a boarding house until a benefactor donated money to the Preservation Society of Newport to restore the building. It reopened in 1953 as a tavern and restaurant.

Today the White Horse dining room serves up local seafood and produce to diners who follow its business-casual dress code.

2. GRISWOLD INN, ESSEX, CONNECTICUT

The Griswold Inn, known as "The Gris," has fed people since it first opened in 1776. Three brothers who were not Griswolds opened the tavern, naming it after the Griswold family (good customers, perhaps?) who lived nearby.

The Griswold is surrounded by the historic hamlet of Essex on the banks of the Connecticut River. The dark wood walls and exquisite marine paintings are exactly what you'd expect from a historic inn that catered to sailors since the American Revolution.

Only six families have ever run it. The British captured The Gris during the War of 1812 and used it for headquarters. It stayed open during Prohibition with entertainment for yachtsmen.

The Griswold Inn entered popular culture over the past fifty years. It was mentioned in an episode of *Mad Men* as a romantic getaway, and the soap opera *Dark Shadows* filmed the exterior as the Collinsport Inn.

3. HANCOCK INN, HANCOCK, NEW HAMPSHIRE

The Hancock Inn became a favorite of U.S. president and New Hampshire native Franklin Pierce when a friend of his bought it in 1830. It's been run continuously as an inn since it opened in 1789.

The tavern and dining room are especially cozy in the winter, heated by a fireplace and wood-burning stove. The Town of Hancock itself was once partly owned by John Hancock, and today nearly every building on Main Street is on the National Register of Historic Places. A Paul Revere bell chimes on the hour from Hancock's meeting house.

4. DORSET INN, DORSET, VERMONT

The Dorset Inn sits on the spine of the Green Mountains near three ski resorts. Well before skiing became popular, its restaurant started serving food around 1796. The first chef raised his own chickens, cows, and vegetables, and bought milk from the farmer next door. Today the Dorset Inn serves bistro food with as many local ingredients as possible.

Ye Olde Tavern in nearby Manchester opened in 1790 and beat out the Dorset Inn as the oldest restaurant in Vermont. However it lost its liquor license—and a "continuously operating" claim—in 1904, not reopening until 1924.

5. UNION OYSTER HOUSE, BOSTON, MASSACHUSETTS

When the Union Oyster House first opened its doors as the Atwood & Bacon Oyster House in 1826, the building already had been around for a century. It was likely built in 1704, and Hopestill Capen's dress goods business first occupied it. In 1771, Isaiah Thomas published *The Massachusetts Spy* from the second floor.

The second floor was also home to the exiled French king Louis Philippe in 1796. Daniel Webster used to consume six plates of oysters and a tumbler of brandy for lunch at the oyster house, and Sen. John F. Kennedy liked to read his Sunday paper there. Today the highly atmospheric Union Oyster House serves traditional New England fare.

6. PALACE DINER, BIDDEFORD, MAINE

Right in the center of Biddeford's Historic District is the Palace Diner, serving up comfort food for breakfast and lunch since 1926.

The Pollard Co. built the Palace Diner in Lowell, Massachusetts, and today it's one of two Pollard cars left in the United States (the other is in Bristol, New Hampshire).

You might have to hunt for the Palace Diner. At 18 Franklin Street it's hidden behind a large brick building that faces Main Street. It belongs to the historic district, a collection of brick nineteenth- and twentieth-century commercial buildings. Biddeford began its rise as a textile-mill city in the 1840s, and the historic district used to function as the city's central business district.

As a postscript, the Cliff House in Ogunquit can also contend for oldest restaurant, but it hasn't been continuously operated since it opened in 1862.

OLDEST HOUSES

To make a claim for the oldest houses in New England is also to invite controversy. The region has plenty of very old houses, but few of them survive intact. Some were built over several years, which raises the question of how to date them: From the start of construction or from completion?

Many old houses have been remodeled over the years. One in Rhode Island was burned during King Philip's War, while another in Maine was restored and modernized by a wealthy pop star.

A survey of the field of New England's oldest houses results in at least six with valid claims to be the oldest in their state. Of course, some may beg to differ.

1. HENRY WHITFIELD HOUSE, GUILFORD, CONNECTICUT

The Henry Whitfield House is believed to be the oldest house in Connecticut and the oldest stone house in New England. On Old Whitfield Street, it was built for Puritan minister Henry Whitfield, a descendant of Geoffrey Chaucer. The walls are nearly two feet thick, held together with mortar made of yellow clay and crushed oyster shells.

The first settlers of Guilford began building the home in September 1639, shortly after they arrived. They started too late in the year, and all they finished was the great hall and north fireplace. They completed the house in the summer of 1640 with the help of the Menunkatuck Indians.

Henry Whitfield, his wife Dorothy Shaeffe Whitfield, and their nine children moved into the house in 1640. But after all that work, he returned to England in 1650. Ten years later, Roman Catholics used the house as a chapel, no doubt to the dismay of the local Puritans.

The house was remodeled in 1868 and opened to the public in 1899 as Connecticut's first museum.

2. FAIRBANKS HOUSE, DEDHAM, MASSACHUSETTS

The Fairbanks House is said to be the oldest timber-framed house in North America. It was built for Jonathan and Grace Fairbanks, Puritans from Yorkshire, England, who had six children. Tree ring dating confirms the house was built in the late 1630s and early 1640s. English carpenters from East Anglia built the house.

The house stayed in the Fairbanks family through eight generations, and the Fairbanks family still owns it. Perhaps that's why the house never had a mortgage on it. One of Jonathan and Grace's descendants, Charles Warren Fairbanks, was Teddy Roosevelt's vice president and had a city in Alaska (Fairbanks) named after him.

What's remarkable about the house, according to Yale professor Abbott Lowell Cummings, is that no other mid-seventeenth century house in New England survived in such "unbelievable unspoiled" condition.

The Fairbanks House, at 511 East Street, is now a historic house museum open seasonally.

3. STEPHEN NORTHUP HOUSE, NORTH KINGSTOWN, RHODE ISLAND

In 1645, Stephen Northup came from England at about the age of fifteen. At the age of thirty he started building his house, now 99 Featherbed Lane.

Most of the original house was probably burned in King Philip's War (1675–1676), along with everything south of Providence. Northup rebuilt the house, possibly with parts from the original building. Additions were made around 1712 and 1850.

Northup was married with six known children and lived until at least 1687. An enterprising fellow, he built the first dam at the home where

Gilbert Stuart later lived. Stuart painted the portrait of George Washington that appears on the dollar bill.

Stephen Northup is also an ancestor of Stephen Douglas, who famously debated Abraham Lincoln and lost to him in the 1860 election for U.S. president.

The Northup House is now a private residence.

4. RICHARD JACKSON HOUSE, PORTSMOUTH, NEW HAMPSHIRE

The Richard Jackson House, the oldest house in New Hampshire, sits on the banks of the Piscataqua River across from the oldest house in Maine. Richard Jackson built it in 1664 in the English style, but Americanized it with an extravagant use of wood.

He was a mariner, farmer, and cooper who outlived his two sons, dying in 1718. The house was divided in 1727 among his daughter-in-law and her children. Five generations of men named Nathaniel Jackson owned and occupied the house from 1727 to 1897.

The fifth Nathaniel Jackson bequeathed the house to his daughter, Mary E. Jackson, and her son, also named Nathaniel. They rented the house to an African American couple, Clarence and Belle Tilley.

Then the house in 1924 was sold to William Sumner Appleton, founder of the Society for the Preservation of New England Antiquities (now Historic New England). Appleton allowed Belle Tilley to continue living in the house. Meanwhile, he restored the property, removing modern modifications and replacing the windows with leaded diamond-paned windows. Appleton's restoration became the basis for Historic New England's preservation philosophy of keeping generations of changes intact.

The house is now a museum.

5. JOHN BRAY HOUSE, KITTERY, MAINE

The John Bray House qualifies as one of Maine's oldest because it was built on the site where wealthy shipwright John Bray first erected a dwelling in 1662. An Englishman from Devon, he chose the most pleasing spot in Kittery Point, one with a panoramic view of Portsmouth Harbor.

The current house, a two-and-a-half story wooden frame building, was probably not built before 1720. Parts of the original house were incorporated into it. It's set on the south side of Pepperell Road (Maine State Route 103).

Daryl Hall of the pop duo Hall & Oates bought the house in 2008 and restored it, saving it from destruction. He later sold it for $1.6 million.

Hall saw an ad in *Antiques and Arts Weekly* that said the house was up for auction. He sent his architect to look at it. Then he sent his assistant to the auction. Hall's money went far enough to buy the house after fifteen minutes of bidding.

Hall restores antique houses as a hobby, and has also restored houses in London and Upstate New York.

6. MOOAR-WRIGHT HOUSE, POWNAL, VERMONT

The oldest house in Vermont is believed to be the enigmatic Mooar-Wright House in Pownal, a town in the far southwest of the state. There is no documentation of its early ownership.

Some date the house to 1750. According to local legend, the house was built on Main Street as a tavern by Charles Wright in the 1760s. Others speculate the house was built by Dutch settlers who thought the land was part of the New York colony.

People sometimes call the house the Defoe-Mooar-Wright House. Some historians believe it was built by John Defoe, imprisoned in 1776 for his Loyalist sympathies. He escaped and fought on the side of the British at the Battle of Bennington. Then he was captured, imprisoned again, and escaped again, this time to Canada.

The people of Pownal remember the Mooar family visiting in the summer during the 1950s. Since then, it's been used as a law office, and one owner tried to renovate it. The Mooar-Wright house, which sits next to the Solomon Wright Library in North Pownal, is not open to the public.

GENERAL STORES

New England's general stores had their heyday between 1820 and 1860, when income was rising and the population was growing. Like the Hope General Store in Maine, they generally stood at crossroads. They were informal—some might say barebones—with wood floors, a hodgepodge of goods along wooden shelves, a cat cuddled up by the stove, and smells of apples, cheese, coffee, and tobacco.

Town life revolved around the general store, where regular customers exchanged gossip and opinions. The storekeeper often doubled as the postmaster and provided a link to the outside world.

Dozens of the old general stores survive in New England, making visitors feel they've entered a Norman Rockwell painting.

In recent years, general stores have experienced something of a revival. The *Wall Street Journal* called them "one part country store, one part concept shop" with a personal take on merchandise.

The exact age of a general store is often hard to determine. Records are sketchy and claims sometimes exaggerated. For example, one general store that dates to 1788—Gray's, in Little Compton, Rhode Island—has an uncertain status. It closed in 2012 when its owner died, but then reopened as an antique shop.

1. OLD COUNTRY STORE AND MUSEUM, MOULTONBOROUGH, NEW HAMPSHIRE

The Old Country Store and Museum in Moultonborough in New Hampshire's Lakes Region may be the oldest general store in the country. The Holden family, which runs the historic store, has records dating to 1781.

Town founder Jonathan Moulton got a deed for the land on which the store stands as a reward for his service in the American Revolution. He sold the land with a barn frame on it to Samuel Burnham in 1777. Burnham sold it two years later to a trader named George Freese.

Now here's the evidence that Freese ran a general store from the building: A fellow named Bradbury Richardson worked for Freese in exchange for goods in 1781. And a map of New Hampshire printed in 1784 shows the store as the only building in that part of Moultonborough. That could lead to the conclusion that Richardson's goods came from the store.

Today the Old Country Store, on the Whittier Highway, is a Lakes Region tourist attraction. A wooden Indian stands guard at the entrance to the store chockablock with bobblehead dolls, coffee mugs, T-shirts, shoes, maple syrup, and the inevitable candles.

2. DAVOLL'S GENERAL STORE, DARTMOUTH, MASSACHUSETTS

Davoll's General Store stands at the mercantile center of the Russells Mills historic district in Dartmouth. Past owners included a series of prominent Dartmouth families named Howland, Russell, Allen, Slocum, and Tucker.

William Howland bought the building in 1792, and opened a general goods shop a year later. After changing hands in the nineteenth century the Davoll family bought it in the next. Wilfred and Virginia Morrison and their daughter Beverly bought Davoll's in 1974, and kept the name. Wilfred told the local newspaper, "We stand around and solve all the problems of the world."

Kim Arruda and Jim Chouinard bought the store in 2016, and then spent a year and a half renovating it. They found boat knees and a felt hat from the nineteenth century inside the walls of the old building. Today they sell penny candy, maple syrup, bread, jewelry, and beach towels from the store, located on Russells Mills Road, right next to the Wild Honey Café.

3. BROWN & HOPKINS COUNTRY STORE, GLOCESTER, RHODE ISLAND

"A Destination for Generations," boasts the owner of the Brown & Hopkins Country Store. She is named neither Brown nor Hopkins, but Elizabeth Yuill, and she bought the store in 2004.

Located on Putnam Pike, which runs through the village of Chepachet in Glocester, the store is crammed with primitive country wares. It also features a penny candy display on a twenty-four-foot pine checkout counter from the nineteenth century.

Timothy Wilmarth built the wooden building, now painted green, as a home and a hattery. It became a general store in 1809 when Ira Evans bought it, and it's been one without interruption ever since.

Mr. Brown and Mr. Hopkins (James and William) gave the store its present name when they bought it in 1921. For years they sold things like brooms, long underwear, rifles, and coffee.

Then in the 1970s, country decorating became the rage and the store went into the business with a vengeance. It still sells reproduction country furniture and accessories, as well as clothing, local foods, a grab-and-go café, and, of course, candles.

4. COLEBROOK GENERAL STORE, COLEBROOK, CONNECTICUT

The Colebrook Store is the oldest continuously operating general store in Connecticut. Founded in 1812, it operated until it closed in 2007. Then in December 2014 it reopened under new management.

The store was owned by Martin and Solomon Rockwell, who belonged to one of Colebrook's founding families. Julius Rockwell became a U.S. senator from Massachusetts in 1854. The Rockwells also built the Colebrook Inn, which now houses town offices and the historical society.

The Colebrook Store changed hands several times. In July 2007, the owner put out a sign that said, "closed for vacation." She never reopened.

Then in 2003, the Colebrook Preservation Society bought the building for eighty-five-thousand dollars. Five years later, Jodi Marinelli signed a lease on the building and moved with her family into the second floor above the store. Today the store serves breakfast and lunch, and sells groceries, candy, baked goods, and knick-knacks.

5. DORSET UNION STORE, DORSET, VERMONT

On the outside, the Dorset Union Store looks the same as it did in 1816, the year it opened. And it still has the same bell above the door that announces customers, the way it did two centuries ago.

The store presides over Dorset Green in the center of the town, which overlooks the Taconic Mountains. Not surprisingly, the Dorset Union store belongs to the Dorset Historic District, notable for its uniform white clapboard buildings. Some of the sidewalks are made of marble from the nearby quarries.

During a hiatus from 1955 to 2007, the store was called Peltiers, but new owners restored the original name. They also expanded the wine room and added a bakery and deli. You can buy fresh produce as well as Vermont products at the store, or grab a sandwich and eat outside at a picnic table on the green.

6. HOPE GENERAL STORE, HOPE, MAINE

At the Hope General Store you can get much of what you need and learn most of what's going on in the small farming community of Hope, Maine.

The store sits at the crossroads at the center of town, just outside of Camden. There's a blacksmith across the street and a carpenter next door. Built in 1832, it's been a Grange hall, an antique store, and a post office.

The store closed in the late 1990s, but a new owner brought it back to life. It changed hands in 2014, but kept its small-town feel. An updated menu features sandwiches made with brie and caramelized onion, and the beverage selection runs from champagne to Pabst Blue Ribbon beer. Also for sale: the requisite penny candy, maple syrup, candles, and local honey.

COLONIAL HOMES PHOTOGRAPHED BY WALLACE NUTTING

WALLACE NUTTING, A PEEVISH MINISTER, MADE A FORTUNE IN FASHION, a fashion called the Colonial Revival. People caught up in the craze began to preserve old houses and collect antiques. They saved countless old buildings from the wrecking ball and turned them into house museums.

The Colonial Revival started sometime in the nineteenth century, when Americans began to value old American things and to put them in their homes. It peaked in the 1920s, when the Rockefellers rebuilt colonial Williamsburg in Virginia and Henry Ford restored the Wayside Inn in Sudbury, Massachusetts. The Colonial Revival had a huge impact on architecture through World War II, as many architects looked to the old New England houses for inspiration.

Wallace Nutting had a lot to do with popularizing colonial antiques, homes, and even landscapes. He longed for a simpler time, so he naturally embraced America's past. A nervous breakdown forced him to retire from the pulpit around 1904, when he was still in his early forties. To earn a living, he took to selling photographs of peaceful rural scenes, colonial homes, and period bric-a-brac. The public loved his photographs of cozy hearthside scenes and old home exteriors.

He ultimately sold ten million of them, he estimated.

Before Martha Stewart ever brandished her glue gun, Wallace Nutting created an empire of hand-tinted photographs, books, reproduction furniture, and experiences, all evoking a better, happier time. By 1915, he was earning a thousand dollars a day.

1. ELEAZER ARNOLD HOUSE, LINCOLN, RHODE ISLAND

Before he retired around 1905, Nutting had his final pulpit at the Union Congregational Church in Providence. He hated the city, but he soothed his jangled nerves with bicycle rides in the countryside.

On those bicycle trips, he began to take photographs of birches and blossoms. He then made a deal with a local printer to print platinotypes of landscape photographs he'd taken in Northern New England. Nutting had so much success he opened a studio in New York City, but soon moved to Southbury, Connecticut.

It wasn't until 1919 that he came back to Rhode Island and photographed the Eleazer Arnold House in Lincoln. Wheeler, a tavern owner, built the house in 1693. It's a rare example of a seventeenth century "stone-ender," a house with fieldstone side walls and chimney and wooden end walls.

The Eleazer Arnold House on Great Road was donated to the Society for the Preservation of New England Antiquities (now Historic New England) the year Wallace Nutting took the photograph. The public can visit on weekends year-round.

2. DANA'S HOUSE, WOODSTOCK, VERMONT

As his preaching career wound down, Nutting began vacationing in and near Woodstock. He took many photographs of the surrounding scenery and houses. Some of those appeared in 1922 in the first of his "beautiful" book series: *Vermont Beautiful.*

In 1909, Nutting dressed two women in colonial garb and photographed them in front of the Dana House. Then he hand colored the photograph and put it up for sale. Or he may have hired someone to color the photographs. At one point he employed two hundred colorists to keep up with demand.

The Dana House is now a small house museum.

3. WADSWORTH-LONGFELLOW HOUSE, PORTLAND, MAINE

Elizabeth and Peleg Wadsworth built the house in 1785–1786, after Peleg served as a general in the American Revolution. It was the first brick building in Portland, and is now the oldest building still standing on the Portland Peninsula.

The Wadsworths raised ten children in the house. Their grandson, Henry Wadsworth Longfellow, lived there from the age of eight months until he was thirty-five. Henry's younger sister Anne Longfellow Pierce was the last family member to live in the house. When she died in 1901, she left it to the Maine Historical Society, which has run it as Maine's first house museum since 1902.

In 1914, Wallace Nutting came to Maine and photographed the Wadsworth House, now known as the Wadsworth-Longfellow House.

Located on Congress Street, it opens to the public seasonally.

4. JOSEPH WEBB HOUSE, WETHERSFIELD, CONNECTICUT

In 1914 Wallace Nutting began buying a series of colonial homes he called "The Wallace Nutting Chain of Colonial Picture Houses." They allowed him to create "a proper setting for quaint pictures with attractive background and furnishings." But they also gave him flexibility, because he didn't have to adapt to the schedules and room arrangements of the new house museums coming into vogue.

One of the links in his chain of homes was the Webb House in Wethersfield. Joseph Webb, a successful merchant, built it in 1752. He died at thirty-four, leaving six children and a widow. Diplomat Silas Deane, executor of the estate, later married Webb's widow and built a house next door.

Webb's son Joseph, Jr., inherited the house. In 1774, he hosted Gen. George Washington for five nights while he planned the Siege of Yorktown with the Comte de Rochambeau. The house changed hands several times before Wallace Nutting bought it in 1916 as a sales office, studio, and tourist attraction.

For a time the public flocked to it, paying twenty-five cents for admission. But then World War I and gas rationing interrupted the nostalgia business.

Nutting sold the house to the National Society of the Colonial Dames of America in 1919. Today it belongs to the Webb-Deane-Stevens Museum.

5. WENTWORTH-GARDNER HOUSE, PORTSMOUTH, NEW HAMPSHIRE

The Wentworth-Gardner House in Portsmouth was another link in Wallace Nutting's chain of colonial picture houses.

Mark Wentworth, a member of the powerful Wentworth family, had built the Georgian mansion in 1760 as a wedding gift for his son Thomas. He hired skilled local craftsman to carve woodwork in the style of the English aristocracy. After the Wentworths moved on, a well-to-do Revolutionary War veteran named Richard Gardner lived in it.

By the second half of the nineteenth century, the neighborhood around the house deteriorated into a slum. The owners cut up the house into tenements.

Nutting bought the Wentworth-Gardner house in 1915, removing later additions and returning it to its eighteenth-century appearance. Three years later, he sold it to the Metropolitan Museum of Art, which intended to move it to New York City. But the museum changed its mind, and the Wentworth-Gardner house stayed in Portsmouth as a house museum.

Today it is open to visitors on Mechanic Street.

6. HAZEN-SPILLER HOUSE, HAVERHILL, MASSACHUSETTS

Wallace Nutting was born in the village of Gleasondale, Massachusetts, in 1861. His father died in the Civil War when he was eight months old.

As a boy, a story about his ancestor resonated with him. The forebear was killed in an Indian raid in Groton, Massachusetts, in 1639, and his head stuck on a pole to warn off new settlers.

Nutting returned to Massachusetts again and again. He bought the Cutler-Bartlett House in Newburyport and the Ironmaster's House in Saugus. He moved to Framingham in 1912, and lived there for the next three decades until his death.

In 1917 he bought the Hazen-Spiller House in Haverhill, where Indian raiders burned many wood houses. That may have contributed to Richard Hazen's decision to have the house made of brick. The house is unusually large and has fireplaces at either end of the building.

Nutting dated the house to sometime before 1700, and he speculated the early settlers used it as a garrison to escape Indian raids. But Nutting was more into aesthetics than history, and today historians date the Hazen-Spiller house to 1724—well after the Indian raids stopped in Haverhill.

Wallace Nutting operated the house as a museum in 1918, though it was not one of his more successful properties. Today the house at 8 Groveland Street has private ownership.

HISTORIC VESSELS

Most newcomers came to New England by boat, whether as well-to-do religious dissenters in barques, kidnapped Africans in clipper ships or fishermen in shallops. Once the English got here, they started chopping down trees for the king's masts, and then they kept on building more boats.

Pirates and privateers patrolled the seas in sloops, schooners, and brigantines. Merchant vessels made traders wealthy with cargo from the West Indies and, after the Revolution, China. Whaleships sailed the world bringing home sperm oil and whalebone.

George Washington believed the fledgling nation needed naval power to defend its independence from Britain. He turned out to be right.

1. USS *CONSTITUTION*, BOSTON, MASSACHUSETTS

The USS *Constitution*, better known as Old Ironsides, is one of the most famous boats—if not the most famous boat—in the world.

George Washington named her in 1797, and today she is the world's oldest commissioned naval vessel afloat.

During the War of 1812, Old Ironsides defeated four English warships of the supposedly invincible British Royal Navy. On August 19, 1812, she earned her nickname while quickly winning a one-sided battle with HMS *Guerriere*. *Guerriere* began firing at the Constitution while she was largely out of range near the Nova Scotia coast. As one shot bounced off her hull, a seamen reportedly shouted, "Huzza, her sides are made of iron!"

The U.S. Navy considered Old Ironsides a piece of junk in 1833. Then a Harvard student named Oliver Wendell Holmes found out the plans to use her for target practice.

Holmes, indignant, wrote a poem about her and sent it to the Boston *Daily Advertiser*. A storm of protest saved the old warship. Today you can visit Old Ironsides, now even older, in Boston.

2. CHARLES W. MORGAN, MYSTIC, CONNECTICUT

In the mid-nineteenth century, whaling was the fifth biggest sector of the U.S. economy. The United States had more than three times as many whaling ships as the rest of the world combined. That explains why New Bedford, the center of the whaling industry, was the richest city in the country.

The *Charles W. Morgan*, a whaling ship built in 1841, is the oldest surviving merchant vessel in the United States. She was designed to catch whales and harvest the whale blubber on deck for oil—a messy, smelly business. But whale ship crews shared in the earnings from a voyage, so it was worth it.

From her home port of New Bedford, the *Charles W. Morgan* made thirty-seven voyages, usually lasting about three years each. During her active lifetime, she had a thousand crewmen. Sailors knew her as a lucky ship, having survived Arctic ice, a South Pacific cannibal attack, hurricanes, and Cape Horn roundings.

After harvesting 2,500 whales over eighty years, it took eighty-seven years to fully restore the old vessel. The Mystic Seaport Museum finished restoring the *Charles W. Morgan* in 2013. Today you can walk on her decks at the museum.

3. LEWIS R. FRENCH, ROCKLAND, MAINE

The *Lewis R. French* launched in 1871 from Christmas Cove in South Bristol, Maine. She made the list because she represents two of the most important things the ubiquitous two-masted schooner did: fished and carried cargo.

Coastal schooners like the *Lewis R. French* were the eighteen-wheelers of the sea. They were fast and easy to sail and cheap to make and operate.

Well into the twentieth century they hauled commodities like wood, coal, fertilizer, and grain.

For the first six years of her working life, the *Lewis R. French* carried cargo up and down the Atlantic coast. Then she switched to seining off of Maine.

The *Lewis R. French* went back to hauling freight, for years carrying lumber and coal to her homeport of Vinalhaven, Maine. Then she brought canning supplies to the sardine factories in the Maine towns of Eastport and Lubec—until 1972, and still with no engine.

But the *Lewis R. French* was in bad shape. By that time, the old schooners were being restored and used to carry tourists in waterborne versions of the dude ranch. A new owner brought the *Lewis R. French* to Rockland and repaired her for just that reason.

Since then, the *Lewis R. French* has operated as a windjammer along the Maine coast, carrying tourists around Downeast in the summertime.

4. S.S. *TICONDEROGA*, SHELBURNE, VERMONT

Steamships eventually replaced schooners as freight carriers. The *Ticonderoga*, a side-paddle-wheel lake boat, carried both freight and passengers on Lake Champlain.

Paddle steamers had been around for a century when the *Ticonderoga* was built in 1906 at the Shelburne Shipyard on Lake Champlain. In 1950, the historic boat returned to Shelburne—to the Shelburne Museum, where she sits on dry land.

At two-thirds the length of a football field, she required a crew of twenty-eight to operate. In the early days, she met the evening train from New York in Westport on the lake's east side and steamed to St. Albans. She carried passengers, farm produce, livestock, and dry goods. During both world wars she carried soldiers between Plattsburgh, New York, and Burlington. Later she ran from Burlington west to Port Kent, New York, until her retirement in 1953.

The museum restored her interior, with original furniture and appointments in the dining room, captain's quarters, promenade deck, and barber shop. She is now open to visitors.

5. YACHT *WEATHERLY*, NEWPORT, RHODE ISLAND

During the Gilded Age, the America's Cup yacht race ranked as the premier sporting event in the world. Ever since 1851, when the United States beat Great Britain in a race around the Isle of Wight, the event has drawn international attention. Today the America's Cup is one of the oldest sporting trophies in the world.

Watery Rhode Island for decades has played a major role in the race, with Newport often hosting the Cup. A Bristol shipyard, the Herreshoff Manufacturing Company, designed and built every America's Cup winner from 1893 to 1920.

Some of the America's Cup yachts still survive, including *Weatherly*, a twelve-meter yacht that successfully defended the trophy in 1962. Today she sails out of Newport—from America's Cup Avenue—for the America's Cup Charters.

6. THE *PISCATAQUA*, PORTSMOUTH, NEW HAMPSHIRE

The gundalow, like the two-masted schooner, was a workhorse of the waterways. Homely and homemade, the gundalow was a flat-bottomed scow that carried cargo up and down the rivers and lakes of Maine, New Hampshire, and Vermont.

Gundalows carried produce, rock, and timber to oceangoing schooners. The gundalows could carry a lot, as some of them were seventy feet long and nineteen feet wide. They hauled granite, lumber, and coal as well as farm produce and fish. Then they returned upriver with imported goods like cotton, spices, sugar, molasses, and coffee.

At first, around 1650, gundalows were just simple barges that rode up and down river with the tidal currents. Poles and oars helped them along.

By 1700, gundalows had cabins and single sails for auxiliary power. The gundalow mast could be lowered to make it under bridges.

Gundalows lasted for a long time, into the twentieth century. One of the last, the *Fanny M.*, was launched from Durham, New Hampshire, by Captain Edward H. Adams in 1886. The Smithsonian Institution has drawings of the *Fanny M.*, which inspired the Gundalow Company to build a replica gundalow. Today you can buy tickets to ride in the gundalow *Piscataqua.*

COVERED BRIDGES

Covered bridges have been around in the United States since the late eighteenth century. Uncovered bridges had short lifespans of about fifteen to twenty years. So people started to cover them to protect the timbers underneath from the wind, rain, and snow.

Today covered bridges are more about rural charm than practicality.

Pennsylvania, Ohio, and Indiana each has more covered bridges than any New England state. Pennsylvania, with 219, has the most. But Vermont can claim the densest concentration of the old timbered structures, with 106.

New Hampshire once had close to four hundred covered bridges, but that number has dwindled to fifty-four. Rhode Island is the only New England state with fewer than eight covered bridges, with but one.

1. WEST CORNWALL COVERED BRIDGE, WEST CORNWALL, CONNECTICUT

There are about ninety covered bridges in Connecticut, where Ithiel Town invented the lattice truss in 1820. His design used latticework to carry a bridge's load and allowed unskilled workers to build covered bridges quickly with local materials. Town, by the way, also designed the Wadsworth Athenaeum in Hartford and Trinity Church on the Green in New Haven.

In 1864, the current incarnation of the West Cornwall Covered Bridge was built of red spruce and held together with wooden pegs. It's one of the oldest covered bridges in the country. The key to its longevity was Town's lattice truss design—and some heavy metal later in its life.

As more and more automobiles and trucks crossed the bridge, the West Cornwall Covered Bridge was closed to pedestrian traffic in the

1920s. In 1945, an oil truck weighing twenty tons fell through the bottom of the bridge. The State of Connecticut decided to replace it in 1968, but a local group persuaded the state to save the bridge. Connecticut built a steel support deck that saved the bridge and won a Federal Highway Administration award.

The West Cornwall Covered Bridge wasn't painted red until 1957, which gave it iconic status. It's featured in the opening scenes of the 1967 film *Valley of the Dolls*.

The bridge carries the Sharon-Goshen Turnpike (now Route 128) over the Housatonic River in West Cornwall.

2. BURKEVILLE COVERED BRIDGE, CONWAY, MASSACHUSETTS

Timothy Palmer built Massachusetts' first covered bridge in Amesbury in 1792, though it didn't get its roof until 1810. Timber-covered bridges were revived in the second half of the twentieth century, and a handful of "Massachusetts Modern" covered bridges replaced historic wooden bridges that couldn't be saved.

The Burkeville Covered Bridge is beloved in Conway, where it has been the site of fundraising dinners, memorial services, and weddings (not to mention wedding photos). Built in 1870, it measures 107 feet long and is considered a fine example of state-of-the-art wooden bridge building of the era.

The previous bridge was washed away in a flood. The roof caved in under a heavy load of snow in 1975, but volunteers restored it. In 1985, the Burkeville Covered Bridge was closed for safety reasons, but renovated and opened to vehicles in 2013. It is located on Main Poland Road just off of Route 116 in Conway.

3. SUNDAY RIVER BRIDGE, OR THE ARTISTS' BRIDGE, NEWRY, MAINE

Maine once had 120 covered bridges, but fire, flood, development, and the great freshet of 1896 reduced their number to eight.

The Artist's Bridge is deep in Maine's back country on Sunday River Road in Newry. Some say the name of the bridge reflects its position as Maine's most photographed and painted covered bridge. Others suggest it was *plein air* master painter John Enneking who gave the bridge its name because he was seen so often painting it. Artists may have put more paint on their canvases to illustrate the bridge than was ever put on its sides.

It's also one of the oldest bridges in the country, dating to 1872.

The Artist's Bridge is in Newry, northeast of the Sunday River Ski Resort, next to the crossing of the Sunday River by Sunday River Road.

4. HONEYMOON BRIDGE, JACKSON, NEW HAMPSHIRE

Think a bridge can't be romantic? Think again. The Honeymoon Bridge in Jackson, New Hampshire, got its name because it was such a popular spot for couples to share a kiss—and take photographs of themselves doing so.

The bridge dates to 1876 when Union Army Sgt. Charles Austin Broughton and his son Frank built it to access their dairy farm on Route 16A. Broughton was land agent for the Swift River Lumber Company in Albany, New Hampshire, an avid bear hunter, an accomplished fiddler, and a carpenter. Today the bridge ranks as one of the most photographed—and photogenic—covered bridges in New England.

The Honeymoon Bridge carries Village Street over the Ellis River in Jackson.

5. MOUNT ORNE BRIDGE, LUNENBERG, VERMONT

Dating to at least the 1870s, the Mount Orne Bridge was built in the days when people could make money charging tolls to cross covered bridges.

The Union Bridge Company operated the span as a link between River Road in Lunenberg, Vermont, and Elm Street in Lancaster, New Hampshire. Then a log jam wiped it out in 1908 and the two towns rebuilt it.

The Mount Orne Bridge enjoyed a small spot of notoriety in 1969 when a fully loaded salt truck tried to test its limits and plunged through the bridge deck. The truck was a sight, with its rear-end caught on the bridge and its nose resting on the frozen river below. Rescuers dislodged the truck and scooted it off to the shore before the salt that spilled from the truck could melt through the ice and plunge it into the river.

The Mount Orne Bridge joins Elm Street (New Hampshire Route 135 in South Lancaster) with River Road (Town Highway 1) in Lunenberg.

6. SWAMP MEADOW COVERED BRIDGE, FOSTER, RHODE ISLAND

Rhode Island has but one covered bridge on a public road: The Swamp Meadow Covered Bridge in Foster.

Foster proposed building a covered bridge in honor of Rhode Island's 350th anniversary in 1986. Volunteers began building the bridge in September 1992, using an Ithiel Town lattice truss on top of an existing steel bridge. The bridge was dedicated in May 1993, but vandals burned it four months later. The Foster Town Council immediately voted to rebuild it, and it was dedicated on November 5, 1994.

The Swamp Meadow Covered Bridge, in the rural northwest corner of the state, crosses Hemlock Brook on Central Pike.

SAY YOU WANT A REVOLUTION

GEORGE WASHINGTON KNEW IF THE PATRIOTS HUNG ON LONG ENOUGH, they'd win the War of Independence. He was right. But eight years was a long time to keep the powerful British military at bay, and the signs of that struggle can still be seen all over New England.

Technically, the war started in New England with the shot heard 'round the world, but even before that the incendiary rhetoric and clandestine plotting of the Sons of Liberty gave it a good nudge.

The war affected all of New England, even New Hampshire, which had no military action on its soil. It changed the landscape with forts built up and down the coastline. Some people got rich off of it, some lost all their possessions, and some died in battle or in prisons. Women got involved in the fight for independence, if it meant nursing the sick or dressing up as a boy and enlisting.

REVOLUTIONARY WAR
BATTLEFIELDS

New England during the early years of the war was a hotbed of conflict. The British occupied Boston until the patriots kicked them out. They also occupied Newport, until the patriots and the French kicked them out. They cut a swath of destruction through Connecticut and tried to invade from Canada through Vermont. They even established a beachhead in Maine and attacked the Maine coast.

1. FORT CONSTITUTION,
NEW CASTLE, NEW HAMPSHIRE

A skirmish before the war broke out in New Castle as tensions rose between England and the colonies. In 1774, a handful of British soldiers manned Fort William and Mary, a stone fort at the mouth of the Piscataqua River. The fort guarded access to the harbor and to Kittery, Maine (then part of Massachusetts).

In December of that year, Paul Revere rode to New Hampshire to warn patriots that British troops might seize powder and guns at the fort. John Sullivan, later a Continental Army general, led a raiding party of four hundred men. They stormed Fort William and Mary, subdued all six soldiers inside, and took the gunpowder, muskets, and cannon.

Another future general, Alexander Scammell, famously hauled down the British flag, the first patriot to do so.

The fort, renamed Fort Constitution, now belongs to the State of New Hampshire, and it surrounds the Portsmouth Harbor Lighthouse.

2. MINUTE MAN NATIONAL HISTORIC PARK, MASSACHUSETTS

It doesn't get much better for Revolutionary War buffs than Minute Man National Historic Park in Lexington, Lincoln, and Concord. The 970-acre park memorializes the opening battles of the American Revolution —and then some.

Around 9 p.m. on April 18, 1775, seven hundred British regulars started heading out of Boston on a mission to capture arms and gunpowder. They boarded naval barges that took them to Cambridge, and then, wet and muddy, they marched seventeen miles west to Concord. Paul Revere and others, of course, had warned the local militias, and about eighty of them assembled at Buckman Tavern in Lexington, on the road to Concord.

The British advance guard reached Lexington at sunrise. The militia stood in parade formation on the village green, allowing the British to pass if they chose. Amid some confusion, that famous shot rang out, and the British fired a volley in response. The redcoats then charged the militia men with bayonets. When the smoke cleared, the militia suffered eight dead and nine wounded. Only one British regular was wounded.

The Town of Lexington still owns the Lexington Battle Green, a grassy park with monuments and the graves of seven of the eight felled militiamen. The Buckman Tavern sits on the green, which leads to the five-mile-long Battle Road Trail, part of Minute Man National Park.

The British, joined by more troops, reformed into a column and marched onto Concord along the Battle Road. Four hundred militiamen from Concord and nearby Lincoln heard about the skirmish, and gathered on a hill above the North Bridge in Concord to watch the redcoats as they arrived. British companies fanned out in the town, looking for military supplies for about four hours. Most of the arms and provisions had been hidden.

Then the British set fire to the meeting house, and the militiamen on the hill thought they would torch the whole town. So the militia marched down the hill to challenge the ninety redcoats guarding the bridge. The British fired off a volley but the militiamen shot back. Men were killed on both sides and the redcoats fled.

The British then decided to return to Boston, but two thousand militiamen had streamed into Concord. As the redcoats retreated along the battle road, the militia shot at them from behind trees and stone walls.

Their route is now a restored colonial landscape that includes the Hartwell Tavern. Daniel Chester French's famous Minute Man statue stands by the North Bridge, where the colonial militia shot back at British soldiers in the second battle of the day. The park also includes 'witness houses'—homes that had a vantage point of the action—and Barrett's Farm, which the British had unsuccessfully searched for military supplies. Two visitors' centers and The Wayside, home to Louisa May Alcott and Concord's muster-master Samuel Whitney, complete the park.

3. HUBBARDTON BATTLEFIELD, HUBBARDTON, VERMONT

The Hubbardton Battlefield in Hubbardton is the site of the only Revolutionary War battle fought on Vermont soil. (The Battle of Bennington was actually fought in New York State.) It's also one of the best preserved battlefields in America.

The battle started on July 7, 1777, when British forces caught up with the American rear guard retreating after they withdrew from Fort Ticonderoga. The Americans, led by Seth Warner, fought with discipline and inflicted heavy casualties on the British. Though they lost the battle, they halted the British advance and prevented them from pursuing the main American army.

The battlefield itself and the small museum that explains it lie off the beaten path, but they feature stunning views of the Vermont landscape. It's off Exit 5 on Route 4, between Rutland and New York State.

4. FORT GEORGE, CASTINE, MAINE

The Penobscot Expedition has been pretty much forgotten, and that's probably a good thing. It ended in the worst U.S. naval disaster until Pearl Harbor.

In 1779, the British sent troops to occupy Castine with the hope of establishing a colony called New Ireland. They built a fort and named it after King George III.

Massachusetts, alarmed by the British occupation of its eastern district, sent nineteen warships and twenty-four troop transports to Castine. Though the patriots outnumbered the British, the siege failed and all the ships sank. Paul Revere, in charge of ordnance, ended up court martialed for cowardice and insubordination. He fought the charges and won his acquittal.

Some of Fort George still remains. So does the British canal built in 1779, gravesites of Revolutionary War soldiers, and historic houses, taverns, and churches.

5. BATTLE OF RHODE ISLAND, PORTSMOUTH, RHODE ISLAND

The most famous Rhode Island battle of the American Revolution is called the Battle of Rhode Island or the Battle of Quaker Hill.

By August of 1778, the British had occupied Newport, on Aquidneck Island, for almost two years. That month, Continental Army troops led by General John Sullivan sailed from Tiverton to Portsmouth and set up a siege on Aquidneck. They planned to drive the British soldiers back to Newport and then recapture the town with the help of French naval forces.

But a hurricane prevented the French naval commander, Count d'Estaing, from attacking the six thousand entrenched British soldiers. D'Estaing instead sailed his fleet to Boston for repairs.

Sullivan's forces tried to withdraw, but the British attacked in a valley among three hills.

The 365 acres of the battlefield had no structures on them at the time of the conflict, but since then thirty-six houses and a barn have been built.

At the bottom of the valley runs Barker Brook, halfway between the two armies. It ran red after the battle and thus earned the name Bloody Brook. Today most of the brook is hidden.

The Americans retreated to Tiverton without a single soldier killed. The 1st Rhode Island Regiment, comprised of African American and Native American soldiers, took part in the action.

At the intersection of Route 24 and West Main, the state chapter of the national Association for the Advancement of Colored People put up a marker to commemorate the 1st Rhode Island's role in the battle. And a granite memorial stone on the corner of Union Street and Route 138 marks the Battle of Rhode Island.

Nearby on Butts Hill stands an oval earthen fort called Butts Hill Fort, which wasn't involved in the battle but provided supplies and communications.

6. FORT GRISWOLD, GROTON, CONNECTICUT

The Battle of Groton Heights was a shameful affair, but unlike the Penobscot Expedition, it has not been forgotten.

Connecticut built Fort Griswold in Groton in 1775 to defend the supply depot at the mouth of the Thames River. The fort also protected privateers raiding British ships from the harbor.

In 1781, the traitor Benedict Arnold led a company of British soldiers in a raid on New London directly across the river from Groton. Meanwhile, another British commander, Edmund Eyre, attacked Fort Griswold. The British had the advantage because Arnold had inside information. He knew the angle to attack so the American gun positions couldn't fire effective shots.

The British forces infamously massacred the American soldiers. After Colonel William Ledyard surrendered his sword, they ran him through with it. The surrender left six Americans dead and twenty wounded. The British continued to slaughter eighty-three more men and wounded thirty-six.

Benedict Arnold supposedly watched it all from across the river next to the tomb of Jonathan Brooks. Then he went on to burn New London.

The earthen walls of the fort still stand. The Ebenezer Avery House, which sheltered the wounded after the battle, has been restored, and a museum depicts the era.

REVOLUTIONARY-ERA TAVERNS

THE AMERICAN REVOLUTION PROBABLY WOULDN'T HAVE HAPPENED had it not been for the Revolutionary taverns. Sam Adams famously haunted the taverns of Boston, honing his political skills and making his political connections. His cousin John Adams, who began his day with a tankard of hard cider, called taverns places where "bastards, and legislators, are frequently begotten."

1. PELEG ARNOLD TAVERN, NORTH SMITHFIELD, RHODE ISLAND

At 4 Woonsocket Hill Road in North Smithfield stands an apartment house that was once the center of civic life in Union Village. Richard Arnold built the first part of the house around 1690. His descendent, Peleg Arnold, expanded the building into a popular tavern.

Peleg was a Brown-educated lawyer who served as colonel in the Providence County militia during the American Revolution. In 1775, the village decided to keep one hundred arms at his tavern in case of a British invasion (it never came to North Smithfield). Peleg, an ardent patriot, was also said to be an ardent lover of New England rum. He served in the Continental Congress after the war and as chief justice of Rhode Island's Supreme Court.

The building itself is a large two-and-a-half story structure with two chimneys.

2. KEELER TAVERN, RIDGEFIELD, CONNECTICUT

Timothy Keeler somehow obtained the Keeler Tavern in Ridgefield from his uncle in 1769, more than fifty years after his grandfather built the structure as his family home. In 1772, just before the American Revolution, Keeler and his wife Ester converted the house into a tavern. At first the tavern sign featured a portrait of King George III, but Keeler, a patriot, painted it over with an image of a horseman.

During the Battle of Ridgefield in 1777, British troops fired on the tavern, but a relative of Timothy Keeler convinced them not to destroy it. When asked if he'd thank his relative, Keeler retorted, "No sir! I will not thank a Tory for anything! I would rather thank the Lord for the north wind." A British cannonball that struck a corner post of the building can still be seen.

The Keeler family ran the tavern and inn on the site until 1907. That year, celebrity architect Cass Gilbert bought the inn from Timothy Keeler's granddaughter. Gilbert, who designed the U.S. Supreme Court, turned the old tavern into a summer home. Local preservationists purchased it in 1965 and began running it as a museum the next year.

3. OLD CONSTITUTION HOUSE, WINDSOR, VERMONT

The Old Constitution House, built in 1768, gets credit for giving birth to the Vermont Republic. Elijah West ran the tavern when Vermont representatives met down the Connecticut River in Westminster. They were already fighting for independence from Britain, but in Westminster they declared independence from the four colonies that claimed Vermont—Massachusetts, Connecticut, New Hampshire, and New York.

About six months later, on July 2, 1777, a constitutional convention met at Elijah West's tavern and drafted a constitution.

The meeting went on for several days even as the British were recapturing Fort Ticonderoga seventy-five miles away. On July 8, the convention at West's tavern got word of the British advance and considered adjourning. A violent thunderstorm, though, kept the delegates at the tavern and they finished the Vermont Constitution. They probably finished a few pints of beer as well.

The Vermont Constitution, in effect for fourteen years, was the first to prohibit slavery, establish universal voting rights for all men, and authorize a public school system.

Vermont was admitted to the Union as the fourteenth state in 1791. The tavern stayed open until 1848. After changing hands many times, it's now a tavern museum.

4. WYMAN TAVERN, KEENE, NEW HAMPSHIRE

Captain Isaac Wyman was an old French and Indian War fighter who built the Wyman Tavern in 1762. His family ran the tavern for forty years, right through the American Revolution, and it became a central meeting spot for Keene revolutionaries leading up to the war.

When news arrived of the skirmishes in Concord and Lexington, Keene's twenty-nine minutemen assembled at the tavern. On April 22, 1775, they begin their march south to join the Revolution.

In later years it served as schoolhouse for Salmon P. Chase, Abraham Lincoln's secretary of the Treasury. Today the tavern is a museum operated by the Cheshire County Historical Society.

5. BURNHAM TAVERN, MACHIAS, MAINE

In June of 1775 the *Margaretta*, an armed British schooner, sat in Machias Bay, its guns trained on the frontier town of Machias. The British delivered an ultimatum: The townspeople of Machias had to ship their lumber to Boston to build barracks for British soldiers if they wanted critical supplies. Otherwise, they could go hungry. The *Margaretta's* captain, Lt. James Moore, also threatened an attack.

What to do? The militia men of Machias debated their course of action in Burnham Tavern, built on Main Street in 1770 by Job Burnham. His brother-in-law, Jeremiah O'Brien, urged an attack on the *Margaretta*.

He led a band of forty men, mostly armed with pitchforks and scythes, in the capture of the British vessel. After the battle, the tavern was used as a hospital to tend to the wounded of both sides. Moore died of his wounds there. There is today a chest in the tavern said to be stained with his blood.

The Hannah Weston Chapter of the Daughters of the American Revolution now runs the tavern as a museum in the summer.

6. WARREN TAVERN, BOSTON, MASSACHUSETTS

Sam Adams, John Hancock, Paul Revere, and the rest of the boys in the band plotted revolution in the taverns of Boston, including the Green Dragon. Today there's a very old tavern in Boston called the Green Dragon, but it's not the same building—nor is it in the same place—where patriots brewed independence.

The Warren Tavern, though, operates from the same building and on the same spot it did during the Revolution.

It was one of the first buildings to rise from the ashes of Charlestown, which the British left in ruins after the Battle of Bunker Hill.

Captain Eliphelet Newell built the tavern in 1780 with beams salvaged from the Charlestown Naval Yard. He named it after his friend, Dr. Joseph Warren, who died a hero at Bunker Hill.

Paul Revere frequented the Warren Tavern, and George Washington stopped by once when he was in town visiting a friend. You can still quaff a brew at the Warren Tavern, located at 2 Pleasant Street.

REVOLUTIONARY
WAR FORTS

SCATTERED THROUGHOUT NEW ENGLAND ARE DOZENS OF FORTS FROM the Revolutionary War. Some, like Fort Halifax in Maine, date to the French and Indian wars. Others, like Fort Washington in Massachusetts, rose during the American Revolution.

Revolutionary War forts range from the extensive remains of Mount Independence in Vermont to mere traces of earthworks in Rhode Island. They were all sited along waterways and harbors, making them pleasant summer destinations today.

1. FORT HALIFAX, WINSLOW, MAINE

In 1754, at the outset of the French and Indian War, Major General John Winslow built Fort Halifax where the Sebasticook River flowed into the Kennebec.

Fort Halifax belonged to a series of fortifications along the rivers to prevent the French and Indians from attacking English settlements.

During the War of Independence, American rebels took over Fort Halifax from the British. They decommissioned it, but then Benedict Arnold used it as a way station for his troops on his failed expedition to Quebec.

Today, a single blockhouse survives. The fort had been gradually dismantled to build the Town of Winslow, Maine, which grew up around it. In 1987, the Kennebec River flooded and washed the blockhouse downriver. Searchers found twenty-two original pine timbers, and used them to rebuild the blockhouse.

Today Fort Halifax belongs to a municipal park.

2. FORT WASHINGTON, CAMBRIDGE, MASSACHUSETTS

Fort Washington Park contains the remains of the only surviving fortification built by George Washington during the Siege of Boston. It's also the oldest surviving fortification dating to the American Revolution.

In November 1775, Washington wrote to his trusted officer Joseph Reed, "I have caused two three gun half-moon batteries to be thrown up for occasional use." About fifty men could find protection behind the earthworks.

Washington had quickly realized his soldiers needed training to fend off the professional British forces. He ordered them to build the small batteries so they could learn to build larger fortifications. His soldiers later built a battery at Dorchester Heights in Boston, fortified them with captured cannons, and forced the British to evacuate.

After the war, seven people held the Cambridge property in common. They deeded it to the city in 1857 on the condition that it "shall forever remain open for light, air, and adornment." Today the grassy embankments on Waverly Street are part of a park.

3. FORT WASHINGTON, PORTSMOUTH, NEW HAMPSHIRE

Close to the mouth of the Piscataqua River lies the Portsmouth Naval Shipyard, which has built and repaired ships since the seventeenth century. The shipyard built the *Raleigh*, the first vessel to go into battle flying an American flag.

Clearly the shipyard needed protection from British warships during the Revolution. General John Sullivan, who commanded Portsmouth Harbor, ordered fortifications to augment Fort Constitution in New Castle. So the New Hampshire militias manned Fort McClary at Kittery Point and built an earthworks on Seavey Island in the middle of the river.

Another fort went up on Peirce Island in Portsmouth, named after George Washington. From 1775 to 1778, 180 men were garrisoned at Fort Washington, and it was also used during the War of 1812.

Eventually a bridge connected Peirce Island with the mainland. The Army used Fort Washington during World War II as a recreation center. Now a public park, its breastworks have been completely overgrown.

4. BLACK ROCK FORT, NEW HAVEN, CONNECTICUT

In early 1776, Connecticut built a three-gun log fort and blockhouse on a rocky point in New Haven Harbor. Called Black Rock Fort, it stood on the site of an old fort built around 1657.

In 1777, British general William Tryon and 2,600 troops ravaged Connecticut towns. They captured Black Rock Fort after its nineteen defenders ran out of ammunition. Then, when the British forces withdrew, they burned the fort's barracks.

In 1807, the abandoned fort was rebuilt and named after Connecticut hero Nathan Hale. Then Fort Nathan Hale II was built during the Civil War, but saw no action. Named a historic site in 1921, it grew neglected and overgrown after World War II.

But then came the nation's bicentennial and the reconstruction of Black Rock Fort and Fort Nathan Hale. Today they belong to Fort Hale Park, and they include a drawbridge, moat, ramparts, earthworks, powder magazines, and bunker.

5. FORT CONANICUT, JAMESTOWN, RHODE ISLAND

Benedict Arnold once owned the land on which patriot forces built Fort Conanicut in 1776. Not the traitor Benedict Arnold, but his great-grandfather, a governor of Rhode Island.

Early in the war, patriots put eight eighteen-pound guns on a rocky outcrop of Conanicut Island and called it Dumpling Rock Battery.

It didn't stop the British army from invading Rhode Island. The British captured the battery in late 1776 after landing at Newport, and used it to bottle up the colonial navy in Providence. But then the French fleet drew near, so the British spiked the guns, destroyed the battery, and retreated to Newport.

The French occupied Fort Conanicut intermittently until they left, finally, for the Battle of Yorktown.

In 1790, a tower was built on the site and called Fort Dumpling, until it was abandoned in 1824. Then in 1898 the tower was dynamited to make way for Fort Wetherill. Rhode Island now operates the site as a state park. It sits atop 100-foot granite cliffs, a favorite spot for viewing Tall Ship events and the America's Cup races.

6. MOUNT INDEPENDENCE, ORWELL, VERMONT

Mount Independence is one of the largest and least disturbed Revolutionary sites in America.

Patriot soldiers built the fort on a mountaintop across Lake Champlain from Fort Ticonderoga. They started building in July 1776, a week after the return of the disastrous Arnold Expedition from Canada. Benedict Arnold's failure to capture Quebec stoked fears that the British would invade Vermont from the north.

For a few weeks the patriots called their fort East Point or Rattlesnake Hill. Then on July 28, 1776, Colonel Arthur St. Clair read the Declaration of Independence to the soldiers. The Fort got a new name: Independence.

Eventually the Americans retreated from Fort Independence. British and German troops then occupied the fort until November 1777. After they abandoned it, cattle grazed on land that held unmarked soldiers' graves.

Today Mount Independence has a museum and six miles of hiking trails that pass the remnants of blockhouses, soldiers' huts, and a general hospital. Trails lead to the remains of the fort, the Great Battery, and the Horseshoe Battery.

LOYALIST HOUSES

PICK THE WRONG SIDE DURING THE AMERICAN REVOLUTION AND YOU likely lost your house. Many colonies passed laws that let them confiscate the property of known Loyalists. It made free speech a crime, but it also raised money for the war effort.

Many Loyalists fled to Canada or England. The British government compensated some for their loss, but tried to pressure the United States into giving restitution. Under the Jay Treaty of 1794, the United States agreed to "advise" the states to return Loyalist property. Some families are still trying to get their property back.

Connecticut was more lenient toward the Loyalists than the rest of New England. It waited until four other states had passed confiscation laws, and then local officials dragged their feet in identifying Loyalist properties.

Vermont, on the other hand, was eager to seize Loyalist property in order to pay for the Green Mountain Boys.

1. KNAPP'S TAVERN, GREENWICH, CONNECTICUT

Knapp's Tavern is better known as the Putnam Cottage because Revolutionary War general Israel Putnam was said to have stayed there. Today it's a Revolutionary-era tavern museum, though Putnam probably didn't stay there after all.

Israel Knapp built the structure on the Kings Highway (now Route 1) around 1731. His son, Timothy Knapp, was a convivial innkeeper who turned it into a popular tavern in 1754. Continental Army officers—including George Washington—liked to stay there while traveling to and from New York City. The local Safety Committee checked the tavern and deemed it "safe."

Legend has it that Israel Putnam was shaving at the tavern in 1779 when he saw British cavalry in the mirror. Cut off from his men, Putnam jumped on his horse and galloped down a long flight of stone steps to the foot of a cliff. He escaped when none of the British cavalrymen dared follow him.

It's doubtful, though, that Putnam stayed at Knapp's Tavern. That's because Timothy Knapp was a secret Loyalist who'd been found out and arrested for spying.

Knapp eavesdropped on Continental Army officers while serving up food, drink, and witticisms. His two sons carried messages for him that possibly contained instructions for raiding and burning patriot farms. Their sister—Timothy Knapp's daughter—probably turned her father in. Timothy Knapp was quietly sent to an old copper mine-turned-prison in Simsbury. Some speculate he wasn't hanged because the Safety Committee didn't want to draw attention to the fact they'd okayed a tavern that Washington visited.

Today, Knapp's Tavern is a tavern museum and host to revolutionary re-enactments.

2. LUCAS-JOHNSTON HOUSE, NEWPORT, RHODE ISLAND

Tucked among the many historic homes in Newport is the Lucas-Johnston house. The house was originally owned by Augustus Lucas, who arrived in Newport from France around 1700 and got wealthy buying and selling people as slaves. Lucas's grandson Augustus Johnston gave the house greater renown—or rather notoriety. He accepted a position as Newport's stamp agent in charge of administering the Stamp Act.

It was a bad career move. Rhode Island patriots hanged Johnston in effigy. A mob drove him from his home into hiding until he agreed to quit his job. In July of 1776 Johnston went to prison when he wouldn't swear allegiance to the revolutionary cause.

Then the British captured Newport and freed Johnson. When the British left, Johnston left with them, leaving his house to be confiscated. A good part of Johnston's life was spent arguing for compensation for his losses.

Today the Lucas-Johnston House on Division Street is privately owned.

3. MARK WENTWORTH HOUSE, PORTSMOUTH, NEW HAMPSHIRE

John Wentworth was a popular and able governor of New Hampshire. He and his family lived in a gracious home built in 1763. Then attitudes against the British hardened, and Wentworth's approval rating fell.

When a mob pointed a cannon at his front door in June 1775, John Wentworth and his family fled to safety. He sailed to Boston about a month later and sent his family on to England. On March 17, 1776, the day the British evacuated Boston, he left for Halifax.

The New Hampshire government seized the Wentworth house, but saved the furniture and portraits for the family. In 1797 the house was sold, but thirteen years later Ebenezer Wentworth bought it back. In 1911, Dr. Charles Wentworth and his sister Susan converted the house into a nursing home. It is now Wentworth Senior Living.

4. ISAAC ROYALL HOUSE, MEDFORD, MASSACHUSETTS

Puritan leader John Winthrop built the first house on land along the Mystic River in 1637. Nearly a century later, Isaac Royall bought a second house on the property with 504 acres. Royall, a rum distiller and slave trader from Antigua, brought twenty-seven slaves with him to Massachusetts.

Isaac Royall, Jr., inherited the house on his father's death in 1739. He and his family were Loyalists who decided to cut their losses early in the Revolution. They boarded a ship in Boston as British soldiers marched to the Battles of Lexington and Concord. The Royalls sailed to Nova Scotia and then to England, never to return.

General John Stark made the house his headquarters after Massachusetts confiscated the estate. In 1806, the commonwealth returned it to Isaac Royall's heirs. They then sold it and gave part of the proceeds to Harvard, which used it to found Harvard Law School. A local chapter of the Daughters of the American Revolution bought the house in 1908 and turned it into a Loyalist house museum, now on George Street.

5. WILLIAM PEPPERRELL HOUSE, KITTERY, MAINE

William Pepperrell was a fisherman who had lived and prospered on the Isles of Shoals before moving to the mainland in 1680. He married the daughter of John Bray, a wealthy shipwright, and went into business with his father-in-law. Soon Pepperrell was one of the richest men in New England and owned most of Kittery Point.

His son, William Pepperrell, was born in the house in 1696. He joined his father in business and continued the family's rise by marrying the granddaughter of Samuel Sewall, one of the Salem witch trials judges.

Pepperrell joined the Massachusetts militia and rose to colonel. He organized the expedition that captured the Fortress at Louisbourg in 1745 during the third French and Indian War. King George II awarded him a baronetcy for the deed.

His grandson, born William Pepperrell Sparhawk, inherited the house after changing his name to William Pepperrell. That William Pepperrell remained loyal to the English king on the eve of the American Revolution. He fled to England with his wife, who died of smallpox on the way. Pepperrell died in London.

Massachusetts deemed the house Loyalist property and put it up for auction. In 1790, Colonel Samuel Smallcorn bought the house and Daniel Frisbee bought some of the property. At 94 Pepperrell Road in Kittery, it is privately owned.

6. DEMING TAVERN, ARLINGTON, VERMONT

During the American Revolution, Gamaliel Deming was a Loyalist cattle drover from New Milford, Connecticut. His loyalty to Britain made him unpopular in Connecticut, so he and his wife Rebekah made a fresh start. They left for the Green Mountains of Vermont, where they settled on a knoll over the Battenkill River. There they built a two-story building, which they ran as a tavern in what is now Arlington.

Arlington's Loyalists, for a time, hung out at the Deming Tavern. One ardent Loyalist, Dr. Samuel Adams, recruited a voluntary military company to support General Burgoyne and called it Adams Rangers. When Burgoyne lost the Battle of Saratoga, Adams and his rangers retreated to Quebec.

Gamaliel Deming, however, changed heart and joined the patriot side. His two sons joined the Green Mountain Boys, and he moderated the first Town Meeting in 1780. The Deming Tavern is now a bed and breakfast.

GRAVESITES OF REVOLUTIONARY WAR HEROINES

1. HANNAH BUNCE WATSON, HARTFORD, CONNECTICUT

HANNAH BUNCE WATSON STEPPED IN TO RUN THE PRO-PATRIOT *COURANT* newspaper in Connecticut when her husband died suddenly of smallpox.

The *Courant* played a crucial role in maintaining popular support in New England for the American Revolution. The British had shut down all the newspapers in Boston, and New York's Loyalist newspapers printed nothing but pro-British news. Only the *Courant* reported reliable news to patriots in the Northeast.

Hannah already had plenty to do, with five small fatherless children. She knew little about printing but kept the presses running, even after Loyalists burned down the mill that supplied her paper. Since the British wouldn't export paper to the colonies, Hannah persuaded the Connecticut Legislature to lend her money to rebuild the mill.

For two years Hannah steered the *Courant*, publishing stories about battles, local news, analyses of colonial politics, and criticisms of the British Parliament.

Hannah Bunce Watson died in 1807 and is buried next to her third husband, Barzillai Hudson, in the Old South Burying Ground in Hartford. The name on her gravestone is Hannah Hudson.

2. LUCY KNOX, THOMASTON, MAINE

Of all the revolutionary heroines, Lucy Knox probably sacrificed the most for her husband. She defied her rich Loyalist parents in 1774 to marry Henry Knox, a mere bookseller. After the Battles of Concord and Lexington, she never saw or heard from her family again.

When Henry left for war, Lucy Knox begged him to let her come along. He finally relented, and she stayed with him through the Revolution—during the brutal winter at Valley Forge, through pregnancies, and through the deaths of her children.

Lucy and Henry Knox lived in borrowed or rented homes for the first twenty years of their marriage. Henry served as the second commander of the Continental Army, first Secretary of War, and founder of the U.S. Military Academy at West Point. They finally settled in their own house, Montpelier, in Thomaston, Maine.

Lucy Knox died in 1824 and is buried along with her husband in Elm Grove Cemetery in Thomaston.

3. DEBORAH SAMPSON, SHARON, MASSACHUSETTS

At five-foot-seven, Deborah Sampson was tall enough to pass as a boy, quite an advantage for a girl who wanted to join the Continental Army and fight in the War of Independence.

She had grown up in indentured servitude after her father abandoned her family. In 1782, she enlisted in Uxbridge in the Massachusetts 4th Regiment as Robert Shurtlieff Sampson, her dead brother's name.

Sampson's undercover act held, for the most part, throughout her seventeen-month service. She had a close call during a skirmish in Tarrytown, New York, when musket fire struck her head and legs. A doctor dressed her head wound, but she left the hospital before he treated her leg. She removed one piece of shrapnel herself, but couldn't get the second and it stayed with her for life.

After a cold winter in which she suffered frostbite, Sampson received a promotion to serve as a waiter to General John Paterson in April of

1783. When she came down with a fever that summer, her doctor discovered her secret. But he kept it. His wife and daughters nursed Sampson back to health.

With the war ended, General Henry Knox honorably discharged her at West Point in October 1783.

Upon returning to Massachusetts, she married Benjamin Gannett of Massachusetts, and raised four children. She gave lectures and sold a book about her wartime adventures. But she struggled financially, and didn't get her military pension until 1816. After that, she lived comfortably until her death in 1827.

Deborah Sampson Gannett is buried in Rock Ridge Cemetery in Sharon, Massachusetts.

4. MOLLY STARK, MANCHESTER, NEW HAMPSHIRE

Molly Stark may be the best known of the revolutionary heroines because of the war cry uttered by her husband, General John Stark. During the Battle of Bennington, Stark told his men, "There are your enemies, the Red Coats and the Tories. They are ours, or this night Molly Stark sleeps a widow!"

But Molly Stark made her own contribution to the revolutionary cause. Born Elizabeth Page on February 16, 1737, she had been married for seventeen years to Stark when the American Revolution broke out. They had eleven children.

When her husband camped near Fort Ticonderoga, smallpox broke out among his men. They were cold, hungry, and disheartened. Molly Stark sent a message to bring the sick home to her. She cared for some twenty patients, including her own children. She saved every patient, but she came down with the disease, which disfigured her for life.

Elizabeth (Molly) Stark is buried in Stark Cemetery in Manchester, New Hampshire. A brass cannon captured at the Battle of Bennington—called "Old Molly"—is fired every year in New Boston, New Hampshire, in her honor.

5. MARGARET CHAMPLIN, NEWPORT, RHODE ISLAND

Many women joined the Daughters of Liberty, who fought the Revolution with their pocketbooks and their spinning wheels. Few of their names are known.

Margaret Champlin is known to have belonged to the Daughters of Liberty in Newport. They were wealthy young women who boycotted British imports—and, if they were lucky like Margaret, danced with George Washington at a society ball.

The Newport Daughters began a few years before the Revolution after Parliament slapped import duties on household items that weren't made in the colonies.

Colonial merchants resisted the tariffs by boycotting British goods. But that caused a shortage of cloth, so the Daughters of Liberty began to spin yarn from wool in very public spinning bees. On one day, ninety-two Daughters brought their spinning wheels to the Newport meeting house and spun 170 skeins of yarn.

They also boycotted tea from England, making their own Liberty Tea from raspberry or mint leaves.

Margaret Champlin married Benjamin Mason, and their daughter Elizabeth married Oliver Hazard Perry, hero of the War of 1812.

Margaret Champlin Mason died at the age of 76 in 1841 and is buried in Trinity Church Cemetery in Newport.

6. ANN STORY, MIDDLEBURY, VERMONT

Ann Story's heroics during the Revolutionary War earned her the sobriquet "Mother of the Green Mountain Boys."

She moved to West Salisbury, Vermont, in 1775 as a new widow with five children. Tall and strong, she could handle an ax as well as a musket.

Many Vermonters left their farms because Loyalists (like Adams Rangers) harassed them. Ann Story not only stayed, but offered to spy for the Green Mountain Boys.

One day, one of her sons discovered a pregnant woman lost in the woods. Indians had captured the woman, but left her behind when she couldn't keep up. Ann Story took the woman in. Later, the newborn baby's crying drew the attention of a Loyalist scout, Ezekiel Jenny. He demanded to know where the Green Mountain Boys' supporters were hiding.

Story defied him. Jenny continued on his way, and Story told the patriots the Loyalists were afoot. Local patriots tracked down Jenny and his scouting party, captured them, and hauled them to Fort Ticonderoga.

Ann Story later married Captain Stephen Goodrich. She is buried at the Farmingdale Cemetery in Middlebury. Her headstone bears the name Hannah Goodrich.

PLACES WHERE REVOLUTIONARY HEROES LIVED

1. ADAMS NATIONAL HISTORICAL PARK, QUINCY, MASSACHUSETTS

John Adams never fired a gun in the cause of liberty, but he fought for American independence with his sharp intelligence and his considerable energy. Adams persuaded Thomas Jefferson to write the Declaration of Independence because he knew Jefferson to be a better writer.

Adams also convinced the Continental Congress that George Washington should command the Continental Army. He knew New England would need to enlist Virginia's support in the war effort, and he correctly saw Washington as the way to do it.

Adams spent five years away from his family in Europe, trying to negotiate an end to the war even as he found lenders to support it.

His home is now part of the Adams National Historical Park. It includes the birthplaces of two presidents—John Adams and his son John Quincy—along with nine other buildings belonging to five generations of the Adams family.

2. NATHAN HALE HOMESTEAD, COVENTRY, CONNECTICUT

Every schoolchild knows the story of Nathan Hale, the young schoolmaster turned spy for George Washington. The famous Indian fighter Robert

Rogers captured him on Long Island, and the British hanged him without a trial. He is remembered for his last words, which he may or may not have spoken: "I only regret that I have but one life to live for my country."

When the Hale family hadn't heard from Nathan in a while, his brother went to Old Saybrook, Connecticut, to track him down. He learned of his brother's death and was given a trunk of his belongings.

The Hale family eventually sold the house and it passed through several hands. Then a Connecticut lawyer named George Dudley Seymour bought it, restored it, and filled it with Connecticut antiques, including Nathan's trunk.

Nathan Hale never lived in the Nathan Hale Homestead, but he did live in a house on the same location in the Town of Coventry. His family tore it down during the war to build the bigger house, which survived. The Hale Homestead grounds are open year round from dawn to dusk.

3. GENERAL JOHN STARK HOUSE, MANCHESTER, NEW HAMPSHIRE

General John Stark gave New Hampshire its motto, emblazoned on its license plates: "Live Free or Die."

The old Indian fighter marched his New Hampshire militia to Boston as soon as he heard about the Battles of Lexington and Concord. During the Battle of Bunker Hill, he led his men to a spot where he anticipated the British would attack. He may or may not have said, "Don't fire until you see the whites of their eyes." Someone did; it just isn't clear who.

Stark was an unsung hero of the Battle of Saratoga, where he and his men prevented the British from retreating north. His heroics at the Battle of Bennington are more widely remembered. Even today, many New Hampshirites know why Molly Stark didn't sleep a widow that night.

Stark famously went home to his farm in Derryfield (now Manchester) after the war and died at age ninety-three. The Stark family sold his boyhood home in 1821, and then the Amoskeag Manufacturing Company bought it in 1835 to use as worker housing. A century later, the company gave the building to the Daughters of the American Revolution, who restored it. They moved it to the original Stark farm in 1968 and turned it into a house museum on Elm Street in Manchester.

4. NATHANAEL GREENE HOMESTEAD, COVENTRY, RHODE ISLAND

Nathanael Greene had asthma, walked with a pronounced limp, and belonged to the pacifist Quaker religion. None of that stopped him from becoming a revolutionary hero doing some of the toughest jobs of the War of Independence.

When Americans despaired of ever evicting the British from the South, Nathanael Greene lured General Charles Cornwallis away from his supply lines and into battles that inflicted heavy casualties. Greene's guerilla tactics helped force the British out of the South. After the war, he returned to his home in Rhode Island.

Nathanael Greene had built his house on Taft Street in Coventry in 1770, and his family lived there through the war. When the war ended, Greene moved his family to Newport, but then relocated to Georgia and died soon thereafter.

He had sold the Coventry house to his brother Jacob, and it remained in the Greene family until 1899. The family, though, rented it as a tenement house and neglected to keep it up.

In 1919, the Nathanael Greene Homestead Association formed to restore the former home of Rhode Island's best known revolutionary hero. Today it's a house museum open seasonally, part of the Anthony Village Historic District.

5. ETHAN ALLEN HOMESTEAD MUSEUM, BURLINGTON, VERMONT

Ethan Allen's capture of Fort Ticonderoga with Benedict Arnold in 1775 certainly qualifies him as a revolutionary hero. But he spent most of the war imprisoned by the British and then, after his release, ferreting out Loyalists in Vermont.

He also pursued politics, wrote books, and speculated in land. He and his family moved to a new house overlooking the Winooski River in Burlington in 1787, but he only lived there until his death in 1789. His survivors sold the house, which passed through several hands. Local people always knew the house had belonged to Ethan Allen, but no one did much about it until a Burlington resident named William J. Van Patten bought it in 1902.

Van Patten donated twelve acres of the property to the Sons of the American Revolution on condition they maintain it as a park and build a tower to Vermont's revolutionary hero. They did, and Van Patten lived in the house and ran the rest of the property as a dairy farm.

In the late 1980s, a surviving remnant of the farm was turned into The Ethan Allen Homestead Museum. It now functions as a house museum, open seasonally, with living history events and lectures on Vermont's history.

6. MONTPELIER, THOMASTON, MAINE

Henry Knox's great achievement was hauling fifty-eight artillery pieces in the dead of winter from Fort Ticonderoga to Boston. When he reached the city, he had the guns mounted on Dorchester Heights and trained them on the occupying British. That convinced them it was time to leave.

Knox then continued to direct the artillery throughout the war, including the successful siege at Yorktown.

Knox had a rags-to-riches-to-rags life. After his service in government ended, Knox moved to Maine where his wife, Lucy, had inherited considerable property. He built the nineteen-room Knox mansion, named Montpelier, in Thomaston. He then set about trying to make a fortune from the Maine woods. Unfortunately, he spent his final years struggling to try to repay his loans, which by the time of his death far exceeded the value of his assets.

Montpelier was torn down but a replica was built to replace it in the 1920s. Now it's the Henry Knox Museum, which is open seasonally.

VINTAGE
NEW ENGLAND

NEW ENGLAND ISN'T ALL COLONIAL HOMES and revolutionary taverns. It's also stretches of roadside kitsch and honky-tonk resorts. Go to Salem, Massachusetts, and you'll find a purveyor of cheesy witch trinkets for every elegant Samuel McIntire house.

New England may have given the world Towle silver, Sperry topsiders, and Southwick suits, but it also contributed the Mickey Mouse watch, the can opener, and the Frisbee. Some of that old New England money that came from fishing and the China trade went into mills and factories. In the nineteenth century, textile manufacturing was the biggest industry in the United States, and most of it happened in New England. The automobile industry even began in New England before migrating west.

Other businesses moved away as well. Textile companies in particular moved south in search of workers willing to work for lower wages. Whaling simply disappeared, replaced by petroleum and electricity. The great downtown department stores are all gone, and even the shopping malls are disappearing.

Some of New England's commercial past has hung on. There are working farms that started before Roger Williams got banished to Rhode Island, and there are still some mills and factories that make things.

NEW ENGLAND'S OLDEST BUSINESSES

FAMILY-OWNED BUSINESSES ARE FADING INTO THE PAST AS AMAZON and Walmart take over the world.

But New England has some holdouts that go back nearly four hundred years. They include farms that survived real estate development, catastrophes, and competition from agribusiness. A tavern that made it through wars and Hooters. A seaside inn near a presidential retreat and a ferry that's been running since Nathaniel Hawthorne took notes.

1. FIELD VIEW FARM, ORANGE, CONNECTICUT

The Griswold Inn in Essex, Connecticut, and the Hartford *Courant* are two of Connecticut's oldest businesses, having opened in 1776 and 1764, respectively. But neither is as old as Field View Farm, which has operated continuously in Orange since 1639.

Thomas Hine established the farm that year, and his descendants have run it for twelve generations. Today it's a dairy farm that sells eggs, milk, and ice cream, and you can pet the cows.

The last remaining farm between New Haven and New York City, it has stayed alive by diversifying. The farm expanded into the trucking business, with tractor trucks and trailers that haul goods throughout the Northeast.

A fire burned down the main barn in 1996, and since then the Hine family has sold agricultural equipment and rented vehicles to stay in business at 707 Derby Avenue.

2. BARKER'S FARM, NORTH ANDOVER, MASSACHUSETTS

Barker's Farm in North Andover, Massachusetts, has grown corn, strawberries, and apples since 1642. It has been in the same family since then, and is now run by Dianne Barker, the eleventh-generation owner.

When the first Mr. Barker came to America, another old Massachusetts business had been up and running for nineteen years—only in Constantinople. Zildjian didn't move its cymbal company to Quincy until 1928, and later to Norwell.

Today the Barker farm has seventy acres and a farm stand on Osgood Street that sells corn, fruit, butter, and vegetables. Customers can pick their own apples and flowers.

3. EMERY FARM, DURHAM, NEW HAMPSHIRE

The Emery Farm grows hay, corn, pumpkin, and berries on a well-known stretch of Route 4 in Durham. It's across from the old Wagon Hill Farm, known far and wide for the old wooden wagon silhouetted against the sky on top of a hill.

Joseph Smith, the ancestor of Emery Farm's current owners, received a deed to the land in 1655. He started the farm in 1660, and for years it was used for logging, hay, and grain. Then it became a small dairy farm.

Builders couldn't take their eyes off the property and made repeated overtures to buy it for real estate development. David Hills, a tenth generation owner of the farm, protected about sixty acres with conservation easements.

The farm has evolved into a pick-your-own operation, with a café, a petting barn, and a farmstand.

4. SEASIDE INN, KENNEBUNK, MAINE

The town of Kennebunk, Maine, bustles in the summer with visitors seeking lobster, whale watching, retail therapy, and the sight of the summer home of President George H.W. Bush. Visitors have been coming to Kennebunk since 1660, and they've been staying at the Seaside Inn since 1667.

John Gooch was the first member of the family to settle in Kennebunk. He arrived in 1637 as an agent of Ferdinando Gorges, who had the land patent for Maine. Gorges ordered Gooch to operate a ferry across the Kennebunk River. He began running an inn in 1667. The current inn on Beach Avenue has been in the Gooch family since 1756, when Jedidiah Gooch bought the business.

For generations, the business was passed down to the firstborn son. Four generations ago, a daughter finally got it. Today the Seaside Inn and Cottages is run by a ninth-generation member of the family, Trish Mason, and her husband Ken.

5. WHITE HORSE TAVERN, NEWPORT, RHODE ISLAND

The White Horse Tavern is not only Rhode Island's oldest restaurant, it's Rhode Island's oldest business. Frances Brinley built it in 1652, but it didn't sell food and drink until 1683. That's when William Mayes bought the property and enlarged it into a tavern. It took another forty-seven years to be named White Horse.

Since the White Horse makes another list, we'll give a nod to a few other very old Rhode Island businesses. Newport's Caswell-Massey was started by a Scottish doctor as an apothecary in 1752. The company's fine-fragrance soaps and toiletries have been a favorite of George Washington, Cole Porter, and the Rolling Stones. Additionally, John Stevens Stonecutter has been cutting stone in Newport since 1705, and Kenyon's Grist Mill has been grinding meal and flour in West Kingstown since 1696.

6. FORT TICONDEROGA FERRY, SHOREHAM, VERMONT

The trip between Larrabee's Point in Shoreham, Vermont, and Ticonderoga, New York, takes seven-and-a-half minutes, just as it has for more than one hundred years.

A ferry has run from Ticonderoga to ports on the Connecticut River since at least 1759. That's when Lord Jeffery Amherst, governor general of British North America, ordered a ferry service to move armies and supplies in the Seven Years War (one of the French and Indian wars).

Since 1799, a ferry service has run between New York and Larrabee's Point, making it Vermont's oldest business.

Operating from late spring through early fall, the ferry is less important as a vehicle for trade today than it used to be. But it still delights travelers as it did when Nathaniel Hawthorne noted its peculiar charms. He wrote of: "the continual succession of travelers who spent an idle quarter of an hour in waiting for the ferry boat, affording me just enough time to make their acquaintance, penetrate their mysteries and be rid of them without the risk of tediousness on either side."

SIX PRODUCTS AND WHERE THEY WERE MADE

New Englanders used to make things—a lot of things. Clocks and can openers, steam engines and shoes, board games and battleships.

When the early cod fishermen and Yankee traders made their fortunes, they invested them in mills and factories and railroads. Starting with the first water-powered cotton mill in Pawtucket, Rhode Island, New England clothed a good part of the world for many, many years.

Whaling also generated huge profit, and New England's shipyards and chandleries kept the whaling fleet afloat.

Now, as you travel along the highways and railroad tracks you can see the crumbling brick remnants of New England's industrial strength. If you want a glimpse of what it used to be like to make things, you can visit some restored mills that have been turned into historic parks. Or you can visit New England's over-financialized downtowns, where once-productive factories and warehouses are now brew pubs, offices, and condos.

1. MICKEY MOUSE WATCH, WATERBURY, CONNECTICUT

Oh, could Mickey Mouse sell watches. He rescued a floundering clock company as well as Walt Disney studios during the Great Depression.

For years the Waterbury Clock Company was one of the biggest makers of clocks in Connecticut's Naugatuck Valley, known as the Switzerland of America. It also churned out wristwatches during World War I from its huge brick factory on North Elm and Cherry streets in Waterbury.

By the 1930s, the Waterbury Clock Company was on its back. So was Disney. An ad salesman proposed making and selling the Mickey Mouse watch to save them both. Skeptical company executives—including Walt Disney—decided to try it.

The cheap, cheerful watch was just what a depressed public wanted. A Macy's promotion sold eleven thousand Mickey Mouse watches in one day. And by 1957, twenty-five million Mickey Mouse watches had been sold.

In the 1950s, the company took the Mickey Mouse watch off the market and began selling a line of reliable and inexpensive watches. They called them Timex. Today, the Waterbury Clock Company has morphed into the Timex Group, its watch factory an empty hulk. The company started a Timexpo Museum in Waterbury, which traced the company's history, but that, too, closed.

2. BATES BEDSPREAD, LEWISTON, MAINE

For decades, the Bates Bedspread made an ideal wedding gift for discriminating young couples like George and Barbara Bush. In fact, the Bushes posed in a 1948 magazine ad promoting the coverlet.

Bates for years was Maine's largest employer. The giant textile mill complex in Lewiston, opened with one building in 1854 and grew to eleven. In 1940, the company hit on the idea of reproducing colonial-era candle-wicked bedspreads like the one George Washington gave to Martha. It was a hit. By the 1960s, it seemed everyone had a Bates Bedspread.

By 1990, demand petered out and cheap imitators took a big chunk of the market. The company closed in 2001, its mills now part of the Bates Mill Historic District. You can still buy a Bates Bedspread at the Bates Mill Store in Monmouth, Maine, from former employees who started Maine Heritage Weavers to carry on the tradition.

3. MONOPOLY, SALEM, MASSACHUSETTS

In 1888, the Parker brothers moved into an old laundry building and started their eponymous company making board games. First they made board games like *Billy Bumps Goes to Boston*, then they introduced ping pong and tiddledy winks, and eventually they came up with *Monopoly*. They bought more land and built a 35,000-square-foot factory, employing five hundred people.

Hasbro bought Parker Brothers and therefore *Monopoly* in 1991. The game is still actually manufactured in a 1960s-era plant in East Longmeadow, Massachusetts. Hasbro bought the plant from Milton Bradley and then sold it to Belgium-based Cartamundi in 2015. Cartamundi agreed to make *Monopoly* in the East Longmeadow factory, at least until 2020.

The old Parker Brothers factory was torn down, replaced by the Jefferson Street apartment complex. The neighborhood now belongs to the Bridge Street Neck Historic District.

4. LEVI'S DENIM, MANCHESTER, NEW HAMPSHIRE

You can't miss the giant old mill buildings in the center of Manchester. The city grew up around the Amoskeag Manufacturing Company, founded in 1831. The mill yard expanded into the world's largest cotton textile plant, with sixty-four mill buildings stretching a mile and a half along both banks of the Merrimack River.

Among the cloth it produced was denim for the first Levi Strauss "waist overalls." Strauss and his partner Jacob Davis invented the blue jean when they received a patent for the way they riveted their waist overalls in 1873. Amoskeag shipped its nine-ounce XX blue denim to San Francisco, where it was sewn into blue jeans. Until 1915, the Amoskeag mills supplied all the denim for Levi's 501 jeans.

After World War I, the Amoskeag Manufacturing Company suffered from recession, competition, aging technology, and floods, finally closing in 1935. Some textile manufacturing continued in the old mills for a while, but many of the mills were torn down. Today the mill yard is full of offices, restaurants, college branches, and the Millyard Museum.

5. THE CATAMARAN SAILBOAT, BRISTOL, RHODE ISLAND

One of the most talented naval architects in the world was Nathanael Greene Herreshoff, named after the Revolutionary general from his home state of Rhode Island.

After Nat Herreshoff graduated from MIT he opened a boatyard in 1878 with his blind brother, John, in Bristol, Rhode Island. The Herreshoff Manufacturing Company started making steam-powered boats, but during most of its sixty-seven years designed and built yachts for wealthy Americans.

The Herreshoff boatyard built every yacht that won the America's Cup race for three decades. Nat Herreshoff invented new and efficient marine hardware, developed methods to make light wooden hulls, and patented the sailing catamaran.

The Herreshoff Manufacturing Company also built seven catamarans, including *Amaryllis* and *Amaryllis II*. The boatyard closed in 1945 after Nat Herreshoff died, but a museum now stands on the former site. There you can see the *Amaryllis II*, as well as some famous yachts, models, and designs of the Herreshoff Company.

6. FAIRBANKS SCALES, ST. JOHNSBURY, VERMONT

You've probably stood on a Fairbanks platform scale in a doctor's office. For nearly two centuries, Fairbanks scales have been made in Vermont's Northeast Kingdom and sold around the world.

In 1824, Thaddeus Fairbanks, a wheelwright, opened an iron foundry with his brother in St. Johnsbury. They made and sold heating stoves, plows, and farm implements. Around 1830 Thaddeus became interested in growing hemp, but ran into trouble trying to weigh large amounts of the stuff from a balancing beam. So he came up with the idea of the platform scale, which used levers to counterbalance the weight. By digging a pit for his contraption and placing a platform on top of it, an entire wagon could be weighed accurately.

The Fairbanks brothers' company has been bought and sold several times, its headquarters moved to Kansas City, Missouri, and another plant built in Meridian, Mississippi. But they're still making scales in a long, low building in St. Johnsbury, and if you look around the town you'll see many of its public institutions were gifts of the Fairbanks.

PLACES WHERE ICONIC FOODS WERE BORN

WANT A QUICK TEST TO FIND OUT IF SOMEONE GREW UP in New England? Mention fluffernutter sandwiches, and if you get a blank stare they grew up somewhere closer to the Mississippi River.

You can get even more specific by saying "Moxie" or "needham" in Maine, "Del's" or "coffee milk," in Rhode Island, or 'hoodsie" in Massachusetts. You can easily identify a New Haven native by asking, "Pepe's or Sally's?"

Many New England food favorites emerged from teeming immigrant neighborhoods in the nineteenth century. Dishes from the old country combined with American ingredients and voila! Delicacies such as the Fall River Chow Main Sandwich appeared in working-class diners and lunch rooms.

Some iconic New England foods can actually be traced to their place of birth.

1. THE AMERICAN POTATO, EAST DERRY, NEW HAMPSHIRE

In 1718, several shiploads of poor Scots-Irish arrived in Boston, but the Puritan leaders weren't too keen on letting them stay. After all, the town might end up having to support them.

But the Puritans were also worried about threats from the frontier. They realized the Scots-Irish could make a terrific buffer against unfriendly Indians, French Catholics, and other scary things that came out of the wilderness. So they sent the Scots-Irish off to the wilds of southern New Hampshire.

Had they only known what the Scots-Irish brought with them, they might have let them stay.

In 1719, a group of Scots-Irish moved to a settlement they called Nutfield. It later evolved into the towns of Derry, Londonderry, Windham, and part of Manchester.

Soon after they arrived, a momentous occasion took place: They planted the first white potato in North America.

A marker in front of the First Parish Church in historic East Derry notes the historic planting of the noble spud:

"In April 1719, sixteen Presbyterian Scotch-Irish families settled here in two rows of cabins along West Running Brook easterly of Beaver Brook. Initially known as Nutfield, the settlement became Londonderry in 1723. The first year, a field was planted, known as the Common Field, where the potato was first grown in North America."

2. CONVERSATION HEARTS, BOSTON, MASSACHUSETTS

Necco, which stands for New England Candy Company, started in 1847 when a Boston pharmacist invented a machine that cut lozenges from sugar paste. Soon he was making sugar wafers for Union Army soldiers in the Civil War. They were called hub wafers after Boston, the Hub of the Universe (so Bostonians thought).

The company became Necco in 1901, and continued to make Necco Wafers and conversation hearts in a brick complex in South Boston.

You can see where those old-fashioned candies were made if you head to the old Fort Point Channel neighborhood by the Summer Street Bridge. Look for the decaying brick buildings on Necco Court and Necco Street. General Electric was going to clean off the graffiti and spruce up the buildings for a new headquarters, but that didn't happen.

In 1927, Necco moved to the world's biggest candy factory in Cambridge, Massachusetts. By the middle of the nineteenth century, Boston and Cambridge ruled as a candy-making center with 140 candy companies between them.

Eventually Necco moved its manufacturing to Revere, Massachusetts, and still made about eight billion conversation hearts a year. That wasn't enough to save the company, though, and Necco filed for bankruptcy protection in 2018. Ohio-based Spangler Candy bought the company, and production of conversation hearts stopped while production equipment moved out of Massachusetts.

3. THE MODERN DONUT, ROCKPORT, MAINE

In Rockport, Maine, you'll find a historic marker on the parsonage of the Nativity Lutheran Church. It marks the birthplace of a sea captain named Hansen Gregory, who claimed to have invented the modern donut. Enough people believed him that he got the plaque.

Late in life, while living at the Sailor's Snug Harbor in Quincy, Massachusetts, Captain Gregory told the *Washington Post* how he'd come about his invention. As a sixteen-year-old cook aboard a coasting schooner, he had to make something called "twisters." To make them, he took long strips of dough, bent them in half, twisted them into shape, and fried them.

The outsides fried up all right, but the insides remained raw and the bent part sopped up all the grease. Gregory thought a hole in the middle might solve the problem. So he took the top of a pepper pot and, he said, cut into the middle of that donut "the first hole ever seen by mortal eyes."

That was in 1858. He became a captain, and he had a tinsmith make a donut cutter. Then he showed his mother how to make donuts. She served them around Rockport and Camden, and the donut never looked back.

His story does comport with what food historians know about donuts.

4. CABOT CHEDDAR CHEESE, CABOT, VERMONT

In 1919, Vermont cows produced too much milk for Vermont farmers to sell. So ninety-four farmers ponied up $3,700 to start a cooperatively owned creamery in Cabot. They started off making butter and shipping it south. By 1930 they'd advanced to cheddar cheese. Cabot cheeses, butters, and yogurts have since won well over a hundred awards. *Wine Spectator* put Cabot cloth-bound cheddar on its list of the hundred best cheeses in the world.

Cabot expanded in Vermont with creameries in Quechee and Waterbury and a store in Portland, Maine. In 1992 it merged with a southern New England cooperative called Agri-Mark. Today the Cabot Creamery has a visitor's center at 2878 Main Street, where you can buy Cabot cheddar and other Vermont specialty products.

5. WHITE CLAM APIZZA, NEW HAVEN, CONNECTICUT

A peasant meal brought from nineteenth-century Italy evolved into New Haven's famous white clam apizza. It's been praised as an "intoxicating combination of romano cheese, fresh garlic, olive oil, parsley, and clams atop the chewy and charred oblong pies."

Frank Pepe began selling hot pizza—he called it apizza—to fellow immigrants selling their wares in New Haven's open-air market. He had gotten a job at a bakery and sold the "tomato pies" on his own time. Eventually he bought out his employer and in 1925 opened Frank Pepe Pizzeria Napoletana, where he invented the New Haven-style thin crust pizza.

But the landlords kicked him out, so he bought the building next door at 163 Wooster Street. He began selling clams on the half-shell, finally deciding to put them on his apizza. If fresh clams weren't available, he didn't sell white clam apizza.

White clam apizza became a signature New Haven dish, and Pepe's is still serving it up. Frank Pepe died in 1969, but his family carried on the business and has expanded into New York, Massachusetts, Rhode Island, and other Connecticut cities. But only in New Haven does Pepe's compete with Sally's, its rival since 1938.

6. CLAMS CASINO, NARRAGANSETT PIER, RHODE ISLAND

Rhode Island has no shortage of iconic foods. The little state has a big appetite for such local favorites as coffee milk, New York system wieners, Del's lemonade, cabinets, stuffies, and zeppole. But their exact geographic origin is hard to pin down, as they all had peripatetic histories. They either started in food trucks or carts, or emerged simultaneously from a dense immigrant neighborhood.

So clams casino seemed the logical choice for this list, even though their origin is a tad murky. A chef named Julius Keller claimed in 1937 he invented the dish while employed at the Narragansett Pier Casino, a Gilded Age resort. Keller wrote in his memoirs that a Mrs. Paran Stevens had asked for a special clam dish for her eight guests. He came up with a new spin on the old classic of stuffed clams, adding bacon, peppers, and butter to the chopped clams, bread crumbs, and garlic.

Keller's claim can't be verified, but it's certainly plausible. The Narragansett Pier Casino burned down twice, but its stone towers still stand as a recognizable beachfront landmark.

LANDMARK SIGNS

"Sign, sign, everywhere a sign. Blockin' out the scenery, breakin' my mind." To the Five Man Electrical Band singing in 1971, signs were a blight. But today some signs have been with us so long that rather than block out the scenery, they've become the scenery.

When thinking about iconic signs in New England, there is no shortage of choices. But there's at least one in each state that's fun to look at.

1. WEIRS BEACH, LACONIA, NEW HAMPSHIRE

With its tourist history and its attitude toward free expression, the Granite State boasts many iconic signs. Though some have been lost to time, many remain. Nothing tells you you're in New Hampshire's North Country like the Clark's Trading Post sign. And you know you're getting near Portsmouth when you see the giant whale on the Yoken's restaurant sign—still there even though Yoken's is gone.

In late fall, Manchester's Ray the Mover's Florida Express sign also comes to mind. But the winning candidate on the list for New Hampshire's landmark sign is the neon arrow that directs people to the old honky tonk Weirs Beach resort. Built in 1956 to pull in traffic from Route 3, the arrow is as flashy and fun today as it was then.

2. SUPERCOW, NEW BRITAIN, CONNECTICUT

There are dozens of possible iconic images that one thinks of when talking about Connecticut. The carousel at Bushnell Park, perhaps, or one of the many landmark-quality signs along the Berlin Turnpike. But we settled on one unlikely superhero that sits on top of a dairy in New Britain.

Supercow has been poised, ready to take off from the roof of Guida's Dairy, for decades. Why? We don't know. Perhaps to rescue the world from poor nutrition. With roots that go back to 1886, Guida's has been selling milk and juices for longer than any of us has been alive and it hopefully will be long after we're gone. The cow can be seen at Guida's on Park Street.

3. THE BIG BLUE BUG, PROVIDENCE, RHODE ISLAND

Has any kid driven in Rhode Island on Route 95 in the past fifty years and not gawped at the big blue bug sitting right next to the highway in Providence? Originally an ad for New England Pest Control, the company changed its name to Big Blue Bug Solutions because its fifty-eight-foot termite sign became the image everyone associated with the company.

The bug also has a name, thanks to a radio contest: Nibbles Woodway. After doing decades of service promoting the company, Big Blue Bug Solutions also found a way to use the giant insect for charitable work. It offers to promote worthy events for nonprofits for free by placing a banner for an upcoming local auction, dance, or other fundraiser right by the bug's head.

4. CITGO, BOSTON, MASSACHUSETTS

It would be tempting to nominate the Hilltop Steakhouse Cactus on Route 1 as the most well-known Massachusetts sign. For its kitsch and craziness, there aren't many that can match it. But the Kenmore Square Citgo sign has to get the nod.

Year in, year out, Boston Red Sox baseball fans—wherever they may be—are treated to endless television shots of the dazzling lighted sign during breakaways. It's just impossible not to associate it with the lazy, pleasant summer nights spent watching a game.

There was originally a Cities Services (now Citgo) gas station in the building where the sign sits, but it's long gone. As is the original sign, which has been refurbished and updated many times over the years since it first appeared in the 1940s. To see it, you can visit Kenmore Square—or just turn on your television for any Red Sox home game.

5. YOU CAN GET THERE FROM HERE, ALBANY, MAINE

Maine has plenty of iconic roadside signs, including the purple-pink dinosaur of Perry's Nut House in Belfast. The sign for the Goldenrod in York Beach would be a worthy nomination, or pick your favorite from Old Orchard Beach.

But we settled on the small road sign at the junction of Route 35 (Valley Road) and Route 5 (Crooked River Causeway) in Albany Township. It seems to capture both Maine's diverse heritage and its dry humor. It offers the distances to Maine towns that also share the name of foreign locales: China, Poland, Peru, Norway, Mexico, Egypt, Sweden, Denmark, and Lebanon. It always gets a chuckle from people who pass by. And it just goes to show, you can travel around the world and never leave Maine.

6. THE GREAT CHAIR, BENNINGTON, VERMONT

Though Vermont shuns roadside billboards to preserve its natural beauty, there are a few oddities along its roads. Ever since the 1940s, there has been a World's Tallest Ladder-back Chair sign in Bennington. First it stood at the Haynes and Kane Furniture store. The sign was a clear message of what wares the store was hawking. The store refurbished the chair in 1969, but went out of business and left it to fade.

The sign disappeared in 2000 when it had to be torn down, but in 2012 it made its reappearance when new owners, LaFlamme's Furniture, replaced it. Though it's moved around a bit, the chair, proclaimed as the world's largest ladder-back chair, can still be found at the store on West Main Street in Bennington.

DOWNTOWN DEPARTMENT STORES

Downtown department stores used to provide a transcendent shopping experience, offering elegance, convenience, quality, and fashion. People dressed up when they went to shop at downtown department stores, their plastic charge cards in hand. They often stayed for the day, patronizing nearby theaters, banks, restaurants, and other stores like Kresge's or Woolworths.

Downtown department stores offered large selections of the best and latest merchandise. And the truly great downtown department stores prided themselves on gracious service.

At Christmas, downtown department stores took on magical qualities with festive shop windows, patient Santas, and evergreens and twinkling lights everywhere.

They've pretty much disappeared, leaving a hole in shoppers' hearts. Suburban shopping malls took their place for a while, but they're falling prey to Amazon and Walmart.

1. DEPARTMENT STORE HISTORIC DISTRICT, HARTFORD, CONNECTICUT

Customers from the entire region of central Connecticut traveled to Hartford for the city's three leading downtown department stores: Sage Allen & Co., Brown Thomson & Co., and G. Fox & Co.

Hartford's department stores were a treat for all the senses. The aroma of spicy sticky buns pulled customers into Sage Allen's basement. Shoppers also loved G. Fox's cream-cheese-and-date-nut-bread sandwiches.

If you couldn't find an item in one of those stores, you probably couldn't find it. At Brown Thomson you could buy a Cadillac along with a full line of automotive supplies.

G. Fox, probably the most beloved of the old Hartford department stores, prided itself on customer service. If a customer wanted to return a spool of thread, the great G. Fox fleet would pick up the thread. On Christmas Eve, G. Fox kept a small staff and drivers on standby until midnight for desperate parents who needed an emergency Christmas gift.

Everyone in central Connecticut knew exactly where to meet someone downtown—the Sage Allen sidewalk clock. It disappeared after a windstorm damaged it and finally returned in working order in 2007.

All three of Hartford's great downtown department stores disappeared in the early 1990s, felled by two large regional malls. Now, they're part of the Department Store Historic District and home to a community college and retail franchises.

2. PORTEOUS, MITCHELL AND BRAUN, PORTLAND, MAINE

Porteous, Mitchell and Braun opened in 1904 on Congress Street in Portland, the largest department store in Maine. Porteous boasted "lavish and delightful" Christmas decorations of colored lights, thousands of yards of "greenest evergreen," and "truly fascinating show windows."

For decades people did come to see the spectacular store decorations and awe-inspiring toy and doll departments.

In the late 1970s and early 1980s, Porteous expanded to shopping malls in northern New England. The flagship store in Portland closed just short of its 100th birthday in 2003. It's now home to the Maine College of Art.

3. FILENE'S BASEMENT, BOSTON, MASSACHUSETTS

Filene's Basement was perhaps the most famous denizen of Boston's Downtown Crossing, the shopping district that included its rival Jordan Marsh, Gilchrist's, Raymond's, R.H. Stern, and R.H. White. And Filene's upstairs, of course.

William Filene started the store, but his sons made the store a household name after inheriting it in 1901. Edward pioneered the store's basement annex, thronged by bargain-hunters week after week. The annual wedding dress sale inspired local news reports of brides-to-be marauding through the tulle.

Filene's actually sent photographers to customers' homes to take baby pictures—or you could go to the store for that First Communion photo.

At Christmas, the store shook off its humbler aspect and decked itself out for Christmas. In 2006 the name Filene's tragically disappeared from the retail landscape in a merger with Macy's. The former flagship Boston store now houses the fast fashion retailer Primark.

4. VARICK'S, MANCHESTER, NEW HAMPSHIRE

Elm Street was the place to be in Manchester, especially on payday. When the shifts ended at the gargantuan Amoskeag mill yard, workers went to Elm Street to mingle with friends, have a meal, and spend their paychecks at the shops that lined the street.

In the heart of the shopping district was the John B. Varick Co. at 809–819 Elm St. For years it was the largest hardware store outside of Boston, but it also sold a huge variety of merchandise, including sporting goods, jewelry, silver, fishing gear, seeds, toys, luggage, and radios.

Varick's was founded in 1845 by John P. Adriance. His nephew, John B. Varick, came to work in the store at age sixteen, and two years later bought the company. He ran the business for fifty-three years, until sons Thomas and Richard took over the store.

Fire wiped out Varick's in 1888, 1892, and 1914, which is why the store had an early sprinkler system. When John B. Varick's sons died, the business was sold after World War II, then shut down in 1951. Today the building includes retail space and apartments.

5. SHEPARD'S, PROVIDENCE, RHODE ISLAND

The three great Providence stores on Westminster Street—Shepard's, Cherry & Webb, and Gladdings—decked themselves out spectacularly for the holiday, and if you got lost you waited for your parents under the tall, neon-lit Shepard's clock.

Shepard's started in the 1870s, and by 1903 grew to an entire city block as the largest department store in the United States. Its founder, John Shepard, wanted each department to offer a complete selection and a premier shopping experience. Shepard's Tea Room offered a fine dining experience that included its signature chicken croquettes. Not only did it have a letter-writing station, it had Rhode Island's first radio station inside the store.

Shepard's went bankrupt in 1974, and the University of Rhode Island uses its old building.

6. MONTGOMERY WARD, BURLINGTON, VERMONT

Montgomery Ward's fifteenth store opened on Church Street in Burlington on December 28, 1929. The company had an ambitious plan to expand its stores, but fast. Its mail-order sales had dropped, and its rival Sears was opening hundreds of stores on the outskirts of major cities. Montgomery Ward decided to challenge Sears in smaller cities, where country people were driving their new cars to shop.

In 1927 Montgomery Ward had only thirty-six stores. Two years later, it had more than five hundred, two hundred more than Sears. Architects in Chicago probably designed the one in Burlington, which has wide Chicago windows on the second floor.

The Burlington store announced its opening with an ad in the Burlington *Free Press* promoting electric washing machines, men's suits, ladies' dresses, radios, and a "smart three-piece living room suite covered with peach mohair."

The company's timing—the eve of the Great Depression—didn't help the store's survival. It lasted only thirty-two years, closing in December 1961. Various retailers have operated in the building since then, and a bank now uses part of it.

THE FIRST
SHOPPING MALLS

IN 1947, NEW ENGLAND'S FIRST SHOPPING MALL BROKE GROUND IN Stamford, Connecticut. No one knew for sure whether it would even survive. Few had any idea of the love New Englanders would shower on the new shopping meccas with their easy parking, bustling crowds, and seductive merchandise. But then they stopped.

1. RIDGEWAY CENTER, STAMFORD, CONNECTICUT

Alfons Bach understood the future of American consumerism. He had emigrated from Germany well before World War II and wound up in Stamford. Perhaps because of his German roots he had no nostalgia for the old ways of New England. That allowed him to shape the future around the tastes of the generation coming of age in the postwar era.

Bach saw how rapidly the automobile was changing the culture. And shopping, he believed, was bound to change. With cars that needed parking, it made less and less sense to travel to congested cities to shop. Suburban consumers, he believed, would respond to convenient new shopping malls with clean, uncluttered design.

Bach took this vision to Lerner Shops, a chain of women's clothing stores, and suggested they build a modern shopping center. The Lerners, however, did not see his wisdom. So Bach struck out on his own and began work on the Ridgeway Center on fifteen acres of land he owned in Stamford.

Originally opened in 1947 with 110,000 square feet of space, the "motor age merchandising mecca" had such tenants as W. & J. Sloane, Pennsylvania Drug, Deena's, The Lurie Company, Chizzini, a Slenderella figure salon, and a liquor store.

It grew rapidly. In 1951, Bach added a three-level Sears, an office tower, and a cinema—essentially a prototype of today's New England shopping malls. By 1958 he added a Saks 34th Street boutique-type store. The mall went through several renovations and remains in operation today.

2. SHOPPER'S WORLD, FRAMINGHAM, MASSACHUSETTS

In the late 1940s, Bostonians left for the suburbs in droves. New roads and reliable cars created a steady push westward, southward, and northward from the center city. Framingham, on Route 9, was in a perfect position to take advantage of the free-traveling Bay Staters.

Enter Huston Rawls, with his plans for a shopping destination unlike all other shopping malls.

He lured Jordan Marsh to leave Boston for the first time, and he put the store under a giant clear-span dome. His design team created the rest of the mall in the modern Populuxe style, making Boston's downtown seem old and dangerous.

Rawls also plucked at New Englander sensibilities by building the whole thing around an enormous town green.

With forty-four stores and parking for an astounding six thousand cars, Shoppers' World had virtually any product a consumer could think of.

And Rawls's marketing chops were obvious, as he featured the Lone Ranger, Rin Tin Tin, and Rex Trailer to draw crowds. When the grand opening conflicted with the 1951 World Series, Rawls hired "ask me" girls to patrol the shopping center with radios.

The New England weather, however, did not cooperate with his plans. Rain and snow plagued Shoppers' World throughout its life. Poor construction was another problem, and Rawls couldn't bring a second major tenant to the mall.

Still, his vision lasted for forty three years. Shoppers' World was torn down in 1994, and another mall of the same name has taken its place.

3. ETHAN ALLEN SHOPPING PLAZA, BURLINGTON, VERMONT

Ethan Allen, who rode the speculative real estate boom of the late eighteenth century, would probably have built Vermont's first shopping mall had he lived into the 1950s. However, a Vermont real estate developer named Tony Pomerleau built Vermont's first shopping mall in 1951 and named it after the Green Mountain Boy.

The Ethan Allen Shopping Plaza was a simple strip mall in Burlington's North End, a row of stores with a supermarket in the middle and a lot of parking in front. The mall featured the Ethan Allen Bake Shop, Plouffe's Pharmacy, Ben Franklin, Carvel Ice Cream, a bowling alley, and a movie theater.

Pomerleau went on to build about twenty more shopping malls before he died at the age of 100 in 2018. The Ethan Allen Shopping Plaza was torn down and today is a vacant lot.

4. PINE TREE SHOPPING CENTER, PORTLAND, MAINE

The Pine Tree Shopping Center was almost inevitable once Portland abandoned its streetcar service just before World War II. After the war, people moved to the new suburbs and drove their cars to work in the city. Real estate developers seized the chance to build new shopping centers on the edge of Portland.

The Pine Tree Shopping Center opened in 1959 featuring a Zayre, one of the first fourteen stores opened by the Massachusetts retail chain. A favorite with children was Child World, a toy store that looked like a castle (sort of) from the outside. When Marden's replaced it, the crenellated walls and red-roofed turrets remained.

The Pine Tree Shopping Center started out with twelve stores, including W.T. Grant, Woolworth's, Rexall, and Columbia Market grocery store. Air conditioning and late hours attracted shoppers, especially families who could bring their kids after work.

The Pine Tree Shopping Center grew to twenty stores. Then, like so many shopping malls, it lost its anchor tenants and started to look tired. A developer came in, revitalized some of the stores and demolished others to make way for big box outlets.

5. MIDLAND MALL, WARWICK, RHODE ISLAND

When Sears opened Rhode Island's first shopping mall in 1967, it left little to chance. The modern Midland Mall in Warwick benefitted from the collective lessons learned from earlier shopping malls. It hummed from the start.

Victor Gruen, master mall builder, knew the key to success: innovation. Shoppers wanted the latest and greatest. So he built Midland on two floors with an open courtyard—the first such mall in New England. Unlike Shoppers' World, also on two floors, it was fully enclosed. The retailers had learned the importance of keeping that New England weather at bay.

Adding to the contemporary two-story look, the developers also eschewed escalators in favor of "speedramps." Like a moving walkway on a slant, the speedramp looked sleeker and safer than an escalator. It also drew in curious customers to see these innovative people movers.

The developers shrewdly locked in two key anchor stores. Cherry & Webb and the Shepard Company took the key spaces in the mall, and its 450,000 square feet of space filled rapidly. It had a Docktor Pet Center, Orange Julius, Spencer Gifts, Thom McAn Shoes, Flagg Brothers Shoes, and the Midland Cafeteria. The mall survived through 2011.

6. NASHUA MALL, NASHUA, NEW HAMPSHIRE

New Hampshire's status as a no-sales-tax state naturally appealed to developers looking for a way to lure consumers. Less than five miles over the New Hampshire border, they built the state's first shopping mall in 1969 in Nashua. The Nashua Mall offered convenience for Massachusetts shoppers who wanted to make a quick trip for some tax-free shopping.

With 220,000 square feet of space, the mall was one of the many Woolco malls that featured a Woolco Discount Mart at one end and an Almy's at the other.

Woolworths envisioned Woolco as a big brother to the smaller five-and-dime stores, but offering discounted pricing on a large scale. They launched in 1962 with Red Grille restaurant tucked inside most, an update to the Woolworth lunch counter. But by 1982, recession snuffed out all the company's U.S. stores.

In 1969, however, the marketers knew how to bring in the customers in New Hampshire. No celebrities or ultra-modern styling. Instead, the Nashua Mall featured indoor tropical palm trees and the promise of seventy-two-degree temperatures all year round. It finally gave way to more modern retail concepts, such as outlet shopping malls. The Nashua Mall closed in 2003.

CIVIC NEW ENGLAND

JOHN WINTHROP PUT HIS STAMP ON NEW ENGLAND EVEN BEFORE HE set foot in Massachusetts Bay Colony. Winthrop led about a thousand people, mostly Puritans, in a fleet of eleven ships from England. As his ship, the *Arbella*, lay anchored in Salem Harbor, Winthrop delivered a famous sermon on July 2, 1630. He called it *A Model of Christian Charity*, but it has gone down through the ages as the "City upon a Hill" speech.

In the much-copied sermon, Winthrop explained the Puritan ideal: to carry out God's will by settling Christian communities in North America. He tried to prepare his followers to carve a new society out of the wilderness. And he urged his fellow travelers to work together as a community and to do as the Bible instructed.

"For we must consider that we shall be as a City upon a Hill," Winthrop said. "The eyes of all people are upon us."

The Puritans left a legacy of civic involvement, self-government, and self-improvement. It began with militias for mutual protection, courts and Town Meeting for governance, and education for knowing the Bible. Some of the oldest civic institutions in the United States result from those Puritan ideals.

OLDEST COURTHOUSES

The Puritan settlers established tight hierarchies in their communities to maintain order. In their fragile settlements on the edge of the primeval forest, crime threatened their existence. So did blasphemy, disrespect, and dissent.

The Puritans came to New England partly to purge their religion of Roman Catholic, or "papist," excesses. They wanted to banish saints and their feast days, images of the deity, and the pope and his vestments, crosses, and chalices. Those things got in the way of their goal to live according to the Bible. That meant many of the early Puritan laws came directly from the Scriptures, and so did the punishments.

For example, in 1642, a New Haven court found a servant named George Spencer guilty of bestiality with a sow. According to Leviticus 20:15, "if a man lie with a beast, he shall surely be put to death: and you shall slay the beast." Spencer was executed after the pig was killed in front of him.

But John Winthrop and some of the other early Puritan leaders were trained in English common law. So they developed a legal system that took some elements of the Bible and some from the English courts. In the most Puritan colonies—Plymouth, Massachusetts, Connecticut, and New Haven—the laws leaned more heavily toward Scripture.

Rhode Island and New Hampshire law tended to resemble English law more closely. Vermont, claimed by four other colonies, didn't come up with a unified system of laws until founders of the republic drafted a constitution in 1777.

1. PLYMOUTH OLD COUNTY COURTHOUSE, PLYMOUTH, MASSACHUSETTS

When the Pilgrims arrived in the place they called New Plymouth, one of the first things they did was to build a courthouse where the judge, jury, and legislature met. There, they adopted the first written legal code in North America in 1636.

Today the Old County Courthouse, also known as the Old Town House, is the third structure to stand on that spot on Town Square. Built in 1749, it's probably the oldest wooden courthouse in the United States.

The Old Town House was built by Peter Oliver, a Loyalist. His brother, Andrew Oliver, was the tax stamp administrator famously hanged in effigy by the Sons of Liberty. The Town of Plymouth used the building for offices from 1820, when it built still another new courthouse, to the early 1950s.

Now the building is the 1749 Court House and Museum, free to the public and open during the summer. Nearby are the Burial Hill cemetery, The First Parish Church, Brewster Gardens, and Leyden Street, which was laid out by the Pilgrims.

2. POWNALBOROUGH COURTHOUSE, DRESDEN, MAINE

The Pownalborough Courthouse dates to 1761. Located on Courthouse Road, it is the only courthouse that remains from Maine's colonial era.

The town of Dresden was named Pownalborough after Massachusetts governor Thomas Pownall when Maine still belonged to that state. In addition to serving as a courthouse, the building also housed a tavern —as many early courthouses did.

Boston architect Gershom Flagg designed the building, which has hosted such visitors as Benedict Arnold, Robert Treat Paine, and John Adams.

Adams was a circuit rider, which meant he traveled from court to court on a horse or in a wagon. Travel back then was never easy. He complained to Abigail about his "rambling, roving, vagrant, vagabond life."

Adams took ill on his long ride to Pownalborough in 1765 and ran out of food. But he won his case at the Pownalborough courthouse.

"This journey, painful as it was, proved much for my interest and reputation," he wrote, "as it induced the Plymouth Company to engage me in all their causes, which were numerous, and called me annually to Falmouth Superior Court for ten years."

The courthouse today is a museum maintained by the Lincoln County Historical Society and open in the summer.

3. OLD GRAFTON COUNTY COURTHOUSE, PLYMOUTH, NEW HAMPSHIRE

The Old Grafton County Courthouse on Court Street can claim roots dating at least to 1774. It was used as a meeting house during the Revolution and is one of the few eighteenth-century buildings to survive in New Hampshire. Its most famous moment came in 1805 when twenty-three-year-old Daniel Webster pleaded his first court case there. His father, Ebenezer, sat on the bench and praised his son for a "creditable performance" in the civil suit. Daniel Webster never again argued a case in front of his father.

Today the building has been restored, and it is maintained as a museum of the Plymouth Historical Society. It's open for visitors during the summer. The building is not in its original location, however, as it was moved in 1823 when it was converted into a wheelwright's shop. Then in 1876, U.S. Sen. Henry Blair bought it, had it remodeled, and gave it to the Young Ladies' Library Association to use as a library.

4. NEW LONDON COUNTY COURTHOUSE, NEW LONDON, CONNECTICUT

The New London County Courthouse was built between 1784 and 1786 to replace the courthouse burned by the British during the American Revolution. It was an ambitious and expensive building for its time and place. Designed by Isaac Fitch of Lebanon, Connecticut, it was also used as town hall during its early years. Originally it sat at the head of State

Street, but in 1839 it was moved to Huntington Street. It is not only the oldest courthouse in Connecticut, but one of the oldest courthouses continuously settling disputes in America.

Daniel Webster, Marquis de Lafayette, and Horace Greeley all spoke at the New London County Courthouse.

5. KENT COUNTY COURTHOUSE, EAST GREENWICH, RHODE ISLAND

For many years, Rhode Island lawmakers liked to at least give the impression of equal access. So the Legislature sat in each county seat on a rotating schedule. It used the Kent County Courthouse, built in 1805–1806, which resembled the other places the Legislature sat—the Newport Colony House and the Providence Colony House. It also bears a striking resemblance to the New London County Courthouse in Connecticut.

Eventually, all that moving around got too much for the elected representatives, and starting in 1854 they only met in Providence and Newport. The state, however, hung on to the buildings in Bristol, South Kingstown, and East Greenwich.

Then in 1901 when Rhode Island built its statehouse, it finally gave the county buildings back. In 1908, an architectural firm restored the Kent County Courthouse. The outside was historically accurate, the interior not so much—a common practice during the Colonial Revival. For years the courthouse was used as a town hall. Today probate court uses it, which makes it the oldest active courthouse in Rhode Island.

6. WINDHAM COUNTY COURTHOUSE, NEWFANE, VERMONT

The Windham County Courthouse in Newfane, Vermont, dates to 1825, when it was built as a simple box. Additions in 1853 and 1907 gave the courthouse its current Greek revival appearance, with a porch and massive Doric columns.

Still an active courthouse, the Windham County Courthouse sits on Newfane Green, a quintessential New England public common.

HISTORIC ONE-ROOM SCHOOLHOUSES

Thousands of one-room schoolhouses once educated New England children, some well into the twentieth century. Children never walked five miles to them, though, as they may have claimed later in life. Towns built their so-called "district" schools within a one- to three-mile radius, the distance a first-grader could walk.

The district schools were small, utilitarian buildings, usually without plumbing or electricity. An outhouse stood out back, as did a woodshed for the wood-burning stove.

In the early days, one-room schoolhouses were usually built on tiny plots of cheap land in the village center. Dim, cold, and often crowded, one critic called them "juvenile penitentiaries."

In the 1850s, New England's one-room schoolhouses began to change. School reformers like Horace Mann and Henry Barnard argued that schools should have good light, better heat, comfortable seats, and separate entrances and cloakrooms for boys and girls. In their view, schoolhouses should have "civilizing" architectural style and solid construction to uplift and inspire students.

They suggested the two entrances as a way to prevent "much confusion and rudeness" and to promote "orderly habits."

Ultimately, most one-room schoolhouses disappeared—moved, dismantled for reuse, or converted to a new use with additions and alterations. Some survived, however, and some serve as museums today. They remind schoolchildren to be grateful for central heat, electricity, and a ban on corporal punishment.

1. THE SOUTHERNMOST SCHOOL, PORTSMOUTH, RHODE ISLAND

Portsmouth, the second oldest town in Rhode Island, decided three hundred years ago that learning was an "excellent ornament to mankind." It authorized construction of two one-room schoolhouses: the Northernmost and the Southernmost. Built in 1725, the Southernmost still stands, and the Portsmouth Historical Society calls it the oldest schoolhouse in Rhode Island.

The Southernmost's first schoolmaster, James Preston, boarded with another family until he fell ill. The town let him and his family live in the basement of the school. After he died, his widow and her family used the school as their home until the town kicked them out in 1746.

The school was donated to the historical society in 1952, and today serves as a museum. Young visitors today are no doubt intrigued by the school's precise menu for corporal punishment:

Boys and girls playing together—1 lash
Fighting at school—5 lashes
Climbing for every foot over 3 feet up a tree—1 lash
Giving each other ill names—3 lashes
Wearing long fingernails—2 lashes
Boys going to the girls' play place—3 lashes
Girls going to the boys' play place—2 lashes
For not saying yes or no sir or yes or no marm—2 lashes

The worst infractions? You got seven lashes for lying and eight for telling tales out of school. Misbehaving to girls got you ten lashes if you were a boy, while swearing at school got both sexes nine lashes.

2. LITTLE RED SCHOOLHOUSE, GAYLORDSVILLE, CONNECTICUT

Beginning in 1740, teachers at the Little Red Schoolhouse tried to teach children reading, writing, math, history, and penmanship. They did it for the next 227 years. The little wooden building didn't have electricity until 1935 or running water until 1952. A coal stove provided heat for much of the school's existence.

Over time, the building was moved slightly, expanded, and repaired. It finally closed in 1967 as the school board deemed it no longer practical. The building, however, was preserved, and a plaque bolted to it that says, "This school building preserved in memory of Bessie S. Cornwell who taught here for 42 years, 1915–1957."

It's worth mentioning that Nathan Hale taught briefly in a slightly younger Connecticut schoolhouse. In the fall of 1773, he took his first job after graduating from Yale and taught thirty-three children at the East Haddam Schoolhouse, built in 1750. He complained about living a "remote life in the wilderness," though, and got a new job in the more cosmopolitan town of New London in the spring of 1774.

3. YORK CORNER SCHOOLHOUSE, YORK, MAINE

Maine, a largely rural state, had four thousand one-room schoolhouses in 1900. That number fell to 226 in 1960, and today only a handful remain.

York has one that survived, the York Corner Schoolhouse. It's one of the earliest existing eighteenth-century one-room schoolhouses in the country. The town started building it in 1746, then paid two pounds thirteen shillings to finish it nine years later. The windows had no glass, just oiled brown paper, and the school had no stove, just an open fireplace.

After the schoolhouse closed, a farmer converted it to a chicken coop. Local preservationists saved the building and converted it to a museum. Today it belongs to the Old York Historical Society's nine historic buildings. In season, visitors can tour the Old Schoolhouse and Tavern.

Maine, by the way, has six island one-room schoolhouses where children are still taught.

4. WEST SCHOOLHOUSE, DENNIS, MASSACHUSETTS

The West School in the Cape Cod town of Dennis is the only remaining one-room schoolhouse of the twelve that once educated local schoolchildren. It's also the oldest in the Commonwealth of Massachusetts.

Younger children attended school in the spring and summer, while the older ones went to school in winter when they had fewer farm chores.

The wooden building used to stand at the intersection of Old King's Highway and New Boston Road. It operated as a schoolhouse until 1865, and then moved to 61 Whig Street in 1973. Today it's part of the Josiah Dennis House property, which the Dennis Historical Society runs as a museum.

5. EUREKA SCHOOLHOUSE, SPRINGFIELD, VERMONT

Springfield settlers began working on the one-room schoolhouse in 1785, but didn't finish it until 1790. Today it's the oldest one-room schoolhouse in Vermont. Though built from hand-hewn timbers, the settlers tried to give the primitive structure some style. They finished the walls in rough-cut wooden boards scored to resemble cut stone, and they painted it yellow with a cobalt blue roof.

The first schoolteacher, David Searle, gave the school its name. After he graduated from Yale he headed north to the Vermont frontier, looking for work. When he reached Old Fort No. 4, residents told him Springfield wanted to hire a teacher. He followed the Crown Point Military Road, and when he spotted the new school he said, "Eureka"—Greek for "I found it."

Apparently he did his job well. A number of the students went on to attend Dartmouth College.

The town closed the school in 1900. The abandoned building probably would have crumbled into the earth, but a local preservationist named Anna Hartness Beardsley spearheaded the effort to save it.

Today the Vermont Division for Historic Preservation owns the Eureka Schoolhouse, and the Springfield Chamber of Commerce runs it as the centerpiece of a small historic site.

6. RED SCHOOLHOUSE, CROYDON, NEW HAMPSHIRE

The Red Schoolhouse claims to be the longest continuously used one-room schoolhouse in the United States. Students have been learning the three R's in the little school since 1794. But one room doesn't mean one teacher anymore—Croydon now has at least two.

The tiny town, with fewer than a thousand residents, had to defend its title as the "oldest continuously used" one-room schoolhouse when Franklin, Massachusetts, made a similar claim. Unfortunately for Franklin, its Red Brick School had opened fifty years later than Croydon's.

OLDEST PUBLIC HIGH SCHOOLS

THE PURITAN COLONISTS BELIEVED CHILDREN SHOULD BE EDUCATED SO they could read and understand the Bible. They also needed to train their own ministers for life in their new world. So the Puritans early on established public high schools, with four in seventeenth-century New England. They include Hartford Public High School in Connecticut and three in Massachusetts: Boston Latin School, Cambridge Rindge and Latin School, and Hopkins Academy in Hadley.

Still, they're relative babes compared to schools in England and Germany. For example, the King's School in Canterbury, England, was founded in 597.

Those old European schools provided the model for New England's first public high schools. They mimicked the Latin school of fourteenth- to nineteenth-century Europe, teaching—well, Latin.

That approach made some sense, as Latin was the universal language for academic, legal, government, and liturgical matters. For the children of working families, the Latin schools allowed them to improve their station in life.

1. BOSTON LATIN SCHOOL, BOSTON, MASSACHUSETTS

Founded in 1635, Boston Latin School is easily the most famous of all the old public schools.

After the early Puritans established Boston Latin, it evolved into a bastion for the offspring of Boston Brahmins. A Boston Latin education provided a ticket to Harvard, and its alumni include Saltonstalls, Adamses, Lowells, Phillipses, Winthrops, Eliots, and Danas.

Dropouts include Benjamin Franklin and Louis Farrakhan. Graduates include four Harvard presidents, four Massachusetts governors, and five signers of the Declaration of Independence.

Helen Magill White was the first female student, graduating in 1877. She went on to become the first American woman to earn a PhD. The year she graduated from Boston Latin, the city founded Girls' Latin School (later the coed Boston Latin Academy). Not until 1972 did Boston Latin admit its first coeducational class.

Famous alumni include Samuel Adams, Leonard Bernstein, Cotton Mather, George Santayana, Ed Ames, Ralph Waldo Emerson, Arthur Fiedler, John Hancock, Nat Hentoff, Henry Knox, Theodore White, and Sumner Redstone.

2. HARTFORD PUBLIC HIGH SCHOOL, HARTFORD, CONNECTICUT

Founded as Thomas Hooker's Latin School in 1638, Hartford Public High School is the second oldest public high school in the United States. It sits right next to the Harriet Beecher Stowe House and the Mark Twain House, conveniently for Mark Twain's daughters, Olivia and Clara, who attended the school.

Not until 1847 did the school teach anything other than Greek and Latin, the year it changed its name to Hartford Public High School.

A fire destroyed the school building in 1882, only thirteen years after it was built. The school had better science facilities than those in most colleges, with a chemistry laboratory, a science lecture hall, a Clark telescope, and an observatory.

Hartford built a new school building in 1963 and later renovated it. Today, 1,300 students attend the school known as The Pub.

3. PINKERTON ACADEMY, LONDONDERRY, NEW HAMPSHIRE

The Town of Londonderry established a private, classical high school in 1793. Then in 1814 the wealthy Pinkerton brothers, Major John Pinkerton and Elder James Pinkerton, donated sixteen thousand dollars to make the private high school permanent. It wasn't free, though. Tuition cost two dollars a quarter.

The State of New Hampshire incorporated the school on December 4, 1815. Three years later, the high school admitted the first female student. Coeducation didn't last long, however. In 1821, the Adams Female Academy opened and Pinkerton stopped accepting girls.

Pinkerton remained an independent day and boarding school until it agreed to accept public school students from Derry in 1948.

Robert Frost taught at Pinkerton Academy, and murderess Pam Smart and astronaut Alan Shepard attended it. Now it has thirty-one hundred students, eight hundred more than the next biggest school in the state.

Pinkerton Academy remains a private school, but it serves as the public high school for the New Hampshire towns of Derry, Hampstead, Chester, and Auburn.

4. HAMPDEN ACADEMY, HAMPDEN, MAINE

Stephen King taught English at Maine's oldest public high school, Hampden Academy. It should be no surprise then that he set his novel *Carrie* there.

One of his students remembered him as a great teacher, though he looked a bit like a werewolf. "I will never forget the day he came into class with a dandelion in his sport coat pocket, and announced he had sold *Carrie*, including movie rights," wrote Jim Spohrer. "He was very happy, and we were all happy for him.

"Later that week, everyone in the school was working on their novel :-)"

Hampden was founded in 1803 as a private school, then as a theological seminary, and finally a public high school. Today it has about seven hundred students from Hampden, Newburgh, Frankfort, and Winterport.

It also has a new fifty-two million dollar school built in 2012. The National Register of Historic Places lists the original Hampden Academy building, which also happened to be the site of the Battle of Hampden during the War of 1812.

5. PROVIDENCE CLASSICAL HIGH SCHOOL, PROVIDENCE, RHODE ISLAND

In 1800, Rhode Island's General Assembly ordered each town to open public schools. Most towns couldn't do it, but Providence managed to open elementary schools. For decades Rhode Island had no public high school.

By 1838 a heated debate raged over education. Opponents said a public high school would be "too aristocratic" and would "educate children above working for their support." William Goddard, a prominent Brown professor, led the pro-high-school faction that eventually won.

Providence dedicated Classical High School on March 20, 1843. At first it admitted women and African Americans, then decided to segregate African Americans. Four teachers taught arithmetic, algebra, Latin, English grammar, ancient history, medieval history, modern history, and bookkeeping.

The school quickly grew too crowded and the city built a new one in 1878. By 1963 that building was outdated, and Providence held a competition to design a new one. The local firm Harkness & Geddes won the contest in collaboration with Boston architect Walter Gropius.

The new high school was built in 1970 in the same Brutalist style as the much-hated Boston City Hall. Today, Providence Classical High School is a demanding college preparatory magnet school.

6. WINDSOR HIGH SCHOOL, WINDSOR, VERMONT

Windsor High School in Windsor, Vermont, is the youngest of the oldest public high schools in New England.

Sometime around 1786 a school was built in the village of Windsor. It was used until about 1810, when the villagers decided to build a new brick schoolhouse. Then in 1838 the village decided to divide the younger students from the older, which eventually led to the high school in 1845.

It took a while to get a high school building, though. The village decided to construct a "more pretentious school building," one that would be an "ornament and an honor to the place." After much discussion, the town built it in 1886. Windsor boasted it had a high school "not inferior" to any public high schools in the state.

Today it is a junior and senior high school with three hundred students in grades seven through twelve.

Windsor draws students from the Vermont towns of Windsor, West Windsor, Weathersfield, and Hartland as well as Cornish, New Hampshire.

HISTORIC
POST OFFICES

In the earliest days of European settlement, the mail was delivered to coffeehouses and taverns.

Mail delivery was improved in 1673 with the creation of the Boston Post Road, along which post riders carried letters and guided travelers.

Shortly after the Battles of Lexington and Concord, the colonial shadow government, called the Provincial or Continental Congress, met in Philadelphia. They'd been talking about overthrowing the British Imperial Post ever since Parliament imposed the hated Stamp Act a decade earlier.

Now, if they wanted to win the war, the rebellious colonists needed a reliable way to communicate with each other—free from prying British eyes.

And so the 2nd Continental Congress established the U.S. Postal Service on July 26, 1775, and named Benjamin Franklin the first postmaster.

Franklin, a Boston native, had plenty of postmaster experience on his resume. Franklin had been Philadelphia's postmaster for many years, and in 1753 the king had appointed him deputy postmaster general for the colonies. The Crown let him go in 1774 for "actions sympathetic to the colonies."

Not one to miss an opportunity, Franklin named his son-in-law, Richard Bache, comptroller of the postal service.

Franklin served fewer than four months as U.S. postmaster, and no, he didn't set out the markers on the Boston Post Road. Someone else did.

The revolutionary postal service flourished, though. By Christmas it had driven the British Imperial Post out of business.

Since then, most post offices moved from building to building and became something else. Sadly, the first post office in the United States was paved over and built up with modern commercial buildings.

New England is still home to the oldest and the second oldest continuously operating post office.

1. OLD IPSWICH POST OFFICE, IPSWICH, MASSACHUSETTS

On November 6, 1639, the Massachusetts General Court ordered that "all letters which are brought from beyond the seas" should be taken to a tavern run by Richard Fairbanks. Fairbanks was to take care that they be "delivered or sent according to their directions." He got a penny for every letter he delivered.

The Old Fairbanks Tavern was located approximately at 244 Washington Street in Boston, once known as "Newspaper Row." Today a concrete cavern of commercial buildings stands where letters from beyond the seas were once dropped.

Massachusetts actually has six "first" post offices, according to the U.S. Postal Service historian, in Boston, Ipswich, Marblehead, Newburyport, Salem, Springfield, and Worcester. The historian considers a post office established on the day the postmaster is appointed.

All the Massachusetts post offices got postmasters on that July day when Congress gave Ben Franklin the top job. To qualify as a first, a post office has to operate under U.S. authority within the present-day boundary of the state.

The first post office building in Ipswich still stands. It's a small red garrison built in 1763 across from First Church on North Main Street. Congress appointed Deacon James Foster as the postmaster, but he didn't last long. A few months later Daniel Noyes, a Harvard graduate and representative to the U.S. Congress, got the job. He must have appreciated the value of a steady job, for he kept it for twenty-five years.

2. HINSDALE POST OFFICE, HINSDALE, NEW HAMPSHIRE

Post riders stopped in Ipswich on their route between Boston and Portsmouth, New Hampshire, a trip that took six days. Portsmouth got its first official postmaster on the same day the towns in Massachusetts (and Maine, Rhode Island, and Connecticut) got theirs. There was a war on, and the Congress didn't have much time to quibble over postmasters.

Shortly after the Revolution, New Hampshire expanded its post roads farther north and west from the main post office in Portsmouth. The east-west road reached Hinsdale in the westernmost part of the state, and the town got its post office in 1816. It's been in the same spot ever since.

The clapboard post office on Main Street is the oldest continuously operating post office in the same building in the United States.

Nathan Babbitt became Hinsdale's first postmaster in 1815 and built a general store the next year. He tucked the post office into a corner, and eventually the post office took over the entire first floor. The original brass postal boxes date from the nineteenth century.

In the early twentieth century, the post office survived a fire that destroyed Town Hall next door.

3. CASTINE POST OFFICE, CASTINE, MAINE

Portland used to be called Falmouth, and it belonged to Massachusetts along with the rest of Maine. The Falmouth post office opened on the same day the other six did in Massachusetts.

The postal historian, however, calls the Castine Post Office the "second-oldest post office location" in the United States. Castine is a very old maritime town, settled by Europeans seven years before the Pilgrims arrived in Plymouth. Though remote today, in the eighteenth century Castine was a busy transportation hub at the intersection of the Gulf of Maine and a branch of the Penobscot River.

Its current building went up in 1817, and the federal government in 1833 began using it as a Customs House and post office. That Customs House, by the way, was once the second-busiest in the United States, next to the one in New York City.

4. EAST WINDSOR HILL POST OFFICE, SOUTH WINDSOR, CONNECTICUT

Connecticut has as many "first" post offices as Massachusetts: in Fairfield, Hartford, Middletown, New Haven, New London, Stamford. They all got their postmasters on that fateful July day in 1775.

Some historians call the East Windsor Hill Post Office in South Windsor (go figure) the oldest continuously operated post office in the country. That's because a Connecticut storeowner at the South Windsor shop on Main Street received the first government post rider in 1783.

But does "receiving a post rider" qualify as a post office? The U.S. Postal Service historian doesn't think so. The East Windsor Hill building didn't officially function as a post office until 1837.

Still, it's pretty impressive that the pre-Revolutionary warehouse building is still selling stamps and casing the mail.

5. GRAFTON POST OFFICE, GRAFTON, VERMONT

Grafton's old post office is part of a small cluster of buildings listed on the National Register of Historic Places. It was built in 1855 for the town's third postmaster. The little clapboard building functioned as a post office for 103 years, until 1958. In 1938, a flood lifted it from its foundation during the great New England hurricane and moved it to a new location.

The Grafton Historical Society bought the historic post office in 1962 and ran it as a museum until 1978. Now the historical society leases the building.

6. PROVIDENCE POST OFFICE, PROVIDENCE, RHODE ISLAND

Tiny Rhode Island also got six new postmasters—and hence six new post offices—on July 26, 1775. They were in East Greenwich, Newport, Providence, South Kingston (originally "Tower Hill"), Warren, and Westerly.

Providence has a newish, but still historic post office: the oldest automated postal facility. Built in 1960 at 24 Corliss Street, it was the first to use machines to sort the mail. It also provides an object lesson into the follies of government contracting.

After World War II, the postal service's methods and technology were horribly outdated. The postal service selected Providence for a new sorting and distribution center. A company called Intelex got the contract to build the new system. Theoretically, the post office would turn a key in the door and everything would run smoothly from there. They called it Project Turnkey.

On October 20, 1960, the state-of-the-art machinery started processing mail—sort of. Employees hadn't been trained to run the equipment, which malfunctioned and failed. Much of the new machinery wasn't used at all. Project Turnkey became Project Turkey.

The "first automated post office" was honored with a stamp in 1960 despite criticisms that it was obviously self-serving. The stamp, however, proved popular, and the facility still operates.

OLDEST PUBLIC LIBRARIES

Identifying New England's oldest public libraries is no easy task. That's because book collections took many different forms in the early days of European settlement.

Many New England libraries evolved over time from private collections to public institutions. Philanthropists founded some, while collective town actions resulted in others.

There's no shortage of New England towns that claim to have the oldest libraries in their state. In New Hampshire, for example, the Portsmouth Athenaeum was founded as a private library in 1817, sixteen years before the Peterborough Town Library. But Peterborough, funded by taxpayers from the start, claims to be the oldest tax-supported library.

But this list is limited to the oldest libraries that lend books to the public. So Peterborough in, Portsmouth out.

1. REDWOOD LIBRARY, NEWPORT, RHODE ISLAND

The Redwood Library and Athenaeum started off as a forty-five-member literary society founded by Bishop George Berkeley, the great Irish philosopher. Berkeley moved to Rhode Island in 1729 to start a college. He gave up a few years later and returned to the British Isles, but he left behind a literary society. It morphed into the Company of the Redwood Library in Newport in 1747. As its purpose it had "nothing in view but the good of mankind." Today it calls itself the oldest lending library in America.

Newport merchant Abraham Redwood gave the library five hundred pounds sterling to buy 751 used books (including one on how to build a latrine) from London.

When the British occupied Newport in 1776, they used the library as an officers' club. Many of the books disappeared. In 1806, the library began advertising for their return, but didn't get many back. In 1947, the library staff tried again and recovered 92 percent of the missing volumes, or at least copies of them.

Peter Harrison, the first professionally trained architect in the United States, designed the building. He later designed Newport's Brick Market and Touro Synagogue. Ezra Stiles, who helped found Brown University and served as president of Yale, served as its most well-known librarian.

2. SCOVILLE MEMORIAL LIBRARY, SALISBURY, CONNECTICUT

The Scoville Memorial Library started in 1771 when a local blast furnace owner named Richard Smith offered to buy two hundred books from London. But he said the rest of the town had to chip in, and thirty-nine people contributed. On the third Monday of every third month, patrons could borrow and return books. The library fined them for damaging books. Back then, letting candle wax drip on the pages, or greasing, was a problem for book lovers.

In 1805, another local philanthropist named Caleb Bingham donated the Bingham Library for Youth. Then Miss Harriet Church donated the Church Library. Town Meeting in 1810 voted to authorize selectmen to spend one hundred dollars to buy more books for the town library.

But the town's books were kept in Town Hall, so Jonathan Scoville in the 1890s left fifteen thousand dollars in his will to build a library. Miss Grace Scoville bought a tower clock, which still chimes on the quarter hour. Salisbury Cathedral in England sent the library a fifteenth-century stone carving, presumably because of the town's name.

The library now claims to be the oldest publicly funded library in the United States.

3. PETERBOROUGH TOWN LIBRARY, PETERBOROUGH, NEW HAMPSHIRE

The Peterborough Town Library, founded in 1833, is the oldest taxpayer-supported free library in New Hampshire.

Unitarian minister Abiel Abbot had the idea for a collection of books owned by the people and free to everyone who lived in Peterborough. Luckily, they found some money in the state coffers. A capital stock tax had been levied to build a state university, but it didn't raise enough money. Hence, New Hampshire created a Literary Fund, and Peterborough decided to use it for books.

On April 9, 1833, Town Meeting approved the library on the principle that, like the public school, it deserved maintenance by public taxation. The town bought one hundred books and put them in Smith and Thompson's General Store, along with the post office. The postmaster acted as librarian until 1854, when the town appointed Miss Susan Gates to take care of the town library books. In 1873, the growing collection of books moved to Town Hall.

Within two decades Peterborough had six thousand books and not nearly enough room. So in 1893, the town gave the library its own building designed by noted bridge engineer and summer resident George Shattuck Morison.

4. WITHERLE MEMORIAL LIBRARY, CASTINE, MAINE

The Witherle Memorial Library in Castine, Maine, began in 1801 as a private collection of books that only paid subscribers could use. Then the Town of Castine took over the library in 1827 and established it as Maine's first municipal library in 1855.

Local ship chandlers George and Mary Witherle donated the money for the land and the building's foundation. The building itself was finished in 1913. Today the library has more than thirteen thousand volumes and local history collections, including the story of Castine's founder, Jean-Vincent d'Abbadie de Saint-Castin. It also includes the history of the

Penobscot Expedition; books by and about Civil War journalist Noah Brooks; and the letters of Union Army soldier Henry Butler to his wife during the Civil War.

5. STURGIS LIBRARY, BARNSTABLE, MASSACHUSETTS

The Sturgis Library is the oldest building in the United States to house a public library. The original part of the library was built in 1644 as the house of Reverend John Lothrop (also spelled Lothropp or Lathrop).

Lothrop immigrated to the Massachusetts Bay Colony in 1634, having been imprisoned in England as an outspoken Puritan. He was pardoned after he agreed to leave for the New World. Lothrop landed in Plymouth and settled in Barnstable in 1639, one of the town's first settlers.

He married twice and had thirteen children. Today his descendants number eighty thousand, including six U.S. presidents—the Bushes, Franklin Roosevelt, Millard Fillmore, James A. Garfield, and Ulysses S. Grant.

One of his descendants, William Sturgis, made a fortune in the China trade. When he died in 1863, he bequeathed his family home, fifteen thousand dollars, and his books for a public library.

The first two rooms of the house were used for religious worship, so the Sturgis Library also has the distinction of being the oldest building in the United States used regularly for religious services. The Lothrop Room is quintessential early Cape, with wide pumpkin pine floorboards and a beamed ceiling.

It's located on the Old King's Highway, and has sixty-five thousand books.

6. PEABODY LIBRARY, THETFORD, VERMONT

The Peabody Library in the Post Mills Village of Thetford was built in 1867, making it the oldest active library in the state federation of public libraries. George Peabody gave it to the town as a gift.

In the first decade of the nineteenth century, Peabody was a teenager from South Danvers, Massachusetts, who wanted to visit his grandfather in Post Mills. Too poor to pay for a horse or carriage, he walked for ten days. He chopped wood for innkeepers along the way and slept in their stables. Once he arrived he then spent the winter with his grandfather and became close to his aunt and uncle.

By 1867 Peabody acquired great wealth and gave some of it away from his home in England. He gave the village five thousand dollars to pay for land, building construction, and fifteen hundred volumes from a London book dealer.

Peabody's philanthropy extended well beyond Post Mills. He founded and endowed museums at Harvard, Yale, and Salem, Massachusetts. He also gave a Peabody Conservatory of Music and Peabody Institute Libraries in Baltimore, and in Danvers, Newburyport, and Georgetown, Massachusetts. The town of South Danvers renamed itself Peabody in his honor.

Today in Thetford the one-room library building still has a long wooden table and rows of white bookshelves. Two curved staircases lead to an open balcony. Just about everything in the building is original except for the carpet and the paint.

OLDEST HOSPITALS

Hospitals had been run for centuries by religious orders to care for the poor, not just the sick. They evolved during the eighteenth century into places for the practice and teaching of medicine by trained professionals. Nurses, like Louisa May Alcott, were for a long time untrained workers.

Over time, hospitals became centers of medical innovation and research. They developed specialties and affiliated with medical schools. During the nineteenth century, lunatic asylums were built to take care of mentally ill people outside the family.

After the Civil War, the number of hospitals grew rapidly in the United States, to forty-four hundred by 1910. They became larger, cleaner, and more professional.

New England's oldest hospitals reflect that evolution. One early hospital gave wine to poor people. Another took in the insane. Several were originally named after women, and one was started by a woman who also wrote hymns. One of the oldest hospitals has a unit named after a woman who gave birth to a president in another of the oldest hospitals.

1. BOSTON DISPENSARY, BOSTON, MASSACHUSETTS

One of the five oldest hospitals in the country, the Boston Dispensary was founded in 1796, sixty years after the start of Bellevue Hospital in New York and Charity Hospital in New Orleans.

Boston's civic leaders founded the Dispensary, New England's first hospital, to take care of poor people. Oliver Wendell Holmes and other prominent physicians got their medical training there.

Doctors took care of patients at the Dispensary in Boston's South End or in their homes, and gave them medicine and wine, if they felt it necessary. Clinics were established throughout the city, and eventually so was an evening clinic for the working poor, partially funded by employers.

Subscribers supported the Dispensary by paying five dollars a year for a ticket, which entitled them to recommend two patients to its care. The Massachusetts Historical Society has a ticket signed by Paul Revere.

The Boston Dispensary over the years affiliated with other medical institutions, including Boston's Floating Hospital for Children, Tufts University's medical and dental schools, and the Pratt Diagnostic Clinic. In 1968 those affiliates merged into Tufts New England Medical Center, now Tufts Medical Center.

2. YALE NEW HAVEN HOSPITAL, NEW HAVEN, CONNECTICUT

The old State Hospital is Connecticut's first and boasts many other firsts. It published the first nursing textbook in 1879, produced the first X-ray in the United States in 1896, and used chemotherapy as a cancer treatment for the first time ever in 1942. In 1946, the year future president George W. Bush was born there, Yale New Haven became the first U.S. hospital to allow healthy newborns to stay in their mothers' rooms. In 1975, Lyme disease was identified and named at Yale New Haven Hospital.

Founded in 1826 by the General Hospital Society of Connecticut, it opened in rented quarters. By 1833, founders raised enough money to build the thirteen-bed State Hospital designed by Ithiel Town. (Town also created the plans for many of New England's covered bridges.) The hospital later added east and west wings.

During the Civil War, the U.S. government leased the building as a military hospital. Fifteen hundred beds were set up in the building and in tents on the grounds. The hospital treated twenty-five thousand U.S. Army soldiers during the war. Yale New Haven Hospital has been designated a military hospital in every subsequent war.

Today it has a 1,541-bed hospital, the 168-bed Smilow Cancer Hospital, the 201-bed Yale New Haven Children's Hospital, and the 76-bed

Yale New Haven Psychiatric Hospital. It's also the teaching hospital for the Yale School of Medicine and the Yale School of Nursing.

3. BUTLER HOSPITAL, PROVIDENCE, RHODE ISLAND

Rhode Island's first hospital has the unusual distinction of being a psychiatric hospital. Butler Hospital for the Insane was founded in 1844 with a donation from industrialist Cyrus Butler, along with financial support from Nicholas Brown, Jr.

The hospital's first superintendent, Dr. Isaac Ray, toured the asylums of Europe before Butler received its first patients in 1847. Ray reported his findings in Europe in the *American Journal of Insanity* and is considered a founder of forensic psychiatry.

Today, Butler Hospital is affiliated with Brown's Warren Alpert Medical School and the flagship of the university's acclaimed department of psychiatry.

4. MAINE GENERAL HOSPITAL, PORTLAND, MAINE

The Maine Medical Association proudly claims credit for creating the Maine General Hospital. But the state Legislature had a hand in it too.

The Maine Medical Association had been founded in 1854 to quash the practice of homeopathic and alternative medicines. Among other concerns was the need for a general hospital. The Legislature granted land and funds for the institution, which opened its doors in 1874.

Maine Medical Center in Portland is now the largest hospital in Northern New England, with 637 beds serving Maine, parts of Vermont, and New Hampshire. Like the Yale New Haven Hospital, the Maine Medical Center has a connection to the Bush family: the Barbara Bush Children's Hospital.

Once the teaching hospital for Bowdoin College, it is now affiliated with Dartmouth, St. Joseph's, Tufts, and the University of Southern Maine medical schools.

5. MARY FLETCHER HOSPITAL, BURLINGTON, VERMONT

The first hospital in Vermont opened its doors in 1879 in Burlington, thanks to the generosity of Mary Fletcher.

Mary was born in Jericho, Vermont, to Thadeus and Mary Fletcher in 1830. Thadeus was a successful businessman who left a fortune when he died. Young Mary was the last of the family's five children, and by 1876 she had outlived her siblings and her parents. Though she suffered from tuberculosis, Mary, who never married, worked to realize her parents' philanthropic dreams.

With the family's wealth she established the Fletcher Free Library and the Mary Fletcher Training School for Nurses. Working with her doctor, Walter Carpenter, she spent more than two hundred thousand dollars buying land and constructing and equipping the Mary Fletcher Hospital. She then named it after her mother. She died in the hospital, in 1885.

The hospital has merged with other institutions over the years, but part of the original hospital is still working today as part of the University of Vermont Medical Center.

6. PORTSMOUTH COTTAGE HOSPITAL, PORTSMOUTH, NEW HAMPSHIRE

New Hampshire's oldest hospital was founded nearly a century after Dartmouth Hitchcock—the state's first medical school—opened its doors in 1797. Portsmouth Cottage Hospital admitted its first patients in 1884.

Harriet Kimball, the daughter of a Portsmouth pharmacist, founded Portsmouth Cottage Hospital as a charity, with some help from the city. She was also a published poet and hymn-writer.

The hospital opened in a large house once the home of a famous writer, Thomas Bailey Aldrich. The house now belongs to the Strawbery Banke Museum complex.

In 1889, five years after Portsmouth Cottage Hospital opened, fundraising for a proper hospital building began. A two-and-a-half story brick building opened in 1895 and expanded until 1962, when the hospital moved to a new building next door.

In 1983, the for-profit hospital chain Health Corporation of America bought it and opened a new campus, calling it Portsmouth Regional Hospital. HCA since settled fraud charges with the U.S. government totaling two billion dollars, the largest fraud settlement in history.

WORKING CLASS NEW ENGLAND

MUCH OF COLONIAL NEW ENGLAND HISTORY COMES FROM PURITAN records. The early Puritan settlers were often well-off and well-educated, and they had the time and the means to write down their version of events. The carpenters and farmers and fishermen who kept those settlements going were too busy working to write much.

Since then, generals and presidents have gotten plenty of attention in the history books. You have to look a lot harder for the history of ordinary people—how they got here, what they did, and how they died. But you can find it.

PLACES
WHERE WORKERS
WERE KILLED

JUST GOING TO WORK HAS ALWAYS BEEN A HEALTH HAZARD. THOUSANDS of workers have died on the job over the years, and sometimes not by accident.

Some died slow deaths from their work environments, like the Vermont quarry workers who succumbed to silicosis. Others, like Connecticut munitions workers, perished suddenly in violent explosions.

Sometimes workers were shot to death because they challenged their employers over working conditions and pay. Sometimes they challenged Mother Nature and paid the ultimate price.

1. TRURO, MASSACHUSETTS

In 1841, so many Cape Cod fishermen perished in a deadly October storm that the local women stopped dating men who went to sea.

On Saturday, October 2, 1841, most of the Truro fishing fleet on the Georges Banks left off fishing and made for home. Only two of the nine ships that set out made it.

The wind kicked up that afternoon and reached gale force by midnight. The ocean threw up waves as high as mountains.

In the seven fishing vessels out of Truro, fifty-seven men and boys died at sea, and only a few of their bodies were recovered. All lived within two miles of each other. Eight Snows and eight Paines died. So did three boys not yet thirteen years old.

An obelisk in Truro's First Congregational Parish Church yard commemorates the storm victims.

2. THE PENOBSCOT RIVER, WEST BRANCH

Joe Attien, a Penobscot Indian chief, worked for seasonal wages as a logger and a Maine guide.

Henry David Thoreau wrote about him in his 1864 book, *The Maine Woods*. "He was a good looking Indian, twenty-four years old, apparently of unmixed blood, short and stout, with a broad face and reddish complexion, and eyes, methinks, narrower and more turned up at the outer corners than ours."

On July 4, 1870, Joe Attien led a team of seven log drivers down the river's rough waters in a bateau.

When the river men tried to break up a logjam, the churning water shot the boat across the channel and smashed it against the rocks. The bateau filled with water and hurtled over a waterfall among the rocks and logs. Some of the men couldn't swim, and Joe Attien died trying to save them.

When the river drivers found his body, they cut a cross into a tree by the side of the river and hung his boots in the tree. The boots stayed there until they rotted away.

Today you can learn more about Maine's logging history by visiting the Maine Forestry Museum in Rangeley, Maine.

3. AMOSKEAG MILLS, MANCHESTER, NEW HAMPSHIRE

Ida Cram and Mary Kane worked at the Amoskeag Company's Number Seven mill on October 15, 1891, a day when all hell broke loose.

The Amoskeag, the world's largest cotton textile factory, had installed a mammoth Corliss steam engine to run four of its plants. Steam engines were then relatively new, but maintaining and operating them required a skill that many had not mastered.

That morning in 1891, Amoskeag mill managers noticed the steam engine seemed to be running erratically. An engineer, Samuel Bunker, went to the engine room to find the problem. No one knows if Bunker ever found what went wrong because the giant Corliss engine killed him when its flywheel flew apart.

Ida Cram and Mary Kane also died in the explosion, which showered the mills with debris and sent raging blasts of steam from the broken machinery. Dozens were injured. Investigators never conclusively figured out the reason for the blast that sent three people to the grave.

Today, visitors can tour parts of the historic Amoskeag mills that are home to the Manchester Millyard Museum.

4. PROCTOR MARBLE FACTORY, PROCTOR, VERMONT

On May 22, 1903, Janos Szlaby, a Hungarian immigrant, worked the graveyard shift at the Vermont Marble Company.

A belt that turned the stone-finishing machinery in one of the plants snagged. The supervisor sent Szlaby to free the belt with the factory machinery whirring below. Szlaby slipped and tumbled into the factory's balance wheel, which crushed him to death.

More pernicious than such sudden death were the lung ailments that stone workers suffered from years of exposure to stone dust in the quarries and cutting sheds. Pneumatic tools that replaced hand tools threw off great clouds of dust in enclosed work spaces. Workers who worried about their lungs confronted company managers who wanted the efficiency of modern equipment.

In the early 1900s labor agreements included language about limiting dust on the job, but the methods didn't work. One study of how stonecutting workers were killed in the 1920s and 1930s found silicosis cost them eleven years of their lives.

You can visit one of Vermont's marble quarries at the Proctor Marble Museum.

5. MOSHASSUCK CEMETERY, CENTRAL FALLS, RHODE ISLAND

William Sayles started a bleachery in Lincoln, Rhode Island, which grew into the enormous Sayles Finishing Plants in the 1920s. By then, mill owners were trying to squeeze more work out of their workers because demand for textiles had slackened while foreign mills stiffened competition.

In the fall of 1934, unions organized a general strike throughout the textile industry—the largest in U.S. labor history. From New England to the South, four hundred thousand textile workers walked off the job. The strike lasted twenty-two days.

Strikers stopped work at Sayles, but the company hired strikebreakers to continue production. Several thousand strikers shut down the factory anyway. Rhode Island Governor T.F. Green ordered state troopers and deputy sheriffs to end the strike. They arrived wielding machine guns and tear gas bombs against the unarmed workers.

The police fired on strikers hiding in the Moshassuck Cemetery, killing Charles Gorczynski, a seventeen-year-old textile worker from Central Falls. Workers carried his body through Pawtucket in an enormous funeral procession.

In the end, eight strike sympathizers and four striking workers were killed, and one hundred thirty two people were injured in what became known as the Saylesville Massacre.

Today, you can visit the Moshassuck Cemetery on Lonsdale Avenue in Central Falls. You can also see the Sayles mills and workers housing in the Saylesville Historic District in Lincoln.

6. REMINGTON ARMS, BRIDGEPORT, CONNECTICUT

The *New York Times* called the enormous Remington Arms plant, "the greatest small arms and ammunition plant in the world." It may also have been the deadliest.

At its height, Remington Arms employed more than seventeen thousand workers. Some died on the job. On March 28, 1942, an explosion killed four women and three men and injured eighty others.

The blast "shook the huge munitions plant at about 2 p.m., sent bullets whizzing dangerously through the vicinity, touched off a general fire alarm and brought a rush of ambulances," reported the *Boston Globe*.

Investigators blamed the explosion on a nail that fell into a box of cartridge primers. Today the abandoned Remington Arms plant still sits on Barnum Avenue in Bridgeport.

IRISH LANDMARKS

THE IRISH FISHED OFF THE NEW ENGLAND COAST WHILE THE PILGRIMS struggled to survive in Plymouth Colony. They built Catholic churches in New England when Paul Revere was making bells, and they carved canals when John Quincy Adams was president. They ran the gamut of social class, from household servants to one of Ireland's greatest philosophers, George Berkeley, briefly a resident of Rhode Island.

Between 1815 and 1845, as many as one million Irish immigrants came to "Amerikay," looking for opportunity. Then in 1845, the Irish potato crop failed, and in 1846 it failed again. In the spring of 1847, known as "Black 47," the massive migration began.

More Irish headed to Canada than the United States because the fares were cheaper. The British government imposed heavy tariffs on U.S.-bound ships, but only levied light taxes on vessels heading to Canada. The British reasoned the Irish emigrants would populate the vast Canadian territory, a long-held goal of that expansionist empire.

However, most Irish immigrants wanted to come to the United States, where they believed they could get plenty of work. So they sailed to Canada and then headed south of the border. They were called "two boaters."

Between 1845 and 1855, more than 1.5 million Irish—mostly poor and hungry—immigrated to the United States. So many died while crossing the Atlantic that their ships were called "famine ships" and "coffin ships."

Then as now, Irish-Americans concentrate in the Northeast, where one in five New Englanders claims Irish ancestry.

1. ISLES OF SHOALS,
PORTSMOUTH, NEW HAMPSHIRE

Before England destroyed Ireland's merchant marine, Irish merchants traded with the American colonies as early as the 1630s. Irish fishermen from Galway and Waterford settled the Isles of Shoals, an archipelago of tiny islands nine miles from the coast of Maine and New Hampshire.

By 1645 as many as six hundred people lived on the islands in the warm weather. Soon after, many settled there permanently. Fishermen named Kelley, Haley, and McKenna lived on the islands with their families in a little kingdom that governed itself. By 1680, Roger Kelley was chief magistrate and described as "King of the Isles."

They prospered by catching cod, salting it, and selling it on the world market. They were a hard-drinking lot, and John Winthrop took a dim view of them.

Some of the islanders eventually migrated to the mainland. During the American Revolution, the patriots ordered them to evacuate. Some took their homes with them. During the nineteenth century, the islands then developed into a summer colony for artists and writers.

No manmade Irish structures remain on the islands, but on a summer's day a trip to the Isles of Shoals is a rare delight that evokes the fishermen's past. The Isles of Shoals Steamship Co. offers several kinds of island tours.

2. ENFIELD FALLS CANAL,
WINDSOR LOCKS, CONNECTICUT

In the early nineteenth century, the Connecticut River rapids in Enfield made it tough to travel by water between the burgeoning towns of Springfield, Massachusetts, and Hartford, Connecticut.

In 1824, the Connecticut Legislature gave a charter to the Connecticut River Company to build the Enfield Falls Canal and a system of locks in what is now Windsor Locks. The canal created a detour around the rapids.

About four hundred Irish immigrants, men between the ages of twenty and forty, dug the five-mile canal. In May 1827 they began to shovel out the earth and haul it up steep inclines with wheelbarrows.

After long days of work at low wages, they stayed in cheap boarding-houses along the canal.

After the Enfield Canal opened in November 1829, most of the Irish laborers moved on to work on other canals. But some stayed, forming the nucleus of the Irish community that would swell in Windsor Locks during the Great Hunger.

Most settled in Poquonock, where they worked in the Congress Mill and lived in company-owned apartments and boarding houses. Others worked on farms nearby or as domestic servants. By 1860, twenty percent of Windsor Locks' population was first- or second-generation Irish, and they made St. Mary's Catholic Church a center of community life.

Yankee Connecticut viewed the Irish as dirty drunks who lived in shanties and slept with pigs. Mark Twain, writing at his home in Hartford, used the stereotype to create Pap Finn, Huck Finn's layabout father.

Today you can hike along the towpath in the Windsor Locks Canal State Park.

3. BATTERY STREET HISTORIC DISTRICT, BURLINGTON, VERMONT

Nathaniel Hawthorne visited Burlington, Vermont, in 1832 and wrote down his impressions of the young city. He noted "the great number of Irish emigrants." They were everywhere: "lounging" around the wharves, "swarming in huts and mean dwellings near the lake," and "elbow[ing] the native citizens" out of work.

Burlington had lots of Irish immigrants—30 percent of its population around 1850. They first sailed from Ireland to Canada, then came down Lake Champlain—"the Irish lake"—on steamboats. From 1840 to 1860, the Irish comprised the largest ethnic minority in Vermont.

They came to work on the Champlain Canal, on railroads, and in textile mills. Young women could get decent wages as domestic servants, and men with strong backs could find work in Vermont's quarries.

In Burlington, most lived and worked along the industrial waterfront. Today, a section of that waterfront is known as the Battery Street Historic District, bounded by Main, St. Paul, and Maple streets, and Lake Champlain.

4. GOVERNOR WILLIAM SPRAGUE MANSION, CRANSTON RHODE ISLAND

On New Year's Eve 1843, Amasa Sprague left his mansion to take a walk. His servant later found his dead body, shot and bludgeoned.

The rich and powerful Sprague owned several textile mills, including the Cranston Print Works and the Slater Mill. He had had a dispute with three Irish brothers who ran a saloon in town. One of those brothers, John Gordon, was convicted of his murder.

John Gordon's real crime was to be Irish at a time when hatred of the Irish ran rampant. The judge had actually told the jury to pay more attention to Yankee witnesses than to Irish witnesses.

Circumstantial evidence showed John Gordon was innocent, but the state hanged him anyway. After Gordon's execution, Rhode Island banned capital punishment. Then in 2011, Governor Lincoln Chafee pardoned him.

Today you can visit Cranston to see Sprague's house, the Governor William Sprague Mansion, now a museum named for his son. John Gordon lived above a general store and saloon, a site that is now St. George Maronite Catholic Church.

5. NEAL DOW HOUSE, PORTLAND, MAINE

In Portland, Maine, Mayor Neal Dow didn't just discriminate against the Irish, he attacked them. Dow mounted a temperance crusade against the immigrants he called "rum-swilling foreigners."

Mayor Dow famously feuded with an Irish bootlegger and brothel owner named Mrs. Margaret Landrigan. She was a two-boater from County Cork who arrived in Portland in the 1840s.

Prosecutors hauled her into court for various liquor offenses from 1846 to 1851. Neal Dow's estranged cousin John Neal defended her, and the two men argued over her in the newspapers. Neal called her "a poor, but generous, kind-hearted Irish woman." Dow countered she kept "a notorious groggery" that caused police more trouble than any other.

Her life ended in a shanty where she was found dead, presumably murdered.

In 1855, Portland's Irish working-class residents rioted when they found their teetotaling, saloon-raiding mayor had stashed $1,600 worth of booze at City Hall. Dow called out the militia and ordered them to shoot. They did, killing a twenty-two-year-old sailor on the eve of his wedding.

Neal Dow's house is on the Portland Irish Heritage Trail on Congress Street.

6. MILLVILLE WORKER HOUSING, MILLVILLE, MASSACHUSETTS

By some estimates, Millville, Massachusetts, was 98 percent Irish from the late nineteenth century to the 1980s.

Joseph Banigan created Millville's Irish identity. He fled the potato famine and arrived in Rhode Island in 1847 at the age of eight. He lasted in school for about a year, but before he turned thirty he made enough money to found the Woonsocket Rubber Co. in Rhode Island.

In 1877, he bought some rundown mills and water rights in Millville across the border in Massachusetts. He turned the complex into a state-of-the art mill, adding eighty new houses for workers and a schoolhouse—known as Banigan City and Banigan City School.

Banigan hired hundreds of Irishmen to work sixty-hour weeks making rubber footwear. He was ruthless toward his mostly Irish labor unions. They walked out when he suddenly cut wages 18 percent. Banigan retaliated by firing strikers, evicting them from their homes, and blacklisting them so they couldn't work elsewhere. But he eased his conscience by spending millions on such palliatives as orphanages, hospitals, and churches.

By 1893 Joseph Banigan was New England's first Irish-Catholic millionaire. He sold his rubber company to the U.S. Rubber Co. cartel and became president, but didn't last long. He died in 1898.

Today, some of Millville's worker housing can be found in the Main Street Historic District of Millville, which encompasses the village center of the town.

NEW DEAL
PROJECTS

DURING THE GREAT DEPRESSION, A QUARTER OF THE LABOR FORCE WAS out of work. Those lucky enough to have jobs had their hours and wages cut. Things got so bad that people feared revolution, and when Franklin D. Roosevelt became president he supposedly said, "If I fail, I shall be the last one."

He didn't and he wasn't. His New Deal put tens of millions of people to work and changed the landscape throughout New England. It put sidewalks on streets, bridges over rivers, hiking trails in forests, seawalls on beaches, and public buildings in cities and towns. Much of the New Deal legacy is still in use and still visible today.

Roosevelt intended to revive the ideals of civil society, collective governance, and social well-being. He insisted his New Deal relief programs provide jobs and not handouts. Over eight years, the Works Progress Administration alone employed more than eight million Americans. The Civilian Conservation Corps (CCC) put three million young men to work at a monthly wage of thirty dollars—twenty five of which had to be sent home.

1. ACADIA NATIONAL PARK, MOUNT DESERT ISLAND, MAINE

By the time of the Great Depression, Acadia National Park was nearly twenty years old. Overgrown and inaccessible, it had few facilities, not nearly enough for the park's many visitors.

Superintendent George Dorr dreamed of improving the park, and he saw his chance in the CCC. He asked Roosevelt for a camp at Acadia.

Eventually some three thousand poor boys, mostly from Maine, came to Acadia for six months or longer to work as part of Roosevelt's "Tree Army."

The CCC ran three camps in and around Acadia National Park. They opened new trails and improved old ones, planted thousands of trees, made fire roads, fought fires, built footbridges, and constructed two campgrounds. They built Ocean Drive, which loops around the park with stunning views of the coast, and they opened hiking trails to Echo Lake, Long Pond, and Beech Cliff.

2. CAPE COD BRIDGES, SAGAMORE AND BOURNE, MASSACHUSETTS

When the Cape Cod Canal opened in 1914, its private owners hoped to cash in by charging tolls for shipping traffic. Mariners avoided the canal, though, because three drawbridges over the canal were such a navigational hazard. The canal enterprise lost money.

The U.S. government eventually took over the Cape Cod Canal. In 1933, Public Works Administration workers began building the Sagamore and Bourne bridges for the Army Corps of Engineers. They replaced earlier bridges, and allowed large oceangoing ships to pass below.

Ralph Adams Cram, the most influential architect of his day, designed the structure, including the neoclassical pylons and the Gothic-shaped arches.

The identical bridges both opened on June 22, 1935. A miniature copy of the bridges was used for the John Greenleaf Whittier Bridge, which connects Interstate 95 in Massachusetts from Newburyport to Amesbury.

3. MANCHESTER AIRPORT TERMINAL, LONDONDERRY, NEW HAMPSHIRE

The New Deal brought dozens of improvements to New Hampshire, such as the Hampton Beach seawall, town halls in Dover and Nashua, the Concord Library, and Cannon Mountain Ski Resort.

The New Deal also brought to Londonderry in 1937 an Art Deco airport terminal and control tower. Rural New Hampshire hadn't seen a lot of the Streamline Moderne style of architecture, but it seemed to fit with the glamor and newness of air travel. The terminal, a mere sixteen-hundred square feet, housed a ticket counter, lobby, offices, and a waiting room.

The 1937 terminal continued service until the airport outgrew it in 1995. The sleek Art Deco architecture saved it from demolition. The airport authority, local municipalities, and a new aviation historical society moved it over several runways. It is now home to the Aviation Museum of New Hampshire.

4. MCCOY STADIUM, PAWTUCKET, RHODE ISLAND

Thomas P. McCoy, Pawtucket's colorful mayor, wore shamrock-patterned ties and a red rose in his lapel. He used his political clout to get a baseball stadium from the New Deal, and he laid its cornerstone on November 3, 1940.

McCoy had chosen swampland called Hammond Pond as a building site, which guaranteed years of employment for hundreds of workers. Vehicles and equipment were swallowed overnight in the bottomless muck. In the end, the stadium cost more to build than the assessed value of Fenway Park.

When McCoy died suddenly in 1945, the City of Pawtucket named the stadium for him.

McCoy Stadium struggled for years, intermittently attracting farm teams for the Boston Braves, the Cleveland Indians, and the Boston Red Sox. In 1977, a Canadian businessman named Ben Mondor brought the Pawtucket Red Sox out of bankruptcy and visited McCoy stadium. "What a dump," he said. He turned around the team and the stadium, making it a family-friendly place where Girl Scouts camped overnight on the outfield, children got free medical checkups, and fans saw their birthdays celebrated on the Jumbotron.

McCoy Stadium was renovated in 1992 and expanded to seat ten thousand people in 1999, surviving efforts to abandon it.

5. MOUNT MANSFIELD, STOWE, VERMONT

Vermont's New Deal history—in fact, Vermont's history—can't be told without state forester Perry Merrill. When the CCC started up in the 1930s, few states had prepared projects. Merrill had already drawn up a long list, having led conservation, flood control, and forest management projects following the Great Vermont Flood of 1927.

Vermont was originally scheduled to get four CCC camps. Merrill wrangled thirty camps from Washington, with nearly forty-one-thousand men working in them from 1933 to 1942. CCC crews planted more than a million trees, built dams, and cleared more than one hundred miles of roads.

Merrill had seen how Scandinavian ski areas provided jobs and recreation. On his list of projects were ski trails on Mount Mansfield. The CCC boys built such trails as the Skimeister, the Overland, the Perry Merrill, and Lord.

They also made a large parking lot for several hundred cars. In 1940, state officials signed a lease with the Mount Mansfield Company to build a ski lift up Mount Mansfield. Today, that CCC project is the Stowe Mountain Resort—one of the premiere ski resorts east of the Mississippi.

6. TORRINGTON POST OFFICE MURALS, TORRINGTON, CONNECTICUT

Franklin Roosevelt took a special interest in building post offices because of their importance to community life. He insisted his home post office in Hyde Park, New York, be modeled after a historic house in town. His friend and relative Olin Dows painted the murals, which depicted both Roosevelt and Dows ancestors who lived in the Hudson Valley.

In Connecticut, the U.S. Treasury Department built or expanded more than twenty-five post offices and paid for as many post office murals between 1934 and 1943.

Artists vied for mural contracts in national and regional competitions. The winners were chosen for their skill and for the way they showed ordinary citizens, their community, and their history.

Another goal of the post office mural program was to link people to an earlier time and place when Americans faced great obstacles and overcome them.

Torrington chose to remember its native son who resisted slavery in "Episodes in the Life of John Brown." Arthur Covey painted several murals, which have since been moved to the new post office on Elm Street. They show John Brown leading black pioneers and an ox-drawn wagon. They also depict Brown as a young boy with his mother, supposedly a self-portrait of Covey in drag.

LITTLE ITALYS

SHORTLY AFTER THE AMERICAN CIVIL WAR, a new kind of neighborhood emerged in New England cities: a Little Italy. They were poor, dense, Roman Catholic, and very, very family oriented.

Italians immigrated to the U.S. cities to escape desperate poverty in Sicily and Southern Italy. They followed the Irish, who usually moved out of the neighborhood when the Italians moved in.

Today, the descendants of Italian immigrants make up more than 10 percent of the population of every New England state except Vermont and Maine. A Little Italy survives in Boston, in New Haven, and in Providence, but bulldozers took out the Little Italys of Northern New England to make way for hotels and parking lots.

People still flock to the surviving Little Italys for their buoyant street atmospheres, their summer religious festivals, and most of all for their food.

1. THE NORTH END, BOSTON, MASSACHUSETTS

People have lived in Boston's North End since 1630. Paul Revere lived there on the house site of a prominent Puritan minister, Increase Mather. The Old North Church still stands; Paul Revere saw two lanterns hang from its steeple.

By the late 1840s, the North End developed a red light district and prosperous residents moved away. Irish immigrants moved in and then moved up and out. By the early twentieth century, Eastern European Jews arrived. Then came many, many Italians. At one time forty four thousand Italians lived in the North End, more than three times the number of Irish at their peak.

The Italians took over Protestant churches and built new Catholic ones. They started the first Italian café, Café Vittoria, in 1929. They ran grocery stores and bakeries. Enterprising immigrants started the Prince pasta company on Prince Street, and the Pastene Corporation in a pushcart.

Not all Italian immigrants embraced capitalism. In the early nineteenth century, the North End was a hotbed of anarchists who wanted to violently overthrow all government. In 1920, it became the epicenter of the worldwide controversy over Nicola Sacco and Bartolomeo Vanzetti.

The two immigrants were anarchists accused of murdering two payroll guards in 1920 in Fall River, Massachusetts. Seven years later they were executed as protests erupted around the world. Their defense committee had its office in the North End, and two hundred thousand people watched their funeral procession through the streets of Boston.

Today the North End's narrow streets are crowded with cafes, pizzerias, small grocery stores, and dozens of Italian restaurants. The North End's religious societies sponsor a dozen feasts and processions during the year.

2. LITTLE ITALY, BURLINGTON, VERMONT

Italians arrived in Burlington at the turn of the nineteenth century to work in lumber mills and railroad yards. They created a vibrant little neighborhood along the waterfront east of Battery Street.

Outsiders thought they could improve Burlington's Little Italy with urban renewal. In 1966, the final house was razed to make way for the Champlain Street Project. More than two hundred people were scattered after the city bought their houses at unfairly low prices. The old neighborhood fell to parking garages and lots, concrete-and-glass office buildings, a hotel, and a windowless shopping mall.

Today three interpretive signs are all that's left of Burlington's Little Italy. It is fondly remembered as a place where neighbors shared homemade wine and children ran in and out of their neighbors' houses.

3. FEDERAL HILL, PROVIDENCE, RHODE ISLAND

Italian is still spoken in Providence's Little Italy, alive and well and known as Federal Hill. The neighborhood followed the typical trajectory: A colonial neighborhood became a commercial district, then came the Irish, followed by the Italians in the 1870s.

The gateway arch that welcomes visitors to Federal Hill is one of the most recognizable Providence landmarks. Italian flags decorate the main thoroughfare, Atwells Avenue, lined by more than twenty Italian restaurants. The local eateries attract skilled chefs because they're so near Johnson and Wales University.

In 1954, mob kingpin Ray Patriarca moved from Boston's North End to the National Cigarette Service Company and Coin-O-Matic Distributors on Atwells Avenue. He died of a heart attack in 1984.

Today Rhode Island is the most Italian state in the country, just ahead of Connecticut. More than a third of North Providence residents claim Italian ancestry.

4. LITTLE ITALY, PORTLAND, MAINE

Maine is one of the least Italian states in New England, but nonetheless fifty thousand Italian-Americans live within its borders. They began arriving in large numbers around 1900 and moved to Portland's Little Italy on India Street. They worked as barbers, carpenters, fishermen, longshoremen, railroad workers, and masons.

Life centered on St. Peter's Parish on Federal Street, built in 1929. Eventually Portland's Italian-Americans moved to the suburbs, and Portland's Little Italy is nearly gone. St. Peter's Parish is still active, and Micucci Grocery Co. is still open on India Street. Amato's Italian delicatessen, now a chain, claims to have originated the Italian sandwich.

5. NORTH END, PORTSMOUTH, NEW HAMPSHIRE

Portsmouth once had a tiny version of Boston's North End. And if Paul Revere lived in Boston's North End, Daniel Webster lived in Portsmouth's.

First it was a colonial neighborhood, then Irish. A wave of Italians arrived at the beginning of the twentieth century. They worked in the shoe and button factories, or in construction trades. Later they got jobs at the Portsmouth Naval Shipyard.

It was a crowded waterfront neighborhood with narrow, busy streets and dozens of small businesses. Families sold beer and lobster rolls from their homes, popcorn and ice cream from pushcarts.

By 1920, Portsmouth's Little Italy was 95 percent Italian. Urban renewal in the 1950s and 1960s leveled many of the homes, replacing them with a municipal parking lot, a hotel, and commercial buildings. Daniel Webster's home and the Farragut School next door became an A&P and a parking lot, then a hotel. Only a few of the old buildings survive within the boundaries of Market, High, Congress, Bridge, Maplewood, and Russell streets.

6. WOOSTER SQUARE, NEW HAVEN, CONNECTICUT

Connecticut, the second most Italian state in the United States, has 18.7 percent of its people claiming Italian ancestry. Roughly half the populations of three New Haven neighborhoods—East Haven, West Haven, and North Haven—are descended from Italian immigrants.

Wooster Square is New Haven's Little Italy, one of the oldest and most compact in the country. It has plenty of Italian pastry shops and restaurants, like Tony & Lucille's, Da Legna, Consiglio's, Frank Pepe's, and Sally's.

Revolutionary War General David Wooster owned a warehouse near Water Street, giving the neighborhood its name. Before the harbor was filled, Wooster Square was close to the waterfront. Ship captains and wholesale grocers built large houses near the port. By the end of the nineteenth century, factories moved to Wooster Square, making it a less desirable address.

Sargent Manufacturing, a hardware maker, moved in to New Haven and brought workers from the Amalfi coast of Italy. More Italians followed, to make corsets at Strouse, Adler, boots at Candee Rubber Co., clocks at the New Haven Clock Company, and carriage parts at C. Cowles. Many families opened small shops in their homes.

The neighborhood fell into poverty when factories closed during the Great Depression. The city planned to build a highway through Wooster Square during the 1950s and 1960s, but preservationists rallied to save it.

POORHOUSES

Poorhouses were once a very real and feared part of New England life. They evolved from the English poor laws of the sixteenth and seventeenth centuries, which required communities to take care of poor residents.

In colonial New England, the poor often relied on neighbors for help. Most towns in Plymouth Colony, for example, kept cattle to lend to distressed families who could use the milk and birth the calves.

The cost of caring for the poor caused some communities to warn out people who seemed likely to fall into poverty. Sometimes towns drove entire families away.

Eventually overseers were elected to find work for able-bodied people and help for those too old or feeble to work. A poor tax supported the overseer and the almshouse, poorhouse, or poor farm.

Some towns auctioned off their poor in a system called vendue. In 1786, Malden, Massachusetts, auctioned Mary Degresha off to the lowest bidder, who earned six dollars a week for housing and taking proper care of her.

The Great Embargo, the War of 1812, and financial panics in 1817 and 1837 sent waves of paupers to poor houses. So did the Irish migration of the 1840s and 1850s. The Civil War devoured husbands and fathers, leaving thousands of destitute widows and orphans.

The poor were kept out of sight, on farms down back roads or in walled-off buildings. By the late nineteenth century, states built asylums for the mentally ill. After the turn of the century, poorhouses declined and mostly old people lived in them. But some lasted until the 1960s.

1. MIDDLETOWN ALMS HOUSE, MIDDLETOWN, CONNECTICUT

Puritanical Connecticut thought godliness was rewarded with wealth and moral failure resulted in poverty. In the colony's earliest days, people in need were sent to board with better-off neighbors. The Puritans believed the more affluent family would set a good example and teach the poor boarder to become an upstanding member of society.

By the time of the American Revolution, Connecticut towns began to build alms houses for their paupers. By the nineteenth century Middletown was falling into depression, with more poor people than it could handle. Some came from surrounding farms that had failed, while others were victims of the fall-off in river trade during the Great Embargo and the War of 1812.

So the town voted in 1813 to build an alms house on Warwick Street. The Alms House opened in May 1814 and assigned its able-bodied poor to work on farms or local factories making textiles and gunpowder. Some had tasks in the work house inside the building.

The Alms House also housed the elderly, young, disabled, and insane. Discipline problems arose, and miscreants received harsh treatment. They were isolated in a "dark room" (probably the dungeon described by a local historian) for as long as forty-eight hours, or they were bound in shackles and chains, or fed bread and water.

The town selectmen began to worry about the cost of the Alms House. By 1824, the Alms House started to crack down on its residents. Men were separated from women and fewer people were allowed to work outside the building. As more and more people began to move into the neighborhood, a wall went up around the poorhouse.

A local businessman had his eyes on the property, a good industrial location with water access. He offered to swap a sixty-acre farm in a more remote location for the building. The town agreed, and in 1853 the poor moved to the Middletown Town Farms. The Alms House became a hardware factory.

Today, the Middletown Alms House is one of the oldest poorhouses still standing in the United States.

2. FALMOUTH POORHOUSE, FALMOUTH, MASSACHUSETTS

The Falmouth poorhouse was built as a tavern in 1769. Then the War of 1812 caused a depression across Cape Cod, and the tavern owner packed up and left for Cincinnati. The town moved the tavern about five miles next to the Methodist Cemetery, and turned it into the Falmouth Poor House.

The tavern itself was divided into eight-by-eight foot cells where the inmates lived according to their age, sex, health, level of insanity, and depth of poverty. More tiny cells were added in a new wing. The town fenced the land and later built a barn, which turned the poorhouse into a work house. Anyone who refused to work would be confined in a cell or farmed out indefinitely.

In 1878 the poorhouse became a poor farm, which actually supported itself by selling food. It was turned into an infirmary in 1920, and closed in 1960. The seven people remaining in the poorhouse went on welfare and moved to hospitals. The poorhouse now stands empty, but the graves in the Methodist Cemetery are filled with the paupers who died there.

3. BANGOR POOR FARM, BANGOR, MAINE

Just after the American Revolution, Maine towns put their poor in the hands of overseers, who paid people to take them into their homes for a year.

Mercy Lovejoy and her five children, for example, were auctioned off in 1817 to a farmer who fed and clothed them in exchange for their labor. The town of Livermore paid him $3.95 for the six Lovejoys.

Maine then started putting its poor into poor farms and poor houses.

The Bangor Poor Farm from 1827 to 1948 housed poor, disabled, and mentally ill people. Able-bodied inmates had to work on the farm producing cream and milk, hay, pork, and livestock for sale. Refusing to work got you locked in a cell, unless you were insane, feeble, or lame.

Today the Bangor Alms House is a residential hotel called the Dutton House Inn, and some of the cells still survive in the basement.

4. DEXTER ASYLUM, PROVIDENCE, RHODE ISLAND

A wealthy Rhode Island resident named Ebenezer Knight Dexter bequeathed the funds for the Dexter Asylum when he died in 1824. He left his farm to the Town of Providence and stipulated that a stone wall surround it.

Dexter left oddly specific instructions for the wall, which took eight years and $12,700 to finish.

The Asylum housed the poor, elderly, and mentally ill. By the 1840s most were Irish immigrants indentured for six months to work on the vegetable and dairy farm. Men and women lived separately and only saw visitors once every three weeks. They had bread and tea for dinner.

The Asylum punished those found guilty of drinking, immoral conduct, loud talking, disrespectful behavior, or faking illness to avoid work. They locked miscreants in a cell for three days and put them on short rations. The mentally ill—about a quarter of the population—were confined in "maniac cells."

The Asylum was torn down after its sale to Brown University in 1957. Dexter's old wall still stands next to the Olney-Margolies Athletic Complex.

5. SHELDON POOR FARM, ST. ALBANS, VERMONT

Late in the nineteenth century, the St. Albans *Weekly Messenger* exposed the Sheldon Poor Farm, calling it "a disgrace to humanity."

In 1834, four Vermont towns pooled their money to buy a 150-acre property in Sheldon to run as a poor farm. Four towns later joined in and the farm expanded to 235 acres. By sharing expenses, the towns expected to save money.

By 1897, the eight towns spent about twelve cents a day on food, clothing, and shelter for each of the sixty-two residents, according to the *Weekly Messenger*. Five had died the year before.

Only ten of the twenty-eight children attended school. The inmates had to walk, or hobble, through the snow to a filthy privy, but many didn't make it and so the bedrooms bred disease.

The inmates lived in tiny rooms with broken windows and could only congregate around stoves in narrow corridors. A small boy had fallen on a stove and had a large, runny blister on his cheek. Old Jane Donovan was bedridden with rheumatism. "She groans and moans her life away in a miserable hovel on a filthy bed," reported the newspaper. Her only company was a "quartette of feeble old women who smoke and croon idiotically away around a box stove in an adjoining room."

The Sheldon Poor Farm survived until 1968, and a fire destroyed the main building in 1978.

Today at the end of Poor Farm Road you can visit the Sheldon Home Association Cemetery, where lie the bodies of the poor who died there.

6. STRAFFORD COUNTY ALMS HOUSE, DOVER, NEW HAMPSHIRE

Unlike the other states that made their towns care for the poor, New Hampshire by 1866 required the county to provide for them.

New Hampshire's poor generally had to qualify for help by living in a town and paying taxes for seven consecutive years. Town paupers, except for honorably discharged veterans, went to the county poor farms. They could also be indentured as servants or laborers, and children could be apprenticed.

Strafford County built a new alms house in Dover after a fire in 1881 burned the old one and killed thirteen inmates. The replacement functioned as a large-scale farm, with a slaughterhouse, blacksmith shop, windmill, and a three-story building that could shelter three hundred people. The basement had cells that held petty criminals.

Able-bodied paupers and prisoners had to work the farm together and, by 1910, 90 percent of the Alms House staff were convicts.

Eventually, New Hampshire decided the respectable poor shouldn't have to live with criminals, and in 1907 the county built the House of Correction next door to the alms house. Both still stand.

LITTLE CANADAS

BETWEEN 1840 AND 1930, about nine hundred thousand French-speaking Canadians left Québec to work in New England's mills, potato fields, and logging camps. But mostly the mills. Most who left were young adults fleeing backbreaking toil on subsistence farms.

They were the only major ethnic group to arrive in the United States by train. In one week alone in April of 1869, twenty-three hundred French Canadians rode through St. Albans, Vermont, on the way to jobs and a new life.

Up until 1850, most Franco-Americans lived in Vermont. By 1860, another eighteen thousand Canadian immigrants had moved to New Hampshire, Massachusetts, and Rhode Island to work in the mills and factories. Immigration slowed during the Civil War, but the manufacturing boom that came afterward attracted wave after wave of French Canadians.

French Canadians were a big part of New England's biggest business. Textile manufacturing after the Civil War was the biggest U.S. industry in terms of employment and capital investment. By 1900, French Canadians made up 44 percent of the textile mills workforce. One in ten New Englanders spoke French.

A cousin or a brother would arrive first, get a job in a factory and settle in a French-speaking neighborhood called Little Canada. The Irish, who arrived earlier, viewed them as interlopers willing to work for lower wages. They called them Canucks.

It wasn't just the Irish. The *New York Times* reported in 1881 that French Canadian immigrants were "ignorant and unenterprising, subservient to the most bigoted class of Catholic priests in the world."

Franco-Americans were almost all Roman Catholic, and strict ones at that. They believed abandoning their language meant abandoning their religion, and they clung to their language longer than other immigrant communities. They called it *la survivance*.

Even today, New England's Little Canadas celebrate midnight Mass at Christmas with pancakes afterward and serve poutine—French fries, gravy, and cheese curds—in restaurants and social clubs.

1. WINOOSKI, VERMONT

In the mid-nineteenth century, French-speaking Canadians flooded into Chittenden County, Vermont. Nathaniel Hawthorne visited Vermont in 1840 and thought he'd arrived in Canada because everyone spoke French.

A town called Colchester offered jobs in and around the Burlington Woolen mills. Much of the work was low-paid, unskilled labor, but girls and boys could—and did—work in the mills to support their families.

After the Civil War, a shortage of men and the growth of the textile mills meant plenty of jobs for French Canadians willing to work.

Colchester's Little Canada in Winooski Village got its first French parish in 1868 when St. Francis Xavier Church opened. A parochial school had already started. The bishop insisted that half the classes be taught in English. That bilingual education continued well into the twentieth century.

Around the turn of the twentieth century the Burlington Mill began to fail, and the American Woolen Company bought it. Winooski broke off from Colchester in 1922 and incorporated as a city—the densest in northern New England.

2. WOONSOCKET, RHODE ISLAND

Franco-Americans got an early start in Woonsocket, once the most French city in the United States. French Huguenot families settled in the Blackstone Valley late in the eighteenth century and some of them built textile mills along the river. The Ballous, for example, built the Social Mill in 1810, and it grew into one of the largest textile manufacturers in the country.

As the textile industry grew, so did the need for millworkers, and in the 1840s textile owners began recruiting workers in Quebec. By 1900, 60 percent of Woonsocket residents had French roots, and by the Great Depression French Canadians made up three out of four people who lived in the city.

Nickels and dimes from Franco-American millworkers built St. Ann Roman Catholic Church in 1918. By World War II, they'd raised enough money to have Guido Nincheri paint the interior with magnificent frescoes, earning it the nickname "the Sistine Chapel of Woonsocket."

Woonsocket had five French parishes, French newspapers, French movies and radio programs, while school was taught in French. The mills fielded their own baseball teams, which is where Hall of Famer Nap Lajoie got his start.

The mills are mostly gone, but the Museum of Work and Culture in Market Square introduces the visitor to the experience of Quebecois in Rhode Island's mill towns.

3. NORTH GROSVENERDALE, CONNECTICUT

New England had Little Canadas everywhere, not just in cities. Today the place in Connecticut with the densest Franco-American population is North Grosvenerdale, a village in Thompson. About one in four of the five thousand people who live there has French ancestry.

Small textile mills lined the French River in Thompson until after the Civil War, when a Rhode Island investor named William Grosvener bought the water rights and a mill. He expanded his operation, which made fine cotton fabrics until 1954. Grosvener's enormous brick mill had a tower, from which a bell rang at 6 a.m. to mark the factory's opening and at 9 p.m. for the evening curfew.

Around 1872, Grosvener began recruiting French Canadians to work in his mills. They would ultimately make up 80 percent of his workforce. He built worker housing, mostly multifamily houses in the Greek revival style. The village's Little Canadas were on Market Street and in Three Rows, south of the mill and surrounded by the railroad and French River.

4. MANCHESTER, NEW HAMPSHIRE

Manchester had New England's largest and most cohesive Little Canada on its West Side. Management of the giant Amoskeag mills recruited Quebecois because they worked hard and rarely joined labor unions. They also had large families, which meant more workers—children—for the mill.

French Canadians trickled into Manchester after the Civil War and by 1873 five or six families arrived every day on the Train Du Canada. Ultimately they made up more than a third of the Millyard's workforce. They built parishes, schools, and social clubs on Manchester's West Side, and started La Caisse Populaire, Sainte-Marie, the first credit union in the United States. Middle-class doctors, lawyers, and schoolteachers followed the low-wage millworkers from Quebec.

The Irish, already settled, viewed the French Canadians as potential scabs. Fights broke out frequently between the two groups. A line painted down the street separated the French from the Irish on their way to work and school.

Peyton Place author Grace Metalious and Revlon founder Charles Revson grew up on Manchester's West Side. Rene Gagnon participated in the flag raising on Iwo Jima during World War II.

5. LEWISTON, MAINE

In the wee hours of 1924, the Ku Klux Klan set off a bomb in Lewiston, Maine, and burned a twelve-foot cross on the top of a hill. The bombings and burnings continued for a week to celebrate the victory of Owen Brewster, the KKK's candidate for governor.

No one was killed or seriously hurt, but the nativist terrorists did intimidate Lewiston's Little Canada.

French Canadians already made up half of Lewiston's population in 1920, but their numbers grew even more in the city and throughout the state in the 1920s. Maine's Protestants feared the new arrivals planned to take over and return the state to Canada. The Ku Klux Klan fed off those fears, and beginning in 1922 its membership in Maine exploded.

The *Maine Klansman* in 1924 reported, "If anyone walks down Lisbon Street in Lewiston, he will certainly think that he is in Quebec."

And then just as suddenly the Klan died out. Membership began to fall in 1926, and disappeared by 1935.

The Quebecois created their own distinct community just where they'd arrived—the terminus of the Grand Trunk Railroad along the Androscoggin River. Called the Island, it resembled Quebec City's crooked streets more than the typical millworker housing.

The Institut Jacques Cartier, a fraternal organization, built and bought most of the Island's tenements, and it built the Dominican Building, the center of Little Canada's social life.

6. LOWELL, MASSACHUSETTS

Lowell's Little Canada got its start after the Civil War with a French Canadian named Samuel Marin. A Lowell dry goods employee since 1857, the mill owners hired him eight years later to recruit Quebecois families to work in the mills. He developed tenement blocks on land by the Lawrence Mills, and packed in French Canadian families like sardines.

Marin brought three thousand French Canadians among Lowell's forty-one thousand people in 1870. By 1881, that number had swelled to ten thousand, and doubled again by 1909.

Lowell's Little Canada, like many throughout New England, had its own churches, schools, social clubs, and newspapers.

By the 1920s, mill operations were moving south, where labor was even cheaper. Many millworkers lost their jobs. In 1936, the Merrimack River overflowed its banks, wiping out some mills and many small Franco-American businesses. Jack Kerouac's father lost his printing shop in the flood, and spent the rest of his life in poverty and alcoholism.

Little Canada got too shabby for the city fathers of Lowell. The Lowell *Sun* called it a "dismal proletarian district." And so in the 1960s the bulldozers took out most of it in the name of urban renewal. The University of Massachusetts at Lowell now inhabits the space where hundreds of Franco-Americans lived their lives.

In 1977, a monument was erected on the corner of Aiken and Hall streets to memorialize the "hard working French Canadians (who) came to fill the mills of Lowell and build a tradition of faith, generosity, and pride." It then lists all the streets of Little Canada that no longer exist.

STRANGE NEW ENGLAND

NEW ENGLAND HAS ALWAYS BEEN A BIT STRANGE AND SPOOKY. IMAGINE what it was like when colonists arrived in the early sixteenth century, after a great plague had devastated the Indian population. The land was strewn with bones and skulls. So many Indians died there weren't enough left to bury the dead. English colonist Thomas Morton described the heaps of Indian corpses "a new found Golgotha."

Morton was a free-thinking renegade who infuriated the Puritans in the next town—Plymouth. He had the temerity to put up a Maypole, which so offended Myles Standish he took it down and arrested Morton.

The Puritans had plenty of other oddities in addition to their Maypolephobia. They hated Christmas, enforced a strict dress code, and put people in the stocks for kissing their spouse on Sunday.

The Puritans also liked to put witches to death, and not just in Salem, Massachusetts. So no wonder Halloween has a special resonance in New England. There's even a name for the region's special brand of horror: Gothic New England.

Writers from Nathaniel Hawthorne to Stephen King have recycled New England's strange lore. Ghosts, witches, devils, and monsters in human shape populate their novels and short stories.

Another odd breed, the Boston Brahmin, appears in novels by such writers as John P. Marquand and Henry James. Hidebound to the point of eccentricity, their wealth allows them to indulge their whims and passions, often with strange results.

GHOST TOWNS

THOUGH PEOPLE TYPICALLY THINK OF GHOST TOWNS AS BELONGING TO the Old West, New England has plenty of its own.

A Cape Cod town disappeared for the usual reason coastal villages disappear: A hurricane blew it away. Others vanished because of war, economic downturns, or clearcutting and pollution. Still others were abandoned for reasons that may never be known.

1. HANTON CITY, RHODE ISLAND

Hanton City along Route 116 in Smithfield, Rhode Island, started as a colonial settlement also known as the Lost City.

Its overgrown remains consist of several stone foundations, a defunct dam, scattered stone walls, and a burial site with three readable names: Alfred, Eliza, and Emor Smith.

There's little else to show a town once existed there, save for Hanton City Trail in Smithfield and Hanton Road in North Smithfield.

Some say a small band of runaways from slavery built Hanton City after choosing to live in the wilds of Smithfield. Others say the town quarantined people with a communicable disease.

Still others believe Loyalists founded Hanton City during the American Revolution. The patriots exiled several Tories to Smithfield and Glocester in 1776, and they may have gone to Hanton City. Or perhaps a group of Loyalists decided to form an enclave of like-minded people.

Whatever the reason, the land is now privately owned.

2. WHITEWASH VILLAGE, MASSACHUSETTS

Whitewash Village on Monomoy Island off Chatham was established in 1710 with a tavern for sailors. The town took its name from whitewashed rocks, which people could still see in 1864.

The town grew to about two hundred people, mostly fishermen. They packed and dried cod and mackerel for Boston and New York, and they sold lobster to mainlanders.

The town at its height had a school for sixteen students, cottages, storage sheds perfumed with fish oil, and the Monomoy House, a lodging house and hotel. The sea came partway up the front stairs during some high tides, and the children sometimes waded to school.

Around 1860, a hurricane washed away Whitewash Village's harbor and the town was abandoned. The only evidence of it that remains is Monomoy Lighthouse.

3. GAY CITY, CONNECTICUT

Gay City in Hebron, Connecticut, was anything but. The village survived for eighty years until drunkenness, feuds, business failures, and murder turned it into a ghost town.

Elijah Andrus founded Gay City as a community of Hartford religious zealots in 1796. It attracted about twenty-five families, mostly from the Gay family.

Religious leaders served rum to all male members of the community during religious services, either to lure worshipers or as part of the sect's religious practice. Drunken brawls resulted, and some of the settlement's families left. Andrus abandoned his followers in 1800 and John Gay replaced him as community leader.

In 1804 the settlement earned the name Factory Hollow when it built a woolen mill along the Blackledge River. The mill burned down in 1830, triggering another exodus. A paper mill briefly revitalized the town.

Many of Gay City's remaining young men died in the Civil War. Then the paper mill burned, and the town pretty much disappeared. But not before a human skeleton was found in a charcoal pit and a blacksmith stabbed an apprentice to death—for being late.

Gay City's former existence is suggested by stone foundations, several grass-filled cellar holes, and a few tombstones. Since 1944 it's been Gay City State Park, with ten miles of walking trails through forest and swamp and a small beach.

4. ZEALAND, NEW HAMPSHIRE

Follow Route 302 through Crawford Notch, and you'll come upon what used to be the village of Zealand in Carroll. From 1875 to 1885, Zealand had a post office, a school, and as many as 250 men who cut trees for J.E. Henry.

The relentless Henry was the region's largest lumber operator. His men worked eleven-hour days regulated by forty-seven posted rules. Twenty-eight of them concerned the proper care of horses. Henry paid each of his men in person while carrying a gun on his hip, and he brooked no arguments.

Henry wanted to sell the Zealand Mountain and leave Zealand. At the same time a hotel company planned to build the Mount Washington Hotel facing Zealand Mountain. Henry offered to sell the mountain, but the hotel company balked. Henry then threatened to burn every tree in sight, ruining the view from the hotel. He sent in a crew of men to start cutting trees and hauling bricks for kilns in which to burn the logs. The hotel company paid the timber baron his price.

From 1886 to 1903 fires destroyed the town and the valley. Very little evidence of the village remains among the trails and campgrounds.

5. PERKINS, MAINE

Perkins lay in the Kennebec River between Richmond and Dresden before it was abandoned in the 1940s. It includes Swan Island, Little Swan Island, and some tidal flats.

Perkins once had nearly one hundred residents. They built ships, farmed, and harvested ice. Wealthy summer people then discovered the island and built summer homes there. Thomas Handasyd Perkins, a wealthy Boston Brahmin, was its most famous resident. He paid to have the town incorporated, and so the town took its name from him.

By 1918 the population dwindled to sixty-one, and the town was disincorporated. The Great Depression and pollution in the Kennebec River sent the rest of the population away. No one lived there by 2000.

Preservationists are trying to preserve thirteen of the buildings in Perkins, some of which date to the 1750s. The town is protected as the Steve Powell Wildlife Management Area, named after an island biologist and resident.

6. LEWISTON, VERMONT

Settlers came to Lewiston in 1765 and named it after Dr. Joseph Lewis, who arrived two years later. For many years Lewiston was a thriving village in Norwich, Vermont, with mills and a railroad station across from Hanover, New Hampshire.

Coal was shipped to Dartmouth along the railroad until the college switched to heating oil in the 1920s. By 1930, Lewiston's mills had all closed and commercial activity moved to White River Junction.

In 1950, construction of the Wilder Dam flooded the village's low-lying farms. In 1967, bulldozers turned Lewiston into a ghost town when they leveled it to make way for a feeder road to Interstate 91.

The railroad and the station survive, unused. Dr. Joseph Lewis's house is now a pottery studio owned by Dartmouth College. Lewiston Hill Road comprises what was once the village center.

ABANDONED PLACES

THERE'S SOMETHING STRANGELY ALLURING ABOUT ABANDONED PLACES. To stumble across an old World War II bunker or to explore a house deserted long-ago evokes a sense of mystery and even awe.

Some people are drawn to specific categories of abandonment, and they make a hobby of photographing graffiti-covered mills or empty mansions or derelict shopping malls. You can find them in cyberspace.

New England, sadly, is filled with decaying old mills, mansions with moss-covered floors, and more and more shopping malls that echo.

Tim Edensor, a geography professor at Manchester Metropolitan University, called them "marginal spaces filled with old and obscure objects." People can see and feel things in abandoned places they can't in everyday life. They're about nature and time, surrender and decline.

Others just call it "ruin porn."

1. WPOP-AM STATION, NEWINGTON, CONNECTICUT

An old brick radio station molders away on Cedar Street near the train tracks in Newington. The rounded corners and glass-brick windows give the low-slung building an Art Deco flair. A chain link fence surrounds it, and above the door big white letters proclaim "WPOP."

In 1936, WNBC in New Britain moved its 250-watt transmitter and antenna to that now-empty building in Newington. Over time, the station increased its power to five thousand watts. It also changed hands and call letters frequently, until 1956 when it became WPOP.

In 1958, WPOP started broadcasting rock 'n roll music, one of the first to do so in Connecticut. Legions of Baby Boomers grew up listening to songs on WPOP like *Gloria* by the Shadows of Knight, *96 Tear Drops* by ? Mark and the Mysterians, and *Night Train* by James Brown. Those songs made it onto one of the half-dozen albums that WPOP produced in the 1960s and 1970s.

But then television entertainer Merv Griffin bought WPOP in 1973, which eventually got gobbled up by Clear Channel and moved to an all-talk format. It isn't clear when WPOP abandoned the Cedar Street station.

2. GHOST LOCOMOTIVES, ALLAGASH REGION, MAINE

Deep in the heart of Maine's wilderness sit two abandoned locomotives silently rusting miles from any road or railhead.

An independent logger named King Ed Lacroix put the ghost locomotives there. He built a thirteen-mile railroad in the middle of the Allagash—some would call it nowhere—to haul pulpwood to Maine paper mills in Millinocket and East Millinocket.

By 1933 the Great Depression had depressed demand for paper, so Lacroix abandoned the Allagash, the railroad, the rolling stock, and the ghost locomotives.

When demand for paper finally picked up, trucks hauled logs more efficiently than railroads. The locomotives stayed in the back country.

Today the abandoned locomotives that Ed Lacroix left are part of the remote and scenic Allagash Wilderness Waterway protected by the State of Maine.

3. BOSTON BEAR PENS, BOSTON, MASSACHUSETTS

Abandoned bear pens in Boston? Yup. They're part of Zoo New England, formerly the Franklin Zoo in Franklin Park.

Frederick Law Olmsted was responsible for an open plan zoological park surrounded by the larger park. The free zoo was a huge hit when it opened in 1912. Millions came each year. Bears roamed freely (well, freely-ish) in a large stone enclosure at the bottom of a grand stone staircase. Large bas-reliefs of bears still stand amid the decaying cages.

When the Depression came, so did the wild zoo's decline. In 1958, a city commission took over the zoo and tried to revitalize it. They built a fence around the wild menagerie and charged admission. The bear pens, hard to tear down, were simply left outside to rot.

They appear in the book and film *Mystic River*, where a murder victim was found in the bear pens.

4. HILL VILLAGE, HILL, NEW HAMPSHIRE

Hill was established in 1778 along the Pemigewasset River, and it remained a small mill town for more than a century.

In 1937, the people of Hill learned that the federal government planned to flood their town for the Franklin Falls dam. By January 1940, they formed an association and bought land on higher ground. There they built a new Hill, with thirty houses, a water system, and a Town Hall.

In 1941, Hill started a Town Meeting in its old Town Hall, then recessed, and moved uphill to the new Town Hall. There they finished Town Meeting.

Today the old town floods when the dam is closed to prevent flooding downstream. But when the dam is open, hikers can see the streets, cellar holes, water pipes, railings, stone steps, sidewalks, remnants of the old mill, and a cemetery.

5. PAWTUCKET/CENTRAL FALLS STATION, RHODE ISLAND

The Pawtucket/Central Falls railroad station was once a magnificent Beaux Arts palace reigning high above four railroad tracks. Its huge waiting room had a wainscot of Italian marble and a barrel ceiling that rose thirty feet above the tiled floor. Ticket agents worked from windows framed in inlaid wood and two hundred passengers could wait on large oak benches.

The Pawtucket/Central Falls station still straddles the tracks, but that's about all it does. Well, other than crumble and fall victim to vandals.

When it opened, it replaced two separate stations that serviced the New York, New Haven and Hartford Railroad. The size and elegance of the station expressed the affluence and optimism of Central Falls and Pawtucket. When the station opened in 1916, the two cities together had a population that rivaled Hartford, Bridgeport, and Springfield.

The cities fell on hard times, the building deteriorated, and the railroad closed it. It still used the platforms, though. Then MBTA commuter rail serviced the stop until Rhode Island cut funding in 1981. When the state began to pay for MBTA trains again, they couldn't service the disintegrated Pawtucket/Central Falls station. Today, ivy and graffiti cover the old brick walls of the once-useful—and grand—old building.

6. ABANDONED INTERSTATE-189, BURLINGTON, VERMONT

Once the Federal Highway Administration planned to build an interstate from Exit 13 on Interstate 89 in Burlington to the industrial waterfront. Trucks could take it to bring freight to and from the water's edge. But then a toxic barge canal stopped construction just beyond the US Route 7 interchange, only 1.488 miles from the highway's beginning.

About half a mile of unfinished highway remained, though, so Jersey barriers prevented traffic on the orphaned stretch of pavement.

And then industry disappeared. By the 1980s Burlington's commercial activity mainly involved tourism, so transportation officials abandoned plans to finish I-189, at least for a while.

In 2012, federal highway planners came up with a new scheme to extend I-189 to funnel traffic from Route 7 to downtown. Opposition to the plan halted construction, and the abandoned pavement serves as a pedestrian walkway for aficionados of ruin porn.

MYSTERIOUS STONE STRUCTURES

New England colonists found many stone buildings when they arrived in North America. Typically they were one story high, circular or rectangular, and as long as thirty feet. Many had roof openings that allowed a little light to illuminate the interior.

As a result, early mercenaries to the Northeast wrote about "Indian stone castles." In 1654, John Pynchon sent a letter from Springfield, Massachusetts, to John Winthrop the Younger, who served as Connecticut's governor. Pynchon heard "a report of a stone wall and strong chamber in it, made all of stone, which is newly discovered at or near Pequot."

Speculation now runs rampant about the origins of the mysterious stone structures that dot New England, hundreds of them by some estimates. Did medieval Irish monks, American Indians, or Vikings build them? Or did the English colonists just build them as root cellars?

Some of them are ancient, oriented to the stars and planets. Some stand near megaliths, cairns, or dolmens. A few have what are probably stone beds or sacrificial altars.

1. GUNGYWAMP, GROTON, CONNECTICUT

The hundred-acre Gungywamp archaeological site contains such stone structures as beehive chambers, petroglyphs, a double circle of stones, cellars, and walls. All are hundreds of years old.

Some of the structures are thought to be Native American and perhaps had ceremonial functions. Colonial settlers built others as root cellars and birthing chambers. Some features of the site suggest the walls were originally built as fortifications.

Gungywamp's most famous chamber is the so-called "calendar chamber." A vent at one end of the chamber aligns with the spring and fall equinoxes. It thus allows a shaft of sunlight to fall directly on a smaller chamber within the larger structure. Archaeologists suspect the colonists used it for storage for a nearby tan bark mill.

Many of the Gungywamp's structures stand on private land. Visitors can tour parts of the Gungywamp through the Denison Pequotsepos Nature Center.

2. HIRUNDO STONE STRUCTURES, ALTON AND OLD TOWN, MAINE

The Red Paint people of Maine once settled in the Hirundo Wildlife Refuge, a wetland preserve. Archaeologists discovered artifacts from the seven-thousand-year-old village along the Wabanaki Trail.

Among the bogs and ancient burial grounds are at least eighteen curious stone piles, clearly made by man. But by whom and for what? And when? No one knows. Most are six-and-a-half feet in diameter and a foot and a half high.

The University of Maine owns the Hirundo Wildlife Refuge, which is open dawn to dusk all week long.

3. UPTON STONE CHAMBER, UPTON, MASSACHUSETTS

One of the largest and probably best known stone chambers in New England is the Upton Stone Chamber near Worcester in Upton.

It includes a tunnel, fourteen feet high, connecting to a roundish beehive room that rises twelve feet. A stone slab sits on top. In 1989, two archao-astronomists concluded that people used the chamber between 700 A.D. and 750 A.D. to study the Pleiades. Around 670 A.D., they used it to view the summer solstice. It's part of the Upton Heritage Park on Elm Street.

Thirty miles away in Acton, Massachusetts, an underground stone chamber in the Nashoba Brook Conservation Area is known as the "potato cave." Residents had long assumed the structure was a root cellar. A 2006 excavation found evidence people stored food in it in the eighteenth or nineteenth century. Some argue Indians built it before the colonists arrived. Still others say railroad workers lived in it during the nineteenth century.

4. AMERICAN STONEHENGE, SALEM, NEW HAMPSHIRE

America's Stonehenge is the largest collection of stone structures in North America. A thirty-acre complex of underground chambers and stone walls, it includes megalithic tombs called dolmens and cromlechs. There's a secret bed, an echoing oracle chamber, a sacrificial altar stone, and a stone-lined speaking tube that gives the impression the altar is talking when someone speaks into it.

The site also has monoliths that are astronomically aligned, leading to the conclusion the stones were used as a prehistoric calendar.

Radiocarbon dating confirms that whoever built the structure built it four thousand years ago. Today, nature worshippers perform seasonal rituals at the site.

The written record doesn't mention the ancient stone structures until 1907, in *History of Salem, New Hampshire* by Edward Gilbert. He wrote that a family named Pattee owned the land, called Mystery Hill, and had many of the stones carted away for construction in Lawrence, Massachusetts.

A retired insurance executive named William Goodwin bought the site in 1937. He had it excavated and became convinced Irish Culdee monks built the site about 1000 A.D.

5. QUEEN'S FORT, EXETER, RHODE ISLAND

The Queen's Fort and Queen's Bed Chamber have inspired colorful legends involving hermits, bandits, and King Philip, who led the Indians in a war against land-grabbing Europeans.

Archaeologists and historians associate the fort with a man named Stonewall John, a talented stone mason who may have been Narragansett or English. He may have built the stone fort to protect King Philip during King Philip's War. The colonists made one of their first attacks on the fort during the war, which King Philip lost in 1678, along with his life.

Inside the fort is a six-square-foot chamber with a seven-foot ceiling and a sand floor. It may have been built for the Narragansett queen Quaiapen (also called Matuntuck). She supposedly hid out at the site during King Phililp's War before moving somewhere else, where she died. Some have also suspected that Quaiapen and Stonewall John were lovers.

Many archeologists have since dug at the site. Today the Rhode Island Historical Society owns it. You can get to it via a series of trails in Exeter that surround the property.

6. CALENDAR II, WOODSTOCK, VERMONT

Eastern Vermont has some of the densest concentrations of ancient stone structures in North America. An inventory of Vermont's stone chambers compiled by the New England Antiquities Research Association found fifty-two. They discovered them in twenty-three towns in five Vermont counties, particularly Orange and Windsor.

In 1975, a retired marine biologist from Harvard announced his discovery: On Vermont's stone structures he found inscriptions in a dead Celtic language called Ogam. He concluded Celts from the Iberian peninsula carved them around 1000 B.C. They all faced east and many had inscriptions. Some have symbolic markings, while others have Celtic place names.

But critics say Celts would have left other evidence that they'd settled in New England. No one has found any such evidence.

Still, Vermont farmers told stories of their great-grandfathers' plows uncovering stone huts. So in 1977, the Vermont Division for Historic Preservation studied the stone chambers in the state. They concluded the stone structures did not serve as stone burial vaults, charcoal or lime kilns, potash burners, or iron furnaces.

One of the biggest and best known stone chambers is called Calendar II in South Woodstock. Calendar II measures ten feet by twenty feet on the inside, the same geometrical ratio as the King's Chamber of the Great Pyramid. And the door aligns with the solstice sunrise.

STRANGE ROCKS

New England's stony soil has produced a goodly number of strange rocks with names such as the Devil's Footprint, the Narragansett Runestone, and the Man-eating Stone of Glastonbury.

Folktales grew up around some of New England's strange rocks, like the one about the devil's footprint in Maine. Scientific research explained some of the others, like the dinosaur tracks that have been named the Connecticut State Fossil.

In some cases there has never been a satisfactory explanation for how they got that way.

1. EUBRONTES, ROCKY HILL, CONNECTICUT

In 1802, a farm boy named Pliny Moody came across foot-long dinosaur tracks in Holyoke, Massachusetts. That was the first of many discoveries of dinosaur tracks in the sandstone of the Connecticut River Valley.

Eubrontes describes the footprint, not the dinosaur. Edward Hitchcock, the president of Amherst College, studied fossils in Holyoke, and gave them the name. He concluded, wrongly, the Eubrontes tracks were made by large birds.

On August 23, 1966, Edward McCarthy was bulldozing a path for Interstate 91 in Rocky Hill, when he overturned a block of sandstone imprinted with six three-toed footprints. The land turned out to be a former lakebed riddled with dinosaur tracks, the largest such site in North America.

Scientists confirmed the importance of the Rocky Hill dinosaur tracks. The highway was moved and the lake bed was designated a Connecticut state park. Scientists found about two thousand of the three-toed tracks, which have been linked to the Jurassic-era Dilophosauris. However, the scientists covered up about fifteen hundred tracks to preserve their integrity.

Connecticut established Dinosaur State Park, which opened to the public in 1968. An inflatable dome protected the tracks, but it kept collapsing. So the state removed the dome, closed the park, and put up a geodesic dome over the dinosaur tracks. The park is open year-round, except for holidays.

2. DEVIL'S FOOTPRINT, MANCHESTER, MAINE

Next to the meeting house in North Manchester lies a cemetery surrounded by a wall with a strange rock in it. The rock, in the corner of the wall, has three imprints said to be the devil's footprints. One looks like a cloven hoof, the other two look human. Someone conveniently spray painted them red.

There is a story that goes with the rock, which may or may not be true (probably not). Years ago, a crew of construction workers was clearing a path for Scribner Hill Road when they came upon a boulder that could not be moved. One of the workmen exclaimed he'd sell his soul to the devil to move the rock. The next day, the rock was moved and the construction worker gone. The devil left his footprints on the rock as a reminder of the deal.

The North Manchester Meeting House, built in 1793 on Scribner Hill Road, is still used as a church.

3. DIGHTON ROCK, BERKLEY, MASSACHUSETTS

Dighton Rock has been mystifying people since before America was colonized. The rock is an eleven-foot-high boulder covered with ancient petroglyphs of an unknown origin. It was once on the shore of the Taunton River, but it's now been given its own museum (operated by appointment only) in Berkley, once part of Dighton.

Visitors to the strange rock (now in Dighton Rock State Park) will be in good company. Cotton Mather, George Washington, and dozens of scientists have attempted to decode the meaning behind the writing on it.

Some theories: A message left by Norse explorers, Native American symbols, or a message from God. So far there's no consensus as to the rock's significance, and its meaning remains a mystery.

4. MYSTERY STONE OF LAKE WINNIPESAUKEE, CONCORD, NEW HAMPSHIRE

Seneca Ladd was many things: Piano maker, carriage maker, mill owner, banker, amateur meteorologist, and geologist.

People in New Hampshire's Lakes Region remember his legacy well. But his most unusual accomplishment remains a mystery. One day while workmen were digging on his property in Meredith, sometime around 1872, they uncovered an egg-shaped object buried two feet deep and encased in clay.

The object, by far the smallest of our mystery stones, has carvings that remain unidentified. Ladd himself thought his "egg" was Native American, and he displayed it for the curious for much of his life. The egg still baffles scientists as to what exactly it is. Ladd's daughter gave the object to the New Hampshire Historical Society in 1927, which displays it in its Museum of New Hampshire History in Concord.

5. NARRAGANSETT RUNESTONE, WICKFORD, RHODE ISLAND

Quidnessett Rock, also known as the Narragansett Runestone, is a strange rock in North Kingstown, Rhode Island, with a somewhat shaky pedigree.

The two-and-a-half ton rock was first called to the attention of Rhode Island historians around 1984. The rock bears a series of unusual markings that some claim are reminiscent of markings made by the religious sect known as the Knights Templar. This faction claims the stone is a marker, probably documenting a land claim before Christopher Columbus arrived.

However, Edward Brown of Providence eventually came clean: He and his brother made the markings on the rock as young boys in 1964, though not as a hoax. They did it just for fun, he said.

To others, the rock is a nuisance. A resident of Pojac Point in North Kingstown caused a kerfuffle when he lifted the rock and dropped it farther out to sea to slow the onslaught of visitors making pilgrimages to the stone. He got caught, and he retrieved the stone, which is now on permanent display in Updike Park in the Village of Wickford. It makes as good an excuse as any for a trip to the charming village.

6. MAN-EATING STONE OF GLASTONBURY, VERMONT

Between 1945 and 1950, five people disappeared on Glastonbury Mountain, four without a trace: Middie Rivers (1945); Paula Jean Weldon (1946); James Tedford (1949); Paul Jephson (1950); and Frieda Langer (1950).

Rivers was an experienced hunter who knew the area. Weldon was a Bennington College sophomore who disappeared while hiking the Long Trail. James Tedford, a veteran, vanished on a bus exactly three years after Paula Weldon disappeared. Jephson, an eight-year-old boy, went missing from the family truck while his mother fed some pigs. Langer disappeared on a hike near the Somerset Reservoir; her body was found seven months later in an area already searched carefully.

In 2009, a writer named Joseph Citro suggested an explanation in his book, *The Vermont Monster Guide*: The man-eating stone of Glastonbury Mountain. In it, he wrote, that no one had seen it, but Indians knew of it and warned people away. "We can only imagine it as a sizable rock, large enough to stand on. But when someone stands upon it, the rock becomes less solid, and, like a living thing, swallows the unfortunate trespasser. A number of disappearances have been reported on Glastonbury Mountain. Could all these vanished folks have stepped inadvertently on this hungry stone?"

Citro dubbed the area, part of the Green Mountains, the Bennington Triangle.

HOMES OF NUTTY MILLIONAIRES

New England enjoyed the highest standard of living in the world during much of the seventeenth and eighteenth centuries. Fishing, farming, and trading spread quite a lot of wealth around. Then during the Industrial Revolution, many enterprising Yankees made fortunes for themselves. They usually weren't too keen on sharing it with their workers, though.

Great wealth brought with it great freedom to do as one chose. Many of New England's millionaires chose to build palatial estates. And some of them became monuments to their kookiness.

1. LORD TIMOTHY DEXTER, NEWBURYPORT, MASSACHUSETTS

Timothy Dexter was considered a lucky fool for selling coal to Newcastle and bed warmers to the tropics—and somehow making money on the ventures. But he had no luck in one thing he really cared about: acceptance by Boston's aristocracy. They viewed him as uneducated, boorish, drunk, vain, and ridiculous. They weren't far wrong.

Born in Massachusetts in 1747, Dexter called himself a lord, faked his own funeral, and tried to take liberties with pretty women half his age. He had the Midas touch, though. "Lord" Dexter married a wealthy widow in Newburyport and went about multiplying her money. He rounded up stray cats, shipped them off to the Caribbean, and made a profit. He shipped coals to Newcastle on the eve of a strike and sold at a premium. When he wrote a semiliterate book without any punctuation, it went into eight printings.

"Lord" Dexter bought a Newburyport mansion that now houses the city's public library.

2. WILLIAM GILLETTE, EAST HADDAM, CONNECTICUT

William Gillette was the son of a U.S. senator from Hartford, but he chose acting as his career (probably disappointing Dad). When Arthur Conan Doyle asked him to adapt Sherlock Holmes's stories for the stage, Gillette agreed. Then for many years he starred as Sherlock Holmes—complete with curved pipe, deerstalker hat, and the catchphrase, "Elementary, my dear fellow."

Gillette was already well-to-do, but playing Sherlock Holmes for thirty years made him even richer. He decided to build a retirement home on a hill in Haddam with gorgeous views of the Connecticut River.

He built a stone castle that featured a poorly lit entrance hall. When guests entered, Gillette would startle them by dramatically entering the hall from a secret door. He built a miniature railroad so he could tootle around the grounds, and he filled the house with gadgets, including exquisite cat toys for his many cats. He installed hidden mirrors so he could watch his guests unobserved, and secret back doors so he could leave if he felt antisocial.

Gillette died in 1937 at the age of 83. A few years later the State of Connecticut bought his castle and turned it into a state park and museum. Today it's one of the state's most popular tourist attractions.

3. O. H. P. BELMONT, NEWPORT, RHODE ISLAND

Belcourt Castle was built by Oliver Hazard Perry Belmont, the wastrel son of financier August Belmont and grandson of Commodore Matthew Perry. His more enterprising brother August financed the Cape Cod Canal.

O. H. P. Belmont loved his horses certainly more than he loved his first wife. He told his architect, Richard Morris Hunt, to devote the first floor to stables for his horses. The nags had upholstered teak stalls, steam heat, and coats of pure Irish linen. English grooms changed their bedding three times a day.

O. H. P. Belmont was already divorced when he started building the sixty-room bachelor pad in 1890. He had briefly married Sara Swan Whiting. Belmont spent their Paris honeymoon in gambling dens and whorehouses and then abandoned his wife for a French dancer. When she found she was pregnant he denied the child was his.

After he divorced Sara, he married the ex-wife of William K. Vanderbilt, who became Alva Belmont. She moved from the Newport mansion she'd designed, Marble House, to the one her new husband created. Tour guides brought people outside Belcourt and announced, "She used to dwell in marble halls with Mr. Vanderbilt. Now she lives over the stables with Mr. Belmont."

4. EDWARD SEARLES, WINDHAM, NEW HAMPSHIRE

Edward Searles married one of the great Gilded Age fortunes and spent a lot of it on houses. When his wife died shortly after their marriage, Searles's detractors didn't think he should have that kind of money. They called him a bric-a-brac salesman and a paper-hanger.

They were close to the mark.

Searles started his career as a mill hand in his hometown, Methuen, Massachusetts. He eventually wound up at Herter Bros., the Vanderbilts' interior design firm. In 1881, the forty-year-old Searles, a bachelor, moved to California, where he met Mary Hopkins, the widow of railroad baron Mark Hopkins. They worked together building her mansion in Great Barrington, Massachusetts. Then they built another mansion on Block Island. Meanwhile he turned his childhood home in Methuen into an estate. By 1887, he and Mary had married. By 1891, she was dead.

Mary left most of her money to Edward, which displeased her son Timothy. She had cut Timothy out of much of her will because he had hired a private detective to dig up dirt on Edward. Timothy, unsurprisingly, contested the will. Edward and Timothy settled, probably because the detective had discovered a few things about Edward.

Mary's money let Searles continue his building obsession. He liked to travel southern New Hampshire, looking for a farm that struck his fancy. He would buy it, remodel it to look like an English country cottage, then sell it or rent it.

His final masterpiece was Searles Castle on fourteen hundred acres in Windham. The famous Gothic Revival architect Henry Vaughan designed the citadel. Today it can be rented for corporate functions or weddings.

5. HETTY GREEN, BELLOWS FALLS, VERMONT

You might think one of the richest women in the world would live in a mansion. You'd be wrong. Hetty Green, the Witch of Wall Street, lived like a pauper. For years she frequently moved among cheap apartments in Brooklyn, New York, and Hoboken, New Jersey, to avoid establishing a residence and paying taxes.

The miserly millionaire always wore an old black dress, walked blocks to buy broken cookies in bulk, and once spent hours looking for a two-cent stamp.

She started out in life with a chunk of her family's whaling fortune, and parlayed it into a fortune worth about $3.8 billion in today's money. She managed her investments at the Chemical Bank, where she heated her lunch of oatmeal on a radiator.

Hetty had married Edward Green, a silk-and-tea merchant. During their marriage they lived in his family home in Bellows Falls, Vermont. When he squandered his own fortune and lost some of hers, she walked out on him. Later they reconciled and she nursed him through his final days.

A bank, a parking lot, and Hetty Green Park now occupy the site of the Green home at the corner of Church and Westminster Streets. Hetty, who died in 1916, is buried in Immanuel Episcopal Church Cemetery across School Street from the park.

6. SIR HARRY OAKES, BAR HARBOR, MAINE

When Harry Oakes grew up in Sangerville, Maine, he vowed he would make a million dollars.

It took him decades, but he did it. Oakes discovered the world's second biggest gold mine in western Canada. But unlike most miners, he didn't sell his claim. He extracted his own ore from the ground.

Harry Oakes never lost the crude manners of the mining camp. And yet he aspired to the English nobility. He renounced his U.S. citizenship and moved to Canada, where he hoped to pay lower taxes and win a seat in the House of Lords. Canada wouldn't accommodate him, however, so he moved to the Bahamas. There he spread enough money around to get himself a knighthood. His family didn't like the hot summers, though, so Harry bought a mansion called The Willows in Bar Harbor.

His edges stayed rough, and he annoyed people by eating with his knife at fancy parties and spitting seeds across the table. Once a hotel restaurant refused to seat him where he wanted because of his shabby clothes. Sir Harry bought the hotel and fired the staff.

One day he rubbed one too many people the wrong way. On July 7, 1943, someone clubbed him in his sleep, doused him with insecticide, and set him on fire. There were many suspects, but no one was ever convicted of the murder.

His Bar Harbor home is now the Atlantic Oceanside Hotel & Conference Center.

HAUNTED HOUSES

All haunted houses have histories; in fact, it's a history (and maybe even a ghost) that haunts a house. The stories about particular ghosts haunting particular houses generally have some truth, or even the whole truth, to them.

1. OCEAN BORN MARY HOUSE, HENNIKER, NEW HAMPSHIRE

Mary Wilson was born July 28, 1720 on a voyage from Ulster to Boston. Her Scottish parents, Elizabeth and James Wilson, were moving to New England to escape the violence in Northern Ireland.

While at sea, pirates boarded the immigrants' ship and took them aboard their own. The ordeal caused Elizabeth to give premature birth to her daughter. The pirate captain, a father, took pity on her. He let the captives return to their ship and go on their way. In one version, he asked the parents to name the baby Mary after his mother, or maybe his wife. And he gave Elizabeth a bolt of light green silk. Or so the story goes.

Mary did have a light green silk wedding dress. Parts of the dress are on display in the New Hampshire towns of Londonderry and Henniker and the City of Concord.

The Wilsons settled on the frontier with other Scots-Irish immigrants in Londonderry, and Mary grew into a tall, redheaded, well-liked woman. She married James Wallace and had four sons and a daughter. When her husband died, she moved to Henniker.

A huckster from Wisconsin decided to capitalize on the Ocean Born Mary story. In 1917, Louis "Gus" Roy bought a house that Mary's son Robert had owned on Bear Road, just outside town. He invented tales of pirates seeking buried gold and a tall, red-haired ghost that was probably Mary. He gave house tours and rented shovels to tourists to dig for treasure in the backyard.

There is a plaque in Henniker that reads, "Homestead of Robert Wallace, also known as Ocean Born Mary House, 1784." You can also see Ocean Born Mary's grave in the cemetery behind Henniker Town Hall.

2. BECKETT'S CASTLE, CAPE ELIZABETH, MAINE

The ghost of nineteenth-century writer Sylvester Beckett rips the bed sheets off guests at Beckett's Castle, his former summer home in Cape Elizabeth.

The castle is really a four-bedroom stone cottage with a thirty-foot tower, and it sits on a cliff overlooking Casco Bay. Beckett built it himself, mostly by hand, as a summer home. He finished it in 1874.

Beckett was also a journalist and a lawyer, prominent in Portland literary circles. His guests prized their invitations to his home, where he served expensive dinners cooked over the hearth. Beckett died in 1882, but he reappears as a ball of blue light. He also yanks open doors and rips the paintings off walls. Or so the story goes.

The privately owned Beckett's Castle is on Singles Road.

3. LIZZIE BORDEN'S HOUSE, FALL RIVER, MASSACHUSETTS

Lizzie Borden, a thirty-one-year-old single woman, famously took an axe and killed her father and stepmother at their home. Or did she? The debate continues since the couple was found murdered on August 4, 1891.

A jury acquitted Lizzie of murder nearly a year later. Many thought she got away with the crime. Whatever the case, Lizzie continued to live in Fall River, ostracized by the community, until her death at age sixty-six. The murder scene was turned into a bed and breakfast on Second Street.

Ghost hunters who stay there say a floor will creak in an empty room, or doors will open and close mysteriously. Sometimes the proprietor smells a faint flowery scent, and once the hallway chandelier suddenly turned off and a shadow climbed the stairs.

Today, a rhyme persists about the murders:

> Lizzie Borden took an axe
> And gave her mother forty whacks.
> When she saw what she had done,
> She gave her father forty-one.

4. EVERETT MANSION, BENNINGTON, VERMONT

Edward Hamlin Everett, the Glass Bottle King, got rich by inventing the fluted bottle cap—and by discovering natural gas wells. He grew up in Bennington, Vermont, and in 1886 married Amy King. They lived in a mansion in Bennington.

When Amy King died suddenly, some said she committed suicide. Others said she was murdered. Her obituary said she died after a severe operation following an unnamed illness.

Everett remarried, but his three grown daughters disapproved of the new wife. When he died in 1929, he left most of his wealth to his second wife. The daughters challenged the will in court.

During the trial, the eldest daughter was staying at the house when she said she heard weeping coming from her father's study. She went to the room and found her mother lying on the floor, clearly a murder victim.

The hauntings continued. Today, the mansion is part of Southern Vermont College. Security guards say doorknobs turn in empty rooms and doors close by themselves. Students say they see a woman in white, roaming the house and grounds.

The court, by the way, sided with the Everett daughters and gave them a third of the estate.

5. THE BREAKERS, NEWPORT, RHODE ISLAND

Alice Claypool Vanderbilt had no love for her sister-in-law, Alva Vanderbilt, later Alva Belmont. So when Alva built the exquisite Marble Palace in Newport, Alice went one better and built the Breakers. Many consider the seventy-room Beaux Arts mansion, finished in 1895, as the finest of Newport's Gilded Age.

But Alice endured tragedy and loss during her gilded life. She and her husband, Cornelius Vanderbilt II, had four sons and three daughters. One of their daughters, Alice, died at the age of five, and two of her sons— William and Alfred—died before they reached forty. A third son, Cornelius, was disinherited because he married a woman she and Cornelius hated. Another son, Reginald, died of cirrhosis of the liver at forty-five, nine years before his mother.

Alice Vanderbilt died at the age of eighty-eight, outliving her husband by thirty-five years. Soon after her death in 1934, her family spotted a ghost at the Breakers, and it looked just like her.

Since then, the Vanderbilts turned the house over to a nonprofit to run as a house museum. But they still own the furniture and the right to live on the third floor in summer. Alice's ghost has been seen by her family, tour guides, and visitors. Perhaps she's returning to a place where she was happy. Or perhaps she still grieves over the loss of her children.

6. SEASIDE SANITORIUM, WATERFORD, CONNECTICUT

The ominous Seaside Sanitorium may be haunted by ghosts—or by its past.

In 1936, doctors believed the way to treat children with tuberculosis was rest, sunshine, fresh air, and good food. Seaside was built as a "heliotropic" treatment hospital for children, and designed by famous architect Cass Gilbert. The building faces Long Island Sound, with large terraces and porches for sunbathing.

Drugs made heliotropic treatment obsolete, and Seaside became a geriatric hospital, then a medical hospital, and finally a hospital for the mentally disabled. People accused its staff of abusing the patients, and the death rate was unusually high.

The hospital closed in 1996. It's now dilapidated, creepy, and boarded up, its grounds littered with abandoned playground equipment. The ghosts of abused patients are said to haunt the place.

GREAT ESCAPES

NEW ENGLAND HAS LONG BEEN A HAVEN for the persecuted and the poor. The Puritans first came to Massachusetts and Connecticut to escape oppression in England. Huguenots, Jews, and Quakers found safety in tolerant Rhode Island, following Roger Williams's lead. Williams, of course, needed asylum from the Massachusetts Puritans. The Scots-Irish settled New England's frontiers after escaping their own troubles in Ireland.

In the nineteenth and twentieth centuries, waves of immigrants from all over the world fled to New England, refugees from poverty, war, and natural disasters. Wealthy southerners decamped to the mountains and seacoast for quite a different reason: to get away from oppressive heat. Even feathered and furry creatures found sanctuary in New England's wildlife preserves, some of the first in the United States.

PRESIDENTIAL RETREATS

1. JOHN ADAMS HAS A SPA DAY, STAFFORD SPRINGS, CONNECTICUT

JOHN ADAMS OFTEN WORRIED ABOUT HIS HEALTH, PERHAPS TO THE point of hypochondria. In 1771, he was advised to take a trip to Stafford Springs in Connecticut, just over the Massachusetts border. The suggestion may have come from Adams's friend and fellow revolutionary, Dr. Joseph Warren. Warren planned to develop it as a health resort, but he died at the Battle of Bunker Hill.

Adams recorded the trip (as he did everything) in his diary. On Tuesday, June 4, 1771, he wrote that his hostess, a Mrs. Childs, gave him a glass mug filled with the water. He drank plentifully and noted, "It has the taste of fair water with an infusion of some preparation of steel in it."

A wooden shed had been built over a reservoir of the spring water, about three feet deep, where people bathed, washed, and plunged. Adams paid eight cents for the privilege. "I plunged in twice—but the second time was superfluous and did me more hurt than good, it is very cold indeed."

Whether his spa day helped his health, Adams wasn't sure.

The spring is still gurgling.

2. WILLIAM TAFT SHMOOZES BAR HARBOR, MAINE

As president, William Howard Taft first vacationed in Beverly, Massachusetts, until his hostess got sick and tired of Secret Service interference and nosy tourists. She threatened to tear down her house, but instead she floated it across the harbor to Marblehead and told Taft to find new digs.

Taft then announced with great fanfare in July of 1910 that he would summer in Maine, stopping in Eastport, Bangor, Ellsworth, Rockland, and Islesboro. He'd base his operations in Bar Harbor where he would stay on the presidential yacht *Mayflower*.

He spent much of his time with wealthy summer residents. This caused a bit of a stir among year-round residents, which Taft tamped down by giving a speech on the town bandstand.

"The three days that have passed in Bar Harbor will be red letter days in my life," he told the crowd. "The air is like champagne in a Prohibition state, and without the uncomfortable consequences that follow imbibing that liquor."

Taft had some trouble, though, at the Kebo Valley Golf Club, where he sprained an ankle and shot a twenty-three on a single hole.

3. WOODROW WILSON HANGS OUT WITH ARTISTS, CORNISH, NEW HAMPSHIRE

President Woodrow Wilson spent several weeks in the summers of 1913 through 1915 at a country estate called Harlakenden. Wilson leased his summer White House from Winston Churchill—a bestselling American author, much better known at the time than his English counterpart.

Harlakenden overlooked the Connecticut River in Cornish, an art colony from about 1895 to 1920. Augustus Saint-Gaudens was the central figure in the colony, which included about a hundred artists, theater people, and writers. Ethel Barrymore, Frederic Remington, Daniel Chester French, Isadora Duncan, Maxwell Perkins, and Maxfield Parrish were all part of Cornish.

On September 12, 1913, Wilson watched a play called *Sanctuary: A Bird Masque*. The play dealt with a hot topic: the senseless slaughter of birds for ladies' hats. Wilson's two daughters, Eleanor and Margaret, performed in the play.

Harlakenden burned to the ground, but the Cornish art colony survives as the Augustus Saint-Gaudens National Historic Site.

4. CALVIN COOLIDGE GOES HOME AGAIN, PLYMOUTH NOTCH, VERMONT

Late one night in a simple Vermont farmhouse, Calvin Coolidge took the oath of office as president of the United States by the light of a kerosene lamp.

As vice president, he was vacationing at his boyhood home. His father, a notary, swore him in just hours after President Warren G. Harding died. It was 2:47 a.m. on August 3, 1923.

Though Coolidge spent most of his adult life in Northampton, Massachusetts, he often visited his family home. It is a modest white frame farmhouse in the classic New England style of big house, little house, back house, barn. The Coolidge homestead is such a throwback that some call it "Vermont's Brigadoon."

As president, Coolidge donned overalls and posed for photographers with farm implements in hand. His Secret Service detail had to sleep in tents on the property. In the summer of 1924, a dance hall nearby served as his office.

Today, much of the village now belongs to the Calvin Coolidge Homestead District, a National Historic Landmark.

5. IKE PLAYS GOLF, NEWPORT, RHODE ISLAND

In 1957, President Dwight Eisenhower and his wife Mamie decamped to the Naval Base in Newport, Rhode Island. There he dealt with the crisis over school integration in Little Rock, Arkansas.

He also summered in Newport during his presidency in 1958 and 1960. At first Eisenhower stayed at the Naval War College on Coasters Harbor Island. However, he wanted to be closer to the golf course at the Newport Country Club. So he moved to a mansion at Fort Adams for two summers in Newport.

Now called Eisenhower House, it was built in 1873 for General Henry Jackson Hunt, a Civil War artillery officer. The house has stunning views of Narragansett Bay and Newport Harbor. It now belongs to Fort Adams State Park.

6. JFK REIGNS OVER THE IRISH RIVIERA, HYANNIS PORT, MASSACHUSTTS

The summer cottage that Joseph P. Kennedy rented in Hyannis Port in 1926 would eventually become his son's summer White House. Hyannis and Boston's South Shore were so popular with the Irish that people called it "the Irish Riviera." They still do.

Joe Kennedy's waterfront rental had commanding views of Nantucket Harbor. He liked it so much he bought it in 1928, then enlarged and improved it for his growing family. It had six bedrooms and four servants' rooms on the second floor, a wine cellar in the shape of a ship's hull, and a motion picture theater in the basement.

In 1956, Joseph Kennedy's son John bought a smaller home of his own near the big house. In 1959, the youngest child, Edward, bought a house next to the other two. Edward sold it to his brother Robert and his wife Ethel in 1961, and later bought another home nearby.

John F. Kennedy used the compound as his headquarters for his 1960 presidential campaign. After his election he used it as the summer White House. Kennedy parlayed photos of his outdoor fun on Cape Cod—sailing, touch football, playing with his children—into an image of a vigorous family man.

The Kennedy compound still belongs to the Kennedys, but you can see it from a boat in Hyannis Harbor.

THE *GREEN BOOK* GUIDES AFRICAN AMERICANS TO SAFETY

FROM THE 1930S TO THE 1960S, AFRICAN AMERICANS TRAVELING BY CAR might find themselves in a sundown town. They were municipalities that banned minorities within their boundaries after dark. The practice wasn't limited to the Jim Crow South—it happened in New England, too. Black travelers faced potential embarrassment or danger, so they carried blankets, packed lunch, and even toted cans of gasoline when they took to the road.

And they carried their Bible—the *Negro Motorist Green Book*. It guided them to friendly hotels, restaurants, and service stations.

A New York City letter carrier named Victor Green published the first ten-page guide in 1936. He crowd-sourced the information by asking fellow letter carriers to find out about restaurants, service stations, hotels, tourist homes, taverns, liquor stores, beauty parlors, nightclubs, drugstores, and tailors.

"Let's all get together and make motoring better," he wrote in one edition. Green died in 1960, but the guide continued to be published until 1964, the year the Civil Rights Act passed.

Many of the *Green Book's* listings no longer exist. There's no trace of the Mrs. E. Whittle Tourist Home at 785 Bank St., New London, Connecticut. All that's left of Limberlock Lodge in Manchester, Vermont, is a postcard that sold on eBay. Gone is the Mace Guest House, which in 1956 advertised "Fishing and Bathing" for Christian vacationers willing to pay $5.00 for a room or cottage (with meals).

But some are still left.

1. SHEARER COTTAGE, OAK BLUFFS, MASSACHUSETTS

Oak Bluffs, a dense village of gingerbread cottages, has long hosted a vibrant summer community of African Americans on Martha's Vineyard.

Martin Luther King, Jr., wrote speeches on a cottage porch in Oak Bluffs. Dorothy West wrote a novel about the town's social life, *The Living Is Easy*. Such luminaries as Ethel Waters, Spike Lee, and Henry Louis Gates have summered there.

The Shearer Cottage on Martha's Vineyard catered to black vacationers starting in 1912. Charles and Henrietta Shearer built their wooden tourist home in the Highlands area of Oak Bluffs. Charles had been born into slavery but graduated from Hampton Institute in Virginia, then worked as a teacher.

Shearer Cottage is still in business and still run by the Shearer Family.

Ironically, the *Green Book* didn't list the Shearer Cottage until 1963, along with such establishments as Brownie's Cottage, Cinderella Cottage, and Dunmere-By-The-Sea.

2. CUMMINGS GUEST HOUSE, OLD ORCHARD BEACH, MAINE

Such celebrated musicians as Cab Calloway, Duke Ellington, and Count Basie played to enthusiastic crowds at the Old Orchard Beach Casino. The local hotels, though, wouldn't accommodate them. They stayed with the Cummings.

In 1917, Rose and Edward Cummings, Jr., had bought a Victorian farmhouse on Portland Street. The town's first black residents, they converted their home into a boarding house in 1923 and began catering to black travelers.

The boarding house wasn't listed in the town directory, in the town's promotional materials, or in the *Maine Register*. But you could find it in the *Green Book* as "Mrs. Rose Cumming's" at 110 Portland Avenue.

The Cummings children ran it until 1993, and now it is a private home.

3. MRS. WILLIAM SHARPER'S, BURLINGTON, VERMONT

William Sharper came from a mixed-race—black, native, and white—family. His wife, Jenny, was an African American North Carolinian. After they married they moved from Connecticut to Burlington. Perhaps they knew someone who belonged to the city's small black community descended from the Buffalo soldiers once stationed there.

The Sharpers owned a home in the 1930s and 1940s in Burlington's Old North End. They opened the modest, two-story wood frame house to both black and white boarders. After William died, Jennie continued to run her home as a boardinghouse. Today, 242 North Street is a private home.

4. BILTMORE HOTEL, PROVIDENCE, RHODE ISLAND

Most of the accommodations listed in the *Green Book* in New England were small hotels and tourist homes owned by African Americans. In cities, they were usually found in marginal or minority neighborhoods.

One notable exception was the Providence Biltmore, an elegant nineteen-story hotel in the middle of downtown. It was built in 1922 after the Providence Chamber of Commerce campaigned for a signature hotel where people could gather for important civic and cultural events.

The hotel had an open occupancy policy, accepting both black and white guests. But it took a step further by actually paying for a listing in the *Green Book*. Beginning in 1941, it simply reads, "Biltmore" under the heading "Providence."

The Providence Biltmore closed in 1975, but reopened four years later after renovation and a landmark designation. It changed hands, underwent another renovation, changed hands again, and was renamed Graduate Providence.

5. THE YWCA, BRIDGEPORT, CONNECTICUT

The *Green Book* advised African Americans driving to Connecticut to take the new Merritt Parkway rather than small-town roads "to avoid stop lights"—and, undoubtedly, harassment.

The Bridgeport YWCA began in 1884 to help farm girls who worked in the city's factories and mills. In 1921, it started the Phyllis Wheatley Branch "for women of color." By 1942, it built a big headquarters on Golden Hill and moved the Phyllis Wheatley Branch into it.

The women-led organization had spoken out against lynchings, monitored the trials of the Scottsboro boys, and in 1938 desegregated its first dining room in Ohio.

The YWCA National Convention had pledged that YWCA "will work for integration and full participation of minority groups in all phases of American life."

In 1949, the Bridgeport YWCA on Golden Hill was listed as welcoming African American guests. Today, the Bridgeport YWCA is now the Cabaret Theatre, part of the Golden Hill Historic District.

6. TWIN LAKE VILLAGE, NEW LONDON, NEW HAMPSHIRE

New Hampshire was notably absent from the *Green Book* for most of its existence. But in 1963, a handful of hotels appeared under the guide's first "New Hampshire" heading.

Among them was Twin Lake Village, a New London hotel that still offers visitors an "all-inclusive old fashioned family vacation experience." Think *Dirty Dancing* in New England.

The Kidder family has been running the resort on Little Lake Sunapee for more than a hundred years. It has a large lodge with a wraparound porch, cottages, a golf course, tennis courts, and swimming on its two hundred acres.

GORGEOUS CHURCHES
BY RALPH ADAMS
CRAM

When you think of the picturesque New England college campus, you probably think of Gothic spires and stone chapels among manicured lawns and tall elm trees. But campuses might not be so picturesque if it weren't for Ralph Adams Cram.

The same holds true for the Gothic Revival churches that populate New England's cities and towns. Cram was an architect and a lover of the Middle Ages, and he designed dozens of medieval-style buildings.

He had an outsized influence on architecture during the early twentieth century, which is why he appeared on the cover of *Time* magazine in 1926. Unlike his contemporary, Frank Lloyd Wright, his fame has dimmed except, perhaps, in Episcopal Church circles. The Church celebrates his birthday as a feast day.

Cram was born December 16, 1863, in Hampton Falls, New Hampshire, to an old New England family. His parents named him for Ralph Waldo Emerson and John Adams.

He became not only a prominent architect but an Anglo-Catholic, or High Episcopalian, while co-founding the Catholic magazine *Commonweal*. Though married—happily, by most accounts—to a wealthy Virginia woman, he spent summers at a homosexual monastery in Wales.

1. ALL SAINTS CHURCH, BOSTON, MASSACHUSETTS

All Saints Church began with a poignant meeting of sorrowing parents, and it launched the career of Ralph Adams Cram.

One Sunday a snowstorm stranded Mary Lothrop Peabody and her husband Oliver near the small wooden chapel of All Saints in Boston's Dorchester neighborhood. They had been driving from their estate in Milton to their usual church.

The storm hit them on December 28, 1879, the Feast of the Holy Innocents. The Peabodys had just lost a young child. Coincidentally, so had the rector of the All Saints chapel. His sermon moved the Peabodys deeply.

Oliver was the wealthy co-founder of the Kidder, Peabody investment bank, and he and his wife decided to build a new All Saints church. They hired two young architects, Ralph Adams Cram and his partner Bertram Goodhue. Though Cram was just starting out, he had something in common with Oliver and Mary Peabody: All three were High Episcopalians who had Unitarian ministers as parents.

Cram and Goodhue persuaded the Peabodys to revive the Gothic style in the design of All Saints. Finished in 1892, it was Cram's first church. Cram biographer Douglass Shand-Tucci called it a "masterpiece" and a "model for American parish church architecture for the first half of the 20th century."

2. EMMANUEL CHURCH, NEWPORT, RHODE ISLAND

In the early nineteenth century, many residents of South Newport, Rhode Island, couldn't attend church services because they couldn't afford to buy pew seats. So in 1841, three women from Trinity Church began to hold religious meetings in their homes.

Eight years later, with eighty-eight members, they bought an empty Baptist church and won admittance to the Rhode Island Episcopal diocese. By the turn of the century, their old church needed repair or replacement.

Rhode Island's princely Brown family stepped in and commissioned Ralph Adams Cram to design Emmanuel Church. Finished in 1902, it took two years to build. Cram's partner, Bertram Goodhue, designed the rich interior ornamentation, which went wildly over budget.

Today the monumental granite church towers over its working class neighborhood of small wooden houses. Emmanuel still prides itself on welcoming anyone who wishes to worship.

3. ST. JAMES EPISCOPAL CHURCH, WOODSTOCK, VERMONT

The parish of St. James was organized in the summer of 1826, when Woodstock was a prosperous mill town churning out scythes, carding machines, woolens, and carriages.

The founders of the parish bought stone for the church, but discovered quicksand under the land donated for the site. They built a wooden frame church instead, and put a Paul Revere bell in the tower. It was finished in time for Christmas Eve service in 1827.

In 1907, St. James got the stone church its founders wanted. Ralph Adams Cram designed the building, considered one of his most distinguished smaller churches. He incorporated the brass pulpit and lectern, the marble font, and three stained glass windows, one of which came from Tiffany studios.

4. ALL SOULS CONGREGATIONAL CHURCH, BANGOR, MAINE

In 1911, a great fire destroyed much of Bangor, including the First Congregational Church, which overlooked the central business district. The Third Congregational Church also burned in the fire, so the two parishes joined together to build a new church on the First's land.

Ralph Adams Cram designed an exceptionally creative (some say odd) Gothic Revival church. He incorporated flying buttresses, a rose window, a slender copper-clad spire, a small bell tower, and stone from the Third's building.

The church, which occupies a city block, once faced a row of stately homes. Today it looks across at offices, gas stations, and retail stores.

5. ALL SAINTS CHURCH, PETERBOROUGH, NEW HAMPSHIRE

Some consider the most beautiful church in America to be the Episcopal All Saints Church in New Hampshire's Monadnock Region. Cram set the jewel-like church back from the road on four acres of wooded countryside, modeling it after St. Mary the Virgin Church in Oxfordshire, England.

Cram directed the design of everything—outside, inside, furnishings, glass, and ironwork. Critics consider All Saints a terrific example of a *gesamtkunstwerk*, or complete work of art.

Cram stressed local workmen and local materials. He ordered the building built of granite. Some of the finest Arts and Crafts artisans in the region decorated the interior: woodcarver Johannes Kirchmayer, ironworker Frank Koralewski, and stained glass artisan Charles Connick.

Mary Lyon Cheney Schofield commissioned the building in 1913 to honor her family. In 1897, she had suffered the loss of her husband, Charles Cheney, an American Express heir. Mary would suffer many more losses before her death in 1947: Her second husband died in 1920, and one of her sons died in World War I. They are all interred in the chapel.

6. SEYMOUR ST. JOHN CHAPEL, WALLINGFORD, CONNECTICUT

Ralph Adams Cram didn't design every church in the Gothic Revival style.

In 1924, The Choate School in Wallingford, Connecticut, had 339 male students on its Georgian Revival campus. It also had a pressing need for a chapel.

Then-headmaster George St. John wrote, "To run a school without a chapel seemed like running a line for light and power without a powerhouse."

Cram designed the chapel in the Colonial Revival style. Choate broke ground for the building in May 1924 and dedicated it in 1925.

Choate merged with a girl's prep school in 1971 and became Choate Rosemary Hall. In 1998, the school rededicated the chapel and renamed it after the Rev. Seymour St. John, headmaster from 1947 to 1973.

ISLAND ESCAPES

New England has thousands of islands, and a lot of people inhabit them. Cape Cod, after all, became an island when the canal opened, and about 200,000 people live on it. Its population explodes in the summer, as anyone knows who's tried to cross a bridge to the Cape on a Friday afternoon in July.

Island living has plenty of adherents, though, as more than a thousand people each live on Nantucket, Martha's Vineyard, Mount Desert, Block Island, Aquidneck Island, and Deer Isle.

Some islands are just barren rock, of course. Maine has a lot of those. Maine also has more islands that begin with the letter B than Connecticut has islands. About two thousand islands lie off of Maine's coast, while Connecticut has only about 150, mostly in the Long Island Sound.

Massachusetts is no slouch island-wise, with about seven hundred of them.

Rhode Island, the state, isn't an island, but it was named for an island within its borders that's *officially* called Rhode Island. Unofficially, people call it Aquidneck, home to Newport, Portsmouth, and Middletown. Rhode Island has slightly more than a hundred other islands, not bad for the tiniest state in the union.

New Hampshire has only eighteen miles of coastline, but it also has a Lakes Region and 270 islands. Winnipesauke alone has about a hundred of them. And even Vermont has seventy-six islands (remember Lake Champlain!).

1. THACHER ISLAND, ROCKPORT, MASSACHUSETTS

The Great Colonial Hurricane, probably the worst storm in New England's history, struck on August 25, 1635.

Anthony Thacher had the bad luck to choose that day to relocate his family from the Massachusetts town of Ipswich to Marblehead. The fastest route was by sea, so Anthony and his cousin Avery packed up their families and a family friend—nineteen in all—onto a small ship. Four sailors were to take them out around Cape Ann and into Marblehead Harbor.

The hurricane caught the vessel off Gloucester, so the sailors did what seemed sensible: rode the storm out at anchor.

But no anchor could hold in that hurricane. The wind and waves hung the boat up between two rocks, then smashed it apart and washed everyone on board into the sea.

For a time, some of them clung to a rock, but soon the storm swept them away. The waves carried Thacher and his wife to safety on an island offshore. All the rest drowned, including Anthony's five children.

The Massachusetts General Court granted Anthony Thacher the island, now in Rockport, and it still bears his name. Mariners know it by the twin lighthouses. Thacher ultimately settled in Yarmouth, Massachusetts, where he is buried near a monument named after him.

2. COW ISLAND, TUFTONBORO, NEW HAMPSHIRE

Cow Island, the third largest island in Lake Winnipesaukee, provided shelter for two Guernsey cattle that lived long and multiplied.

In 1830 or 1831, a merchant captain named Prince brought a bull and two heifers from Britain to Boston. He then sent a bull and a heifer to his farm on the 520-acre island. The herd grew to forty, and then spread throughout New Hampshire. By 1899, the Guernsey developed a following that can only be described as passionate.

In 1933, ninety Guernsey enthusiasts made a pilgrimage to Cow Island. They decided to permanently mark the island as the home of the first Guernseys with a model of an old gristmill. Five years later, more pilgrims went to the island and Governor Styles Bridges officiated at the formal dedication of the mill. Today there are three million Guernseys in the United States.

3. CHARLES ISLAND, MILFORD, CONNECTICUT

In 1870, a gang of toughs from New York City decided to escape the law by holding a prizefight on Charles Island in Long Island Sound.

Called the Bowery Boys, they were anti-Catholic street brawlers, gamblers, and thieves. They wore red shirts, black pants, leather boots, and stove-pipe hats. They liked to vote—over and over, in fact, for corrupt politicians. And they really liked prizefighting.

Participating or organizing a prize fight could get you five years in jail. Attending one could get you two. Yet by 1870 the Bowery Boys had repeatedly slipped into Connecticut, staged their fights, run roughshod over the local people, and returned to New York with impunity.

The Charles Island match was to pit Edward Tuohey against James Kerrigan. But Connecticut's governor, Marshall Jewell, decided to put an end to it.

Tuohey and his entourage sailed from Brooklyn, but their steamboat foundered off Bridgeport. Meanwhile, the Bowery Boys and their friends took the train and then made it to the island by a wide sandbar at low tide. When they arrived, they got quite a surprise.

Jewell had called up five National Guard companies and brought over the New Haven police. The militiamen rounded up about a hundred gamblers, pickpockets, street toughs, and fight promoters on the island. They also impounded Tuohey's steamboat.

Some of the rowdy fight fans tried to escape arrest by getting on the New York-bound train in Bridgeport.

When the train hit the Fairfield station, however, it stopped far longer than usual. The militia arrived in another train to arrest the fight fans at gun point, and filled the jails with red-shirted brawlers. The New York *Sun* ran the headline: "Keep Them, Connecticut."

4. LIME ROCK ISLAND, NEWPORT, RHODE ISLAND

Rhode Island was a haven for Roger Williams after the Puritan theocracy kicked him out of Massachusetts Bay Colony. For sailors clinging to life in a storm, Lime Rock Island in Newport Harbor for many years did something similar.

Over forty-six years, Ida Lewis faithfully kept the lamp lit at Lime Rock Light Station and rescued as many as thirty-six people from drowning.

Her father had been appointed lighthouse keeper in 1854, when Ida was twelve. Four months after he moved his wife and four children to the island, he suffered a crippling stroke. Ida and her mother tended the lamp in his place.

Even at the age of twelve, Ida was a strong rower. Shortly after moving to the lighthouse, she rescued four young men who capsized their sailboat by pulling them into her dory.

Officially, she saved eighteen lives during her years at Lime Rock Light. Unofficially, she saved thirty-six. She made her last rescue at sixty-three when a friend fell overboard while rowing out to visit her.

Ida Lewis received the Gold Lifesaving Medal from the U.S. Coast Guard and was called the bravest woman in America.

5. NORTH HAVEN, MAINE

In 1929, a kidnapper threatened Charles Lindbergh's family, or rather his family-to-be. He was engaged to Anne Morrow, daughter of one of New Jersey's richest men. Anne's younger sister Constance, while at prep school, had received an extortion letter threatening harm if she didn't come up with fifty-thousand dollars. And, of course, she should keep quiet and not go to the police.

The Morrows did contact the police, who arranged a drop with a stand-in for Constance. But no one came to pick up the money. The family was terrified that the extortionist had found out they'd called the police.

Now in 1929 Charles Lindbergh was a world-famous aviator, and his impending marriage to an heiress titillated the press. Lindbergh decided to fly the frantic Morrows to the island of North Haven where they had a summer cottage. There, he hoped, they could shun the limelight while the police continued to investigate.

But word leaked out and the media circus moved to North Haven. So the family returned to New Jersey and announced Charles and Anne had already married.

The kidnapper was never caught, but North Haven remains a bucolic island retreat, at least in the summertime.

6. NESHOBE ISLAND, CASTLETON, VERMONT

During the 1920s and 1930s, rumors about the crazy doings on Neshobe Island flew through the resort hotels along Vermont's Lake Bomoseen.

The rumors were correct. In 1924, drama critic Alexander Woollcott had rented seven-acre Neshobe Island just a quarter mile from Lake Bomoseen's shore. He loved the island so much he bought it and turned it into a private club for his closest pals.

They were members of the Algonquin Round Table, and they brought their famous friends—like Vivien Leigh, who showed up after winning her Oscar for *Gone With the Wind*.

Harpo Marx took off all his clothes and waved an ax at snooping tourists. Dorothy Parker drank and then she, too, took off all her clothes.

There were only ten members at any one time, and memberships could be bought and sold. Each member paid $1,000 to spend the summer on Neshobe Island.

Woolcott ruled the island like a benevolent despot. Everyone had to take a morning dip no matter how cold the lake. And when Woollcott wanted to play croquet on Neshobe Island, everyone had to play.

The Neshobe Island Club ended abruptly on January 23, 1943, when Alexander Woollcott died suddenly of a heart attack.

CEMETERIES

THE EARLY NEW ENGLANDERS BURIED THEIR DEAD IN FAMILY PLOTS and churchyards. Epitaphs on gravestones still tell sad and sometimes funny tales of shipwrecked sailors, elderly ministers, smallpox victims, and children who died in infancy. Typical of their epitaphs was this one for six-month-old Bezaleel Shaw in Nantucket's Old North Cemetery:

> My life in infant Days was Spent
> While to my parents I was lent
> One smiling Look to them I gave
> And then descended to the grave.

A Cape Cod fisherman was remembered thus:

> Capt. Thomas Coffin
> Born Jan. 7, 1792 Died Jan. 10, 1842
> He has finished catching cod,
> And gone to meet his God.

Eventually, cemeteries got crowded. Graves were stacked on top of each other, or emptied for new corpses. Before the Civil War, cemeteries stank with decomposing corpses because embalming wasn't practiced. That led to the garden cemetery movement, the first of which was Mount Auburn cemetery in Cambridge, Massachusetts.

The garden cemeteries were built outside of cities, but close enough so city-dwellers could reach them easily. They were designed as parks, with landscape and sculpture for ordinary people to enjoy.

1. MYLES STANDISH BURIAL GROUND, DUXBURY, MASSACHUSETTS

After they arrived on the *Mayflower*, the Pilgrims made their final progress to the Myles Standish Burial Ground. John Alden, Priscilla Alden, and George Soule repose in what is said to be the oldest maintained cemetery in the United States.

Originally, the cemetery belonged to Duxbury's first meeting house. When a new meeting house replaced the old, three-quarters of a mile down the road, the Myles Standish Burial Ground fell into disuse. But in 1887, the Duxbury Rural Society went about reclaiming the burying ground and has maintained it as a historic site ever since.

Four years after the Duxbury Rural Society took charge, a small team exhumed the body of an elderly male. They identified him as Myles Standish, along with his daughter Lora, his daughter-in-law, and one of his sons who died young. Myles Standish was reburied in a pine box and a memorial erected above his grave.

However, Myles Standish's descendants didn't like that. So in 1931 they had their ancestor re-exhumed and re-buried in a copper box, then placed in a cement vault beneath the marker. The previous year, the descendants of John and Priscilla Alden placed slate markers near the spot believed to be their final resting place.

2. NEWMAN CEMETERY, EAST PROVIDENCE, RHODE ISLAND

There are probably more seventeenth-century grave markers in Newman Cemetery than in any other of Rhode Island's historic cemeteries.

Newman Cemetery, part of Newman Congregational Church, offers an encyclopedic history of style and fashion in funerary art.

The crude oldest stones often show only the deceased's initials and year of death. The slate eighteenth-century markers include upright headstones with death heads and cherub heads, along with portrait busts of the deceased and flat slabs decorated with coats-of-arms. Later markers include marble obelisks and slate stones with willow-and-urn motifs.

3. NORTH CEMETERY, PORTSMOUTH, NEW HAMPSHIRE

Most residents of the historic city of Portsmouth don't know about the famous people buried in tiny old North Cemetery.

The one-and-a-half acres of the graveyard sitting on the banks of North Mill Pond get far less attention than some of the other historic cemeteries in New England. It has, however, a number of notable residents, including William Whipple, signer of the Declaration of Independence, and Governor John Langdon, signer of the U.S. Constitution.

Also buried in old North: Prince Whipple, an African American who, according to legend, accompanied George Washington in his crossing of the Delaware. The cemetery also includes Portsmouth's first known Catholic and Jewish residents, as well as Thomas L. Thompson. Thompson commanded the *Raleigh*, the first U.S. navy warship built at what is now the Portsmouth Naval Shipyard (and depicted on the seal of the State of New Hampshire). Hall Jackson, a local doctor who attended the wounded at the Battle of Bunker Hill, also rests in peace at North Cemetery.

4. GROVE STREET CEMETERY, NEW HAVEN, CONNECTICUT

The Yale University campus surrounds the Grove Street Cemetery in New Haven, and many Elis found their last home there. Such notables as Noah Webster, Eli Whitney, Walter Camp, and Roger Sherman await their judgment under the turf of the historic cemetery.

Grove Street Cemetery started as the first nonprofit private cemetery in the world in 1796. Previously, New Haven buried its dead on the New Haven Green. But the Green got too crowded during the yellow fever epidemic of 1794–1795. So prominent New Haven families established the burial ground on farmland on the town's border, just north of Grove Street. The first burial, of Martha Townsend, took place on November 9, 1797.

It was an immediate hit, if that can be said of a cemetery.

The two men who designed the remarkable Egyptian Revival gateway—sculptor Hezekiah Augur and architect Henry Austin—are buried in the Grove Street Cemetery. The inscription on the stone gate reads, "The Dead Shall Be Raised." A Yale president supposedly said, "They certainly will be, if Yale needs the property."

Today, the eighteen-acre Grove Street Cemetery provides a dignified resting place for many of New Haven's elite as well as the indigent.

5. MOUNT HOPE CEMETERY, BANGOR, MAINE

Though Mount Auburn Cemetery in Greater Boston was the first cemetery designed as a park, Mount Hope Cemetery in Bangor came a close second. Architect Charles Bryant designed it three years after Mount Auburn opened in 1831. The Bangor Horticultural Society formed to build the cemetery as a place where the dead and the living could contemplate nature peacefully.

Nearly thirty thousand people are buried on its 264 acres, including Abraham Lincoln's vice president, Hannibal Hamlin, and Public Enemy No. 1, Al Brady, shot to death in broad daylight on a Bangor street.

Two scenes from Bangor native Stephen King's *Pet Sematary* were filmed at Mount Hope. For one shot, the crew had to wait until 2 a.m. to get the perfect moonlight.

6. HOPE CEMETERY, BARRE, VERMONT

Most of the people buried in Hope Cemetery carved their own memorials and tombstones. They were stonecutters who worked in the Barre granite quarries.

During the late nineteenth and early twentieth centuries, skilled stonecutters flocked to Barre from Europe. Many brought their radical socialist and anarchist views with them.

The outdoor gallery of granite artistry attracts tourists with its beautifully carved and sometimes unusual granite memorials. They include a soldier smoking a cigarette, a race car, a bored angel, a soccer ball, and an eighteen-wheel truck.

One master stonecutter, Louis Brusa, discovered he had silicosis and commissioned a memorial of himself dying in the arms of a woman. It caused a local scandal because the woman looked like his mistress rather than his wife.

The sixty-five-acre cemetery has more than ten thousand tombstones and memorials, all made from Barre Grey granite.

WILDLIFE SANCTUARIES

Henry David Thoreau had his Walden and John Muir his Yosemite, but many other conservationists saved their own small pieces of land for the birds, the trees, and the animals.

Between 1830 and 1850, farmers and lumbermen had cut down most of New England's trees. Clearcutting caused erosion and flooding and the loss of wildlife. So restoring forests became a focus of early environmentalists like George Perkins Marsh and Mabel Osgood Todd.

The slaughter of birds for ladies' hats became a special concern for the wealthy ladies who wore them. They not only forswore the fashionable plumage, they warned against the extinction of bird species with their voices and their money. They supported the Audubon Society, wrote books about birds, and donated conservation land for the safety of the feathered creatures.

1. HELEN WOODRUFF SMITH BIRD SANCTUARY, PLAINFIELD, NEW HAMPSHIRE

By the standards of his day, animals never had a better friend than Ernest Baynes. Armed with an outsized reputation as a naturalist, he had a gift for ingratiating himself with powerful people. He used that gift to forever change the fortunes of songbirds in America.

As a young man he floundered until the late 1890s when he settled on nature as his true calling. He started contributing articles on animals to magazines and newspapers. Then he moved to the village of Meriden, in Plainfield, in 1904 and made it his base for promoting conservation through books and lectures.

He enlarged on his efforts by establishing a bird sanctuary in 1910 on an abandoned farm in Meriden. He had persuaded Helen Woodruff Smith of Stamford, Connecticut, to finance the project.

To mark its opening in 1913 he enlisted Cornish poet Percy Mac-Kaye to write the play *Sanctuary: A Bird Masque*. A naked effort at bolstering public opinion against slaughtering birds for their feathers, it toured nationally.

The thirty-two acre sanctuary has paths through deep woods, the Museum of Conservation, and plenty of bird baths.

2. BIRDCRAFT, FAIRFIELD, CONNECTICUT

Mabel Osgood Wright's father didn't want her to go to college and her husband, who she married in 1884, didn't want her to write for publication.

She studied nature, however, from the eight acres of gardens surrounding her eighteen-room summer home in Fairfield. Her husband changed his mind about her writing when he discovered she'd published nature essays in the *Evening Post* and *New York Times*.

Mabel then carved out a career as a pioneering nature writer, educator, and bird conservationist. During her lifetime she wrote twenty-five nature books and novels, nurturing America's passion for birds along the way. She saved the national Audubon Society from extinction, after it had ceased publishing its magazine and disbanded even though it had thirty-eight thousand members.

In 1914, Mabel created Birdcraft, six acres of property with bird-friendly plantings, a pond, and a cat-proof fence. It also includes a Natural History Museum.

3. HOG ISLAND AND THE TODD WILDLIFE SANCTUARY, BREMEN, MAINE

Mabel Loomis Todd during her long and interesting life managed to publish Emily Dickinson's poems, have an extramarital affair with Dickinson's brother, and found a wildlife sanctuary in Maine.

She threw herself into her projects, including, first, her affair with Austin Dickinson, then publishing his sister's poetry. Her marriage to Amherst College astronomy professor David Todd survived the affair, and the Todds visited Hog Island in 1906.

By then she had become passionately opposed to clearcutting trees, and so the Todds began buying up land on Hog Island to save its timber. They created a summer camp on it, which the family visited until the 1960s.

After Mabel died in 1932, her only child, Millicent Todd Bingham, arranged with the Audubon Society to establish a nature study center on Hog Island.

The Todd Wildlilfe Sanctuary in Bremen includes Hog Island, a 330-acre island a quarter mile from shore, thirty acres on the mainland, and the Audubon Nature Camp. Roger Tory Peterson got his start writing the modern field guide in 1936 as a teacher at the camp.

4. MOOSE HILL WILDLIFE SANCTUARY, SHARON, MASSACHUSETTS

One January morning in 1896, Boston Brahmin Harriet Lawrence Hemenway sat in her Back Bay parlor and read a shocking article about the wholesale slaughter of birds. So-called plume hunters were killing millions of birds for the feathers to adorn ladies' hats.

Outraged, Hemenway marched across the street to the home of her cousin, Minna B. Hall. The two ladies decided to hold teas to educate their feather-hatted socialite friends about bird carnage. They persuade some nine hundred women to join together to "discourage the buying or wearing of feathers and to otherwise further the protection of native birds."

They called their group the Massachusetts Audubon Society and worked to pass laws protecting birds. In 1916 a resident of Sharon, Massachusetts, offered to donate his farm to Massachusetts Audubon. They accepted, and the commonwealth's first wildlife sanctuary was created.

Moose Hill Wildlife Refuge today encompasses twenty miles of hiking trails on nearly two thousand acres of forests, fields, and wetlands.

5. NORMAN WILDLIFE SANCTUARY, MIDDLETOWN, RHODE ISLAND

The Norman Wildlife Sanctuary is not only a home for birds, it's a historic district listed on the National Register of Historic Places.

The rich Aquidneck Island soil on the southern tip of Middletown gave the area its nickname, "Paradise." Its farms prospered through the Gilded Age, when they supplied the mansions in Newport next door.

By the turn of the century, the wealthy started buying up old farms and turning them into summer homes. That's what self-made millionaire George Norman did for his family in 1898. After he died two years later, his youngest daughter Mabel, then in her thirties, bought the farm from her siblings. She then hired one of Rhode Island's leading architects to remodel the old farm buildings into a Colonial Revival estate.

Mabel loved birds and intended all along to leave the farm as a bird sanctuary. She had her architects design a bird room and a winter bird room in the main house. When she died in 1949, she bequeathed the property to the community.

Today the Smith-Gardiner-Norman Farm Historic District belongs to the Norman Wildlife Sanctuary. It includes four historic buildings, a prominent local landmark called Hanging Rock, and seven miles of hiking trails on 325 acres.

6. MARSH-BILLINGS-ROCKEFELLER NATIONAL HISTORIC PARK, WOODSTOCK, VERMONT

The Marsh-Billings-Rockefeller National Historic Park was the boyhood home of George Perkins Marsh, a founder of both the environmental movement and the Smithsonian Institute.

As a boy, Marsh had loved watching clear-cutting on Mount Tom, most of which his father owned. He realized how denuding forests caused erosion, flooding, and exhausted fisheries. He decided he didn't want to leave the world worse than he found it, so as an adult he developed principles of land conservation.

In 1864, Marsh wrote a book, *Man and Nature*. Environmental historians call it as important as Charles Darwin's *On the Origin of the Species*. The book made the then-novel connection of human activity with the environment. Perkins showed, for example, how the Parisian fashion for beaver hats nearly killed off all the beavers. But then silk hats became the rage, the beavers returned, and wetlands increased in the United States.

Man and Nature also argued that natural resources are finite, which challenged the prevailing view that the earth would constantly rejuvenate itself.

Frederick Billings, president of the Northern Pacific Railroad, bought the old Perkins farm and managed the forest according to Marsh's principles. Mary and Laurance Rockefeller later bought the farm in 1954 and deeded it to the federal government in 1992.

CRIME AND SCANDAL

CRIMINOLOGISTS CAN'T SAY FOR CERTAIN WHAT CAUSES CRIME RATES TO rise and fall. Puritans, of course, thought it had to do with moral failure, though they didn't view it as a failing when they stole the Indians' corn. Some thought booze caused crime, which led to the various failed temperance experiments culminating in the grandest failure of all, the Volstead Act in 1919.

The expansion of railroads certainly caused an increase in white-collar crime, though few paid any kind of penalty for looting taxpayers and investors.

Over the centuries, the definition of crime has changed, along with its frequency. In 1656, a crime wave hit Puritan New England when dissident Quakers started showing up. One of them, Mary Dyer, went to the gallows in Massachusetts. Then in 1692, another kind of crime wave sent Salem, Massachusetts, into hysteria. More than two hundred people were accused of witchcraft, twenty were executed, and five died in prison.

There have since been three great surges of violent crime beginning in 1850, 1900, and 1960, not just in New England, but around the world.

Punishments for various crimes have evolved over that time. Penalties depended on the perceived damage the crime did to society. Kissing on Sunday, for example, threatened the Puritan ideal of a community that followed the Bible's teaching. Stealing a farmer's horse might handicap his ability to farm or take his produce to market. Penalties were commensurate with the crime: stocks for kissing, the gallows for horse theft.

PLACES WHERE A HANGING TOOK PLACE

BACK BEFORE FILM AND VIDEO PROVIDED VIOLENT ENTERTAINMENT, people had hangings to watch. Typically, festive crowds gathered as a horse-drawn wagon carried the prisoner to the gallows. The hangman bound the prisoner's hands and feet, tied a blindfold around his or her head, and then placed the noose. A trap door would open, the prisoner would fall through, and, theoretically, the weight of the prisoner's body would snap his or her neck.

Often that didn't happen, and the prisoner died a slow gruesome death—tongue protruding, limbs thrashing, bowels loosening. What fun!

Hanging was the main form of execution in the United States until the 1890s, and more than four hundred people in New England have been hanged by the neck until they were dead. Pirates and witches most often died on the gallows, though the early courts didn't mind sending children, mothers, or Quakers to early graves.

1. PROCTOR'S LEDGE, SALEM, MASSACHUSETTS

The nineteen people hanged for witchcraft in the Salem witch hysteria of 1692–1693 died on Proctor's Ledge, now a city-owned woods on Gallows Hill.

The most spectacular hanging took place on September 22, 1692, with the executions of Mary Eastey and eight others. Eastey, a pious wife and mother of eleven, eloquently defended herself and helped turn the tide against the bloodlust. She drew tears from almost all who watched with her last farewell, described as "serious, religious, distinct and affectionate."

The Reverend Nicholas Noyes, who presided over the trials, kept a dry eye as he viewed the eight bodies hanging, probably from the limbs of oak trees. "What a sad thing it is to see eight firebrands of Hell hanging there," he said.

Not until the turn of the twentieth century did a local historian identify the site of the hangings. In 2017, the city marked the spot—a scrubby lot behind a row of houses—with a memorial paid for, in part, by some of the accused witches' descendants. It's a semicircular stone wall with memorial stones for the nineteen victims and an oak tree in the center. (The twentieth victim, Giles Corey, was crushed to death.)

2. GRAVELLY POINT, NEWPORT, RHODE ISLAND

Rhode Island hanged twenty-six pirates on Gravelly Point in one thrillingly violent spectacle on July 19, 1723.

Today, Gravelly Point lies next to a marina, a hotel, touristy restaurants, and bars. But in 1723, the tourists celebrated the deaths of pirates commanded by the notoriously cruel Edward Low.

Low enjoyed burning his captives alive, disemboweling them, and cutting off their heads. He once sliced off a Portuguese captain's lips, broiled them, and forced the victim to eat them while still hot.

A British warship had captured thirty-five of Low's crew and took most of them to Newport. Low himself fled with a skeleton crew, and no one really knows how he met his end.

A court sentenced twenty-six of Low's men to death by hanging. A huge crowd watched and cheered as Rhode Island authorities attached their captured pirate flag onto the gallows.

"Never was there a more doleful sight in all this land than while they were standing on the stage, waiting for the stopping of their breath and the flying of their souls into the eternal world," wrote one witness. "And oh! How awful the noise of their dying moans!"

3. SOUTH CEMETERY, PORTSMOUTH, NEW HAMPSHIRE

Ruth Blay died a slow painful death before a thousand spectators in what is now South Cemetery. On December 30, 1768, a horse cart took her to the highest point on South Street, where an executioner placed a noose around her neck.

She stood on the wagon under a newly built gallows, and the horse pulled the cart from under her feet. It probably took her several minutes to die.

Ruth Blay was hanged because she concealed the death of her illegitimate child. She didn't kill it, she just hid the body of the stillborn infant. Unfortunately for Ruth, concealment was a capital crime in colonial New Hampshire.

A thirty-one-year-old schoolteacher, she ultimately admitted to wrapping her dead baby in a quilt and hiding it under the floorboards of a barn. Children playing in the barn discovered the body three days later.

Ruth was the last of three New Hampshire women hanged for concealment.

4. HEMPSTEAD STREET AND BULKELEY PLACE, NEW LONDON, CONNECTICUT

A statue of Connecticut's first Puritan governor, John Winthrop, Jr., stands near the spot in New London where twelve-year-old Hannah Occuish was hanged on December 20, 1786.

Hannah had murdered six-year-old Eunice Bolles after Eunice accused her of stealing strawberries. The colonial court didn't recognize extenuating circumstances, but it undoubtedly knew a few things about Hannah. Her mother, a Pequot Indian, and her father, an African American, had both died. Shuttled among foster homes, she had to work as an indentured servant. Hannah probably suffered from a mental disability.

On July 21, 1786, Hannah lured Eunice into a wood by promising her a piece of calico. Hannah then beat and strangled her to death, and tried to cover her body with stones.

A passerby soon discovered Eunice's body, and Hannah confessed to the crime. After a swift trial, she was convicted and sentenced to hang.

She cried during much of the day of her execution, which took place on a gallows behind the old meeting house.

"She seemed greatly afraid when at the gallows, and said but little to anyone," according to *The Courant* on December 25, 1786. "She thanked the sheriff for his kindness, and launched into the eternal world."

5. FORT GEORGE, CASTINE, MAINE

In Castine, Maine, a stone marker indicates Fort George once stood on what is now a grassy knoll with a cannon on it. A gallows once stood there, too.

On October 31, 1811, a Deer Isle counterfeiter named Ebenezer Ball met his maker on that gallows. Ball had shot to death a sheriff's deputy, John Tileston Downes, who tried to arrest him near a lily pond.

Ball appealed, claiming he hadn't meant to shoot the deputy. His appeal failed, and a large crowd followed him as he was escorted from the jail to the gallows. A local minister, Jonathan Fisher, wrote two ballads on the hanging and peddled them to the onlookers. Two verses read:

> But oh! The sight—the shocking sight
> This day our eyes did see,
> A sinful and a harden'd wretch—
> Launch'd in eternity . . .
>
> Take warning, then, O my dear friends,
> Let me advise you all;
> Pray shun all vice, and do not die
> Like Ebenezer Ball.

6. CATAMOUNT TAVERN, OLD BENNINGTON, VERMONT

On June 11, 1778, the Republic of Vermont hanged David Redding, but didn't bury his bones properly for nearly two hundred years.

During the American Revolution, David Redding made the mistake of choosing the Loyalist side. He joined the Queens Loyal Rangers, and while out of uniform tried to steal muskets stored in a barn. Locals caught him and put him in a temporary cell in the Catamount Tavern barn.

A jury found him guilty of treason, and he was hanged on June 11, 1778. A local doctor took his body, which ended up as a teaching tool until the doctor died. The bones passed to the doctor's son, who stored them in his attic. Then the Vermont Historical Society got wind of the bones in the attic and took them, only to put them in a drawer. Finally in 1976, the people of Vermont gave David Redding a proper burial in the cemetery of Bennington's Old First Church.

Many important events in Vermont's history took place at the Catamount Tavern. But it burned in 1871, and today a statue of a catamount marks the site.

PROHIBITION-ERA SPEAKEASIES YOU CAN STILL VISIT

When the 18th Amendment to the Constitution took effect on January 17, 1920, New England's taverns suddenly became speakeasies.

Law enforcement couldn't keep up, and alcohol flowed freely on the sly in hotel basements, in curtained restaurant nooks, in bars that straddled the Canadian border, and in commercial buildings turned speakeasies.

1. TK'S AMERICAN CAFE, DANBURY, CONNECTICUT

Connecticut did not ratify the 18th Amendment, and it didn't take long to realize the law was honored more in the breach than in the observance. People could easily get booze from rumrunners or stills within the state. By October 1921, the state Prohibition director estimated there were fifteen hundred speakeasies in Connecticut, four hundred in New Haven alone.

Speakeasies flourished in Danbury as well. TK's American Café, originally built as a car dealership in 1928, became one. When the Volstead Act was repealed, it became the Hat City's first legitimate bar. Called Bennie Pane's Stone Bar, it morphed into Pane's Restaurant in 1937 and served pizza. In 1948 it changed hands for the first of five times.

Tom Kennedy opened the old speakeasy on White Street as a sports bar in 1990. He struggled to keep it afloat until he offered ten-cent wings on Tuesday nights. Patrons say it hasn't changed much—except for the televisions—since it was Bennie Pane's.

2. BRAMHALL, PORTLAND, MAINE

Maine was the first state to outlaw alcohol, and Mainers the first to flout the ban. Drinking went underground and crime flourished. Bootleggers smuggled spirits over the Canadian border, rum runners brought them in by sea, and farmers made it from secret stills.

Maine's thirsty public found a haven in Portland's Old Port District. Scofflaws flocked to the Congress Street bar now known as Bramhall during those wild days of Prohibition.

Still a dim, brick-lined stone vault, it has little natural light. For years it was a basement pub under The Roma Café, now defunct. Bramhall has been refurbished and reopened as a cocktail bar with a reasonably priced menu.

3. HOTEL VERNON, WORCESTER, MASSACHUSETTS

On the eve of Prohibition, Worcester celebrated the death of John Barleycorn with raucous partying. People jammed saloons, which stopped serving liquor at midnight if they hadn't run out already.

The party kept going surreptitiously throughout the city, especially at the Hotel Vernon on Kelley Square. Frank "Bossy" McGady, a state trooper, owned it with his brother Beaven.

Down a long wooden staircase the hotel served liquor in a hideaway where no one was ever caught. "Madame Rhubarb" was the password to get through the secret entrance. Babe Ruth often stopped in for a drink or two.

Just after the end of Prohibition, an artist painted a mural around the bar and a backroom was added, decorated like a schooner galley. Henry Mancini and Burl Ives visited during the 1940s and 1950s, and reservations were sometimes needed two weeks in advance.

The construction of Interstate-290 transformed the neighborhood, not for the better. The Hotel Vernon became a residential hotel and dive bar. Today you can get one-dollar drafts, free peanuts, and a tour of the speakeasy in the basement if the bartender isn't too busy.

4. THE CAVE,
BRETTON WOODS, NEW HAMPSHIRE

Liquor was still legal in Canada and times were hard in Northern New England during Prohibition. So the incentive to smuggle alcohol was strong. Bootleggers brought in illegal booze from Canada along the dark, unguarded, wooded roads crossing the Canadian border into New Hampshire, Vermont, and Maine.

A popular speakeasy among Boston's elite was The Cave, a subterranean vault in the cellar of the Mount Washington Hotel. Patrons drank booze out of teacups. According to legend, Joseph P. Kennedy sold bootleg liquor to the hotel, now known as the Omni Mount Washington Resort.

The Cave was originally set up as squash courts. During Prohibition, the hotel turned them into a speakeasy with a pull-down false ceiling. In the event of a raid, an alarm sounded, the booze would be stuffed in the ceiling, and a game of squash would hurriedly start.

The Cave is now open from 9 p.m. to midnight with a late-night menu.

5. CAMILLE'S ROMAN GARDEN,
PROVIDENCE, RHODE ISLAND

Camille's Roman Garden opened the year before Prohibition as Marconi's, after the inventor of the wireless. It spent its first five years on Atwells Avenue, then moved around the corner to a nineteenth-century mansion on Bradford Street near the entrance to Federal Hill.

Rhode Island, like Connecticut, didn't ratify the 18th Amendment, and pretty much ignored the ban on spirits. Camille's put curtains on the private alcoves that ring the dining area. Illegal booze was made in the cellar and served in coffee cups to patrons seated in the alcoves.

Frank Sinatra was especially fond of Camille's Italian wedding soup, and once burped on stage in Providence. He excused himself and said, "I just had the most wonderful food at Camille's Roman Garden."

6. CANAAN LINE HOUSE, CANAAN, VERMONT

Vermont was never dry, it was damp. Rum runners on Lake Champlain and bootleggers from over the Canadian border supplied all the liquor anyone wanted.

Queen Lill's Bucket of Blood in Richford was just one of the many line houses that dotted the Canadian border. The line houses, built to straddle the border between Vermont and Quebec, often had a front door in Vermont and a bar in Quebec.

One of the most well known was the Canaan Line House, on the border between Canaan and Saint-Herménégilde, Quebec.

Today it's the Canaan-Hereford Road Border Crossing. The abandoned remains of the old Canaan Line House sit between the Canadian and U.S. Customs.

SCANDALOUS
LOVE NESTS

WHAT WAS CONSIDERED A CRIME BY THE EARLY PURITANS WASN'T EVEN close to a scandal today. In 1656, Thomas Kemble spent two hours in the stocks in Boston for kissing his wife on the day he returned from a three-year voyage. He should have known not to engage in such lewd and unseemly behavior on a Sunday.

In New Haven, Thomas Meekes was whipped severely in 1649 for "sinful uncleanness"—premarital sex—with Rebecka Turner, who he married several months later.

Adultery was an even more serious crime. Mary Latham was hanged in 1644 for cheating on her husband and bragging about it. Her boyfriend, James Britton, also hanged for adultery.

The death penalty, though, was rare for adultery in Puritan New England. You were more likely to be whipped, or to be branded with an "A" on your forehead, or made to stand in the marketplace with a sign around your neck that said, "Thus I stand for my adulterous and whorish carriage."

Rhode Island was always more tolerant than the other colonies, and imposed lighter sentences for adultery. Still, when a prominent, married U.S. senator stayed overnight with the wife of a prominent Rhode Island politician, it sent a shock through the state.

But standards loosened, and then they loosened some more, and by the 1940s a married movie star could spend the night with his girlfriend without losing his job. And by the 1950s, writing about scandal could make you rich.

1. CANONCHET FARM STATE PARK, NARRAGANSETT PIER, RHODE ISLAND

Some things just can't be hushed up. Such as a former U.S. senator seen with a shotgun chasing someone through the streets of a wealthy summer resort. Especially when that someone was another U.S. senator.

William Sprague, the man with the gun, was a textile magnate who'd just lost a great deal of money. Roscoe Conkling, the man he chased, had been having an affair with Sprague's wife, Kate.

Kate Chase was the beautiful doyenne of Washington society, the daughter of President Lincoln's Treasury secretary, Salmon P. Chase. On the day of her wedding to William Sprague, their prospects looked bright. Sprague had fought valiantly in the Civil War, served as Rhode Island's boy governor, and recently won election as U.S. senator.

But she spent his money freely and cheated on him, while he abused her, drank heavily, and kept a string of floozies.

Kate took up with U.S. Senator Roscoe Conkling from New York. In August 1879, Conkling came to visit Kate at the Spragues' summer estate in Narragansett Pier. William Sprague had left for Maine on business, but unbeknownst to them he returned at night, earlier than expected, on August 7, 1879.

The next morning, Sprague rose early and went into town for billiards and booze. He returned to find Conkling on his piazza with Kate. He berated Conkling, who wisely decided to leave. But Sprague ran after him with a shotgun. The newspapers had a field day.

Kate left her husband that afternoon and the two divorced. She ended up selling butter and eggs door to door and died a pauper. The mansion burned down in 1909, and today the Town of Narragansett owns the property. It is a 174-acre state park known as Canonchet Farm and home to the South County Museum.

2. EMILY DICKINSON MUSEUM, AMHERST, MASSACHUSETTS

Emily Dickinson's married brother, Austin, carried on an illicit love affair for thirteen years with Mabel Loomis Todd, also married. Shortly after Mabel moved to Amherst, they began flirting, until on September 11, 1882, they crossed the Rubicon—according to Austin's diary.

The whole town of Amherst, Massachusetts, including Todd's husband, knew about the affair. He thought it was okay. Mrs. Austin Dickinson did not.

Austin used to take Mabel next door, where his mother and reclusive sisters Emily and Lavinia lived. They'd then have sex on Emily Dickinson's dining room sofa.

We know because Austin recorded everything in his diary. For example, on January 3, 1886, he wrote, "at the other house 3 to 5 and +=====XXX." Mabel, who also kept a diary, wrote on the same day. "A most exquisitely happy and satisfactory two hours."

Emily Dickinson died in 1886. Lavinia asked Mabel Loomis Todd and Thomas Wentworth Higginson to publish her poems. They did, and Mabel embarked on a lecture tour that made famous the reclusive Emily.

Both Dickinson houses are now a museum.

3. WILLOWBROOK COTTAGE, SOMESVILLE, MAINE

Elinor Hoyt Hichborn was living the life of a young society matron in Washington, D.C., when in 1910 she suddenly ran off with Horace Wylie, a married man seventeen years older than she.

Her elopement shocked Washington, especially since she abandoned her three-year-old son. President Taft threatened to send his diplomatic corps to fetch the runaway bride.

Elinor and Horace escaped detection, though, living under assumed names in England. Neither of their spouses would grant a divorce, so they stayed exiled until World War I broke out and forced them to return home.

Money began to run low, and during one winter they rented a farmhouse in Somesville. Shopkeepers sometimes refused to sell Elinor groceries because she had abandoned her husband and child.

All the while, Elinor honed her poetry. When she and Horace finally married, she published a book of poems under her new married name, Elinor Wylie. She would become the voice of her generation and win the Pulitzer Prize for poetry. She would also divorce Horace Wylie and marry a third time before dying suddenly at forty-three.

The cottage they rented is now known as Willowbrook, and is a bed and breakfast.

4. EQUINOX HOTEL, MANCHESTER, VERMONT

Then (and now) the Equinox House served as the center of activity in the village of Manchester. In the summer of 1926, future New York Congressman Adam Clayton Powell, Jr., worked there as a bellhop.

Powell, in his memoirs, recalled how the newly wed Daddy and Peaches Browning spent that summer at the Equinox.

Daddy was fifty-one-year-old Edward Browning, a real estate developer. Peaches was fifteen-year-old Frances Belle Heenan. In addition to being a millionaire, Daddy was known as a pervert interested in young girls.

Peaches's parents encouraged her daughter's relationship with Daddy, and the two began dating. The story prompted outrage. With decency leagues hot on their tracks, Peaches married Daddy in New York City. They then decamped to Vermont to avoid the paparazzi.

Powell recalled how Daddy gave Peaches a hundred dollar bill to tip the bellhops with. Peaches tried to distract the boys by opening her robe while she passed them a ten dollar bill. They insisted on the full amount.

By October the Brownings' relationship had soured, and they appeared in court for separation. Peaches lost her bid for alimony, though she did develop a stage career. Two husbands later she finally got her due when Daddy died in 1934, and she won an interest in his estate.

5. KATHARINE HEPBURN'S SUMMER HOME, FENWICK, CONNECTICUT

Katharine Hepburn loved her summer home in Fenwick, and she loved her married co-star Spencer Tracy. Lucky for her, she could enjoy both of them together.

She had been going to the Fenwick beach colony in Old Saybrook since 1912, when she was five years old.

She met Spencer Tracy on the set of the 1942 film *Woman of the Year*. Hepburn famously said, "I fear I may be too tall for you, Mr. Tracy." Director George Stevens retorted, "Don't worry, he'll soon cut you down to size."

Instead, they fell in love. They starred in nine movies together, but lived apart and kept their affair private. Tracy was estranged from his wife, but neither sought a divorce. Hepburn and Tracy made Fenwick their summer love nest.

The house, on Mohegan Avenue, is privately owned, but you can visit the Katharine Hepburn Museum in Old Saybrook.

6. GILMANTON WINERY, GILMANTON, NEW HAMPSHIRE

Grace Metalious rocketed to fame in 1956 with her first novel, *Peyton Place*. She'd started life in 1924 on the largely poor, Franco-American West Side of Manchester, New Hampshire. After she married George Metalious, they moved north to the small town of Gilmanton. He taught school, while she drank, swore, wore baggy jeans, failed to keep house, and locked her children outside so she could write.

Peyton Place described the seamy side of a small New England town. It sold 100,000 copies in the first month, and it infuriated the people of Gilmanton. Suddenly, reporters were inundating their town looking for dirt. The townspeople shunned Grace and her children because she'd written a dirty book.

With fame came money, enough to buy a dream house in Gilmanton, today the Gilmanton Winery. Grace and George broke up, but before they divorced she took up with a deejay from nearby Laconia. George sneaked into her dream house one night and photographed them in bed together.

Grace and T.J. the DJ married and divorced, then she and George reconciled. And divorced.

Fame made Grace Metalious rich and reckless; she burned through millions of dollars and died of cirrhosis of the liver at the age of thirty-nine.

ARMED ROBBERY

In November 1620, the Pilgrims came ashore on Cape Cod and stole a cache of buried Indian corn in what is now Truro. That's the first European record of property theft in New England. Many more followed.

In the earliest days of the colonies, servants were most likely to be accused of theft—of livestock, of silver, of clothing, and of food. Miscreants were punished by whipping and time in the stocks. Indians were sent to the gallows or sold to the West Indies as slaves.

Once New Hampshire decided to brand thieves with a hot iron, other colonies followed. A first offender would get a "B" on his right hand. A second offense got a brand on the left hand. Steal on a Sunday and that "B" got burned into the forehead. Thieves could also lose part of an ear for a crime.

As the colonies prospered and grew, so did the opportunities for stealing. By 1711, Massachusetts made it a capital crime for a second offense of highway robbery.

After the American Revolution, horse theft became a serious problem. Not only did horses have considerable value, they had the essential element that allowed a fugitive to put distance between himself and the pursuers.

Bank robbery started to come into vogue around 1840, when states started chartering dozens of banks. Banks were a favorite target because that's where the money was.

A few decades before the Civil War, the number of robberies started to increase, and property crime stayed high except during the war years. In Boston, robberies, burglaries, and larcenies peaked between 1869 and 1871.

1. NORTHERN RAIL TRAIL, BOSCAWEN, NEW HAMPSHIRE

Highway robbery could get you hanged, and in the case of Michael Martin, it did.

Martin held up several travelers at gunpoint in New Hampshire and Massachusetts in the 1820s. He was caught and tried, then hanged on Lechmere Point in Cambridge, Massachusetts.

One of his New Hampshire victims, a man named Huse Karr, was traveling from his home in Lyndeborough to Salisbury on the Fourth Turnpike. He left on horseback on the morning of August 9, 1821. By nine in the evening he reached his brother's house in Boscawen. He realized his brother was still at work in Salisbury, so he proceeded north along the turnpike.

Karr saw a man sitting by the side of the road and, thinking it was his brother, slowed down and called to him. That turned out to be a big mistake. The man seized his horse's bridle, drew a pistol, and demanded his money. When Karr handed over his purse, the man demanded his watch, then ordered him to dismount. Then the highway robber climbed on Karr's horse and rode off.

Days later, the same man stole a horse in the town of Palmer, Massachusetts. Horse theft was such a problem then that horse owners formed mutual aid societies to go after the thieves. Palmer apparently had one such group, which formed a posse and caught the thief. He was identified as Michael Martin, the man who had robbed Karr and several others.

Martin claimed several aliases and may have been John Martin, a twenty-six-year-old Irish immigrant. Had he left his gun at home, he would have been sentenced to life in prison. But he was sent to the gallows for using his pistol, and launched into eternity on December 20, 1821.

The Fourth Turnpike later became the Northern route of the Boston and Maine Railroad from Concord to White River Junction, Vermont. It is now the Northern Rail Trail from Lebanon to Boscawen.

2. AMERICAN MUSEUM OF TORT LAW, WINSTED, CONNECTICUT

Between 1845 and 1860, thirty-nine new banks were chartered by the state of Connecticut—and that was a lot back in those days.

State bankers could score by getting federal charters. In 1848, that's what the shareholders of the Winsted Bank hoped to do. But a robbery sometime between Friday night, November 9, and Monday morning, November 11, crushed those hopes.

The Winsted Bank had a granite vault to safeguard its deposits. On the second floor of the bank building a lawyer named V. R. C. Giddings rented office space.

Over that weekend, robbers had entered Giddings's office, carefully removed the floorboards above the vault, and drilled through its granite roof. They made off with $60,000, worth close to $2 million today. But they didn't take everything, which showed they knew something about banking. Back then, banks printed their own money. If they'd taken everything, the bank would have failed and the banknotes would have been worthless. So the thieves took only about half the Winsted banknotes, about $50,000 worth. They also took notes from other banks and gold and silver.

The Bank never recovered, closing in 1864. But a local legend persists that the robbers planned the heist in a cave near town, now known as Robbers Cave.

Another legend, crusading lawyer Ralph Nader, a Winsted native, bought the old Winsted Bank Building and turned it into the American Museum of Tort Law.

3. TD BANK, ST. ALBANS, VERMONT

Toward the end of the Civil War, Confederate soldiers raided the northern Vermont city of St. Albans. They had hoped to divert Union troops and to raise money for the Confederacy by robbing and harassing northern towns.

Between eighteen and twenty-two men, led by Lieutenant Bennett Young, filtered into St. Albans in October 1864. They scoped out three banks in the city: the Franklin County Bank, the First National, and the St. Albans Bank.

At 3 p.m. on October 19, 1864, the town was largely emptied of working men. Bennett Young stepped onto the common and declared he was taking possession of St. Albans. The soldiers made residents swear an oath to the Confederacy, and Young and his raiders looted the three banks, making off with $208,000 in just fifteen minutes.

The raiders torched one house as a distraction and fled the town unharmed. They killed a man—Elinus Morrison—who tried to interfere with their getaway. But their plans to set fire to much of the town failed when the bombs they brought did not work.

Once people in St. Albans figured out what was happening, they quickly formed a posse to pursue the raiders into Canada. Within a day they had captured fourteen of the raiders and eventually recovered $87,000. The rest of the money, however, was never seen again. At least by them.

The three banks are gone, but a plaque on the TD Bank commemorates the raid and the original site of the Franklin County Bank.

4. DEXTER BANK BLOCK, DEXTER, MAINE

On February 22, 1878, the treasurer of the Dexter Savings Bank, John Barron, was found lying in front of the bank vault tied and gagged, his head bleeding. Carried to his home in Dexter, Maine, near death, he opened his eyes just long enough to gaze at his wife and smile. Then he died, a victim of an eighteenth-century criminal mastermind.

At first John Barron was viewed as a hero who died rather than give up the bank's funds. But then a year later, the bank's officers began to think he embezzled funds and committed suicide to avoid disgrace.

Nine years later a petty crook named Charles Stain was serving time in the Norridgewock, Maine, jail. He confessed that his father and three accomplices had robbed the Dexter Bank. Two were tried and convicted, but they were freed in 1901, and Charles Stain recanted his confession.

No one else was ever convicted for the Dexter Savings Bank robbery. Detectives, though, believed the man who planned the crime, George Leslie, had been murdered shortly after it happened.

Leslie was a wildly successful bank robber, a one-man crime wave. Well-born in Cincinnati, he'd been trained as an architect, and he moved to New York to rob banks. He planned his crimes with meticulous attention to detail. Gangs across the country hired him as a consultant on their own bank heists.

Shortly after the failed attempt on the Dexter bank, Leslie's gang pulled off one of the biggest bank heists in history. The Manhattan Savings Institution robbery netted three million dollars. But Leslie didn't see a dime of it. He was found dead before the robbery. His murderer was never discovered, though police believed an accomplice killed him.

As far as the Dexter heist, they thought John Barron had agreed to help Leslie, then changed his mind during the attempted theft.

The Dexter Bank Block is on the National Register of Historic Places, though not for that reason.

5. FORMER HOWARD JOHNSON'S, PROVIDENCE, RHODE ISLAND

Shortly after World War II, Providence police got a tip that a robbery was planned at the Howard Johnson's on Main Street. So four police officers staked out the restaurant. On March 9, 1947, just after 3 a.m., three thieves broke into the darkened building. The officers ordered them to surrender. Instead, one of the robbers fired his gun twice. The police opened fire, immediately killing two of the men. The third fled, breaking through a plate glass door. He didn't make it, as the police shot him dead.

The leader of the gang turned out to be a career criminal, but his two accomplices had no police records. Both had served in the war.

The building, no longer a Howard Johnson's, is still at 1303 North Main Street.

6. 600 COMMERCIAL STREET, BOSTON, MASSACHUSETTS

The 1950 robbery at the Brink's Armored Car depot in Boston was almost the perfect crime. However, the thieves fell out over dividing the spoils, and police arrested them all five days before the statute of limitations ran out.

The eleven robbers planned the crime for two years, watching the depot for eighteen months to figure out when it held the most money.

The gang stole plans for the depot's alarm system, and then returned them undetected. They also removed the cylinders from locks, one by one, and had a locksmith duplicate the keys.

At 6:55 p.m. on January 17, seven of the gang members entered the counting room. They bound and gagged the five employees, then cleaned out everything except the General Electric payroll. It took them only thirty-five minutes to load fourteen canvas bags with a half ton of loot. Two gang members, waiting outside in the getaway truck, whisked them away.

One gang member blew it for all of them. Joseph "Specs" O'Keefe, serving a prison sentence for another crime, wrote to his cohorts demanding money and suggesting he might talk. A hit was ordered on him, but O'Keefe escaped with minor wounds. He made a deal with the FBI to testify against the gang. All eight were caught and convicted. Two died before they were tried.

Police recovered only fifty-eight-thousand dollars of the $2.7 million stolen.

Today the Brink's depot is a parking garage at 600 Commercial Street.

CORRUPTION,
RAILROAD STYLE

Visitors to New England's railroad depots and rail trails enjoy a step back in time via an earlier form of transportation. But railroads were far more than just a means of transportation to the men who owned them. They were the source of vast wealth as the owners of rail lines collected money for every passenger and every pound of freight that passed over them.

As railroads required land and rights of way to operate, the entire industry sat squarely at the intersection of commerce and government, making it a perfect petrie dish for government corruption.

Over the decades, flim-flammers have found countless ways to make fortunes out of railroads: inflated stock prices, fake construction projects, privatization scams, self-dealing, double books, and bogus investments. They caused a never-ending skein of bankruptcies to clear the decks for the next set of investors to be bilked. But to keep control of the rails, the owners needed cooperative politicians who wouldn't force regulation onto them.

This meant spending money, and lots of it, to keep the politicians bribed and happy.

Today, New England is still dotted with remnants of the railroad era. Quaint old rail stations, rail trails, and bridges all hark back to the golden age of rail. Most have a scandal of two built into them.

1. CENTRAL VERMONT RAIL DEPOT, NORTHFIELD, VERMONT

If you planned a rail line from Burlington to Windsor, a stop in the state's capital, Montpelier, might seem logical. Not to Charles Paine, the founder and president of the Vermont Central Railroad. That's because Paine owned land in the small town of Northfield.

A former governor, Paine won a state charter for a railroad in 1843. He decided to run trains through Northfield so they could bring his hometown freight, passengers, and their money.

The decision showed a lot about Paine's greed and shortsightedness. He quickly rounded up investors for his new venture. And that seems to be about the last thing he did well. In 1851, Paine assured stockholders of the success of his great enterprise.

But by 1852, investors were outraged and publicly calling for investigations into everything from the decision to route the railroad through Northfield to the handling of the company finances.

Boston newspapers portrayed the railroad's directors as incompetent self-dealers. Critics charge the railroad put its headquarters and maintenance facilities in Northfield to benefit individual directors.

Meanwhile, company treasurer Josiah Quincy, Jr., died and his estate made claims against the railroad. Quincy had used company assets—over which he had control—to guarantee his debts.

In the spring of 1852, the railroad appointed an investigating committee to sort through the mess. The investigating committee found the railroad's books were a shambles, it had overstated its income, and it was undoubtedly poorly run. But the committee cleared Paine and other directors of any deliberate malfeasance.

The committee's report was too little, too late. By 1853, the railroad was in bankruptcy. Paine's defenders noted that he did, indeed, improve rail access for Vermonters. They also noted that he, too, lost heavily in his venture. It mattered little to Paine. He died in 1853 in Waco, Texas, trying to find new investments.

The remnants of Paine's folly can still be seen in Northfield, where the Vermont Central Railroad's home depot is still standing.

2. NORWALK RIVER RAILROAD BRIDGE, NORWALK, CONNECTICUT

When it comes to the men who masterminded railroad scandals, none were more audacious than Robert Schuyler. A grandson of Philip Schuyler, hero of the Battle of Saratoga, Robert Schuyler was chosen to be the president of the New York and New Haven Railroad because of his impeccable lineage and history. He was beyond reproach. And he used that reputation to carry out a swindle impressive even by today's standards.

Schuyler's scheme started to unravel in 1853 with a catastrophic train crash. An NY&NH train failed to stop for an open swing bridge and plunged into the Norwalk River, killing fifty people. The accident put the rail line in the spotlight and left Schuyler settling claims for damages.

At first things seemed fine, but in 1854 the company's stock took a nosedive. Rumors circulated that the railroad had problems. And then, Schuyler disappeared amid a flurry of rumors that he was ill or had gone to Canada to escape the heat. In truth, he fled to France.

Schuyler packed up more than $100,000 in cash and left the country to avoid a collapse he well knew was coming. Soon the extent of his stock manipulations became clear. Schuyler had sold fraudulent stock shares to raise millions. He operated three sets of books for the company, employing separate clerks for each to keep everyone in the dark.

Bewildered holders of stock—both real and fake—descended on the company to demand an accounting. The case would be tied up in courts for more than ten years. As for Schuyler, he would return to America—in a box. He died in France and was shipped home in 1855, though one of his Harvard classmates questioned whether Schuyler (or anyone else for that matter) was even in that coffin, or if Schuyler had actually gotten away with his fraud.

The New York and New Haven Railroad connected the two cities that make up its name, and train travelers between the two cities today pass over the same ground that carried the old railroad. The railroad bridge over the Norwalk River, where the train derailed, replaced the previous bridge in 1896.

3. CONWAY SCENIC RAILROAD, NORTH CONWAY, NEW HAMPSHIRE

In New Hampshire, the Boston and Maine Railroad bribed virtually the entire New Hampshire Legislature, or at least as many as were needed to support 100-year leases for the railroad lines throughout the state. That was an astounding feat, considering the Legislature had more than four hundred members.

It all came about in 1887, when the Boston and Maine and Boston and Lowell vied to win control over the railroad lines in New Hampshire.

The affair came to a head when Senator Oliver Sawyer publicly charged that fellow senator Kirk Pierce offered him a $500 bribe at Sawyer's summer home on Lake Sunapee if he would give a speech in favor of the Boston and Maine. Senator Pierce dismissed the allegation, claiming he was only joking. Nevertheless, the Senate appointed a committee to investigate. House members and senators came out of the woodwork to announce that they, too, had been offered bribes—though no one admitted to taking any money.

The Boston and Maine, meanwhile, simply said that no one was officially authorized to buy any votes in New Hampshire.

The Senate committee concluded that Sawyer had been telling the truth. A bribe had been offered. The Senate, however, declined to adopt the findings, infuriating Sawyer.

"A dastardly attempt was made to bribe me, and an equally dastardly attempt has been made to smirch my good name," he said. "If our legislation is to be tainted with fraud, if the crime of bribery is to be practiced under the shadow of our halls of legislation, if a great and powerful corporation is to be permitted without rebuke to violate law and tempt men to criminal acts, then, surely, the very foundations of our government are in danger."

His speech fell on deaf ears. The Legislature granted the leases to the Boston and Maine. Governor Charles Sawyer, however, vetoed the bill because of the evidence of bribery. He did note, wryly, that both railroads were probably equally guilty.

The veto was merely a temporary delay for the Boston and Maine, which controlled virtually all the rail lines in New Hampshire within ten years. Many stations served by the Boston and Maine remain in existence today, including the Conway Scenic Railroad. Visitors can not only get a taste of what the old-fashioned stations were like, but also ride the train.

4. UNION STATION, PROVIDENCE, RHODE ISLAND

Rhode Island trolleys made Senator Nelson Aldrich a millionaire. Though such scandals seem quaint by today's standards, the nation was appalled at the political chicanery of the Rhode Island senator.

Aldrich was born poor in 1841 and started his career in the grocery business, but before long he entered politics. First elected to the Providence City Council in his twenties, he rose steadily in the state's Republican machine, winning election to the U.S. House of Representatives in 1878. Three years later, he persuaded the Rhode Island Legislature—which chose the state's U.S. senators—to give him the office.

But as his second term in the Senate was ending in 1892, Aldrich was getting tired of public service. In short, it didn't pay well enough. Enter the Sugar Trust—a group of sugar companies that desperately needed a friend in the Senate—a friend like Aldrich—to help them write more favorable sugar tariffs.

In that era, winning elections required cash. It went to mill owners and other businesses, then from there into the hands of the state's voters. For as little as three dollars, a vote could be purchased. But without cash, voters stayed home. Aldrich lacked the cash as well as the drive to continue his career. The Sugar Trust solved his problems. Not only did it give him the money to buy the votes he needed, its head lobbyist went into business with Aldrich—the rail business.

In Washington, Aldrich worked to squeeze the sugar tariff through the Senate. Back home, he and his partners hatched a secret plan to acquire new leases to run trolley lines. With his connections, Aldrich had no difficulty getting them. Some of the leases, acquired without competition, extended as long as 999 years. With money from the sugar companies he and his partners refurbished the old horse-drawn trolley lines into new electrified systems.

Most of the lines operated under a corporate shell known as the Rhode Island Company. Aldrich was accused of corruption in trading his influence for the Sugar Trust's backing. He flatly denied it. Historians, however, have documented that, in fact, the Sugar Trust funded his rail ventures.

When he finally sold out of the business, Aldrich was a millionaire many times over. Providence's Union Station was a one-time hub for the Rhode Island Company trains.

5. AROOSTOOK VALLEY RAILROAD DEPOT, PRESQUE ISLE, MAINE

What was it about senators and railroads? The Aroostoock Valley Railroad terminal in Presque Isle was once the property of businessman Arthur Gould. Gould built the railroad, which operated between Presque Isle and Caribou, Maine, to haul timber to his sawmill. It also shipped potatoes and a few passengers.

The AVR started running in 1910. Gould had plans to eventually expand into Canada, but later dropped them. He ended up selling the railroad outright to Canadian Pacific Railway.

But nothing came without strings when it came to building a railroad. Gould needed the government in New Brunswick, Canada, to guarantee bonds to cover the cost of constructing the Aroostook Valley Railroad. To get it, he paid $100,000 to J.K. Flemming, the man who would become New Brunswick's premier.

The bribe caused a minor headache for Gould in 1917 when Canadian authorities examined the matter. And it dogged him later on when Maine elected him to the U.S. Senate. The Senate held hearings into the corrupt practice on the laughable pretext that engaging in bribery was conduct unbefitting a senator. (Perhaps to the senators of the day it was acceptable to take bribes, but not pay them out.) Regardless, Gould survived the inquiry by explaining the $100,000 was a campaign contribution and not even his idea.

The Aroostook Valley Railroad operated into the 1960s before it closed down and its rolling stock was auctioned off. Today visitors can walk, bicycle, or ATV over the Aroostook Valley Trail, which runs over some of the old railroad's bridges and rights of way. And the old AVR depot in Presque Isle is still standing, too. If you go, perhaps tip your hat to some of the Canadian taxpayers who helped make Arthur Gould's vision of a railroad a reality.

6. STEAMING TENDER RESTAURANT, PALMER, MASSACHUSETTS

To railroad aficionados, the town of Palmer, Massachusetts, is anything but an unfamiliar spot. It's nicknamed "The Town of Seven Railroads" because it once served as a hub for many rail lines. But for our purposes, we'll discuss the one dubbed by the Palmer Historical Commission as "The Railroad That Never Was"—the Hampden Railroad.

The object of the Hampden railroad was to connect the Central Massachusetts Railroad of the Boston and Maine Railroad at Palmer with the New York, New Haven and Hartford Railroad at Springfield. That would create a through route from New York to North Station in Boston for the B&M.

About four million dollars were raised from investors and construction started in 1910. The bulk of the line was built and track laid by 1912. But the project ran into political headwinds. It couldn't get approvals for a lease on one section of the track. The backers ran out of money. The president of the railroad died. The project devolved into lawsuits between the Hampden and the Boston and Maine.

In 1914, prosecutors issued eighteen indictments against the individuals and banks involved in the Hampden fiasco. They alleged that the bankers fraudulently secured investments in the railroad, and that certain individuals—including Charles Mellen, a protégé of J. P. Morgan—had conspired to steal from the banks. They got off, but the whole train line wound up being sold for scrap. Some of it was used in the World War I effort.

Visitors to Palmer today can stop and reminisce about the Railroad That Never Was at Palmer's Union Station, which houses the popular Steaming Tender Restaurant. Rail lovers can watch the trains that still pass as they dine. (The station, by the way, was designed by Henry Hobson Richardson, who also designed Trinity Church in Boston.)

PLACES WHERE PEOPLE WERE MURDERED

JOHN BILLINGTON WAS THE FIRST EUROPEAN TRIED AND EXECUTED FOR murder in New England. He crossed the Atlantic on the *Mayflower* with his family, but apparently had little interest in establishing a godly community. He was a knave, wrote Plymouth Colony governor William Bradford. After he waylaid his neighbor and shot him to death with a blunderbuss, the Pilgrims hanged him on September 30, 1630.

Violent crime wouldn't really take off until the middle of the nineteenth century. Irish immigrants took most of the blame for it. Police records during the era indicate the ethnicity of a suspect, and in many cases he (or she) came from Ireland. But the Civil War's orgy of bloodshed should also take some of the blame for the rise in violent crime.

Another great wave of violent crime began in 1900 with another tide of immigrants. Perhaps the pressures of factory discipline or adapting to life in a crowded city caused an increase in murder and assault.

Sometimes, people stuck on the bottom rung of the economic ladder will lash out when everyone else seems to be enjoying their prosperity. Some criminologists believe that's what caused the murder rate to start rising again in 1960. Then the economic tide lifted many but not all boats, especially not for African Americans.

1. TOWER HILL ROAD, SOUTH KINGSTOWN, RHODE ISLAND

For many years Thomas Carter's rotting corpse dangled in chains from a tree, a terrifying reminder to the people of South Kingstown that he'd murdered William Jackson.

In 1751, the murder took place on a deserted stretch of the Post Road. Details vary on what actually happened, but it seems Carter, a ship captain, was shipwrecked somewhere off the Atlantic Coast. Heading north he met fellow traveler William Jackson, who gave him money and let him use his horse. Around New Year's Day, 1751, they stopped at a tavern. Then they pushed on along the Post Road until Carter turned on Jackson, stabbing him with Jackson's own sword. Carter stripped Jackson of his clothes and threw him in the Pettaquamscutt River.

Jackson's body was soon discovered and identified by the keeper of the tavern where they'd stopped. Carter was arrested, tried, and sentenced to be hanged and gibbeted. People in South Kingstown for many years remembered the caged corpse dangling from a tree. Wrote Joseph Peace Hazard, "the shrieking—as it were—of its chains, &c., during boisterous winds at night, were the terror of many persons who lived thereto."

Hazard in 1889 marked the murder scene with a stone pillar that today stands on Tower Hill Road in South Kingstown, across from the state government center.

2. FAIRFIELD POND, FAIRFIELD, VERMONT

Around 1840, Eugene Clifford, who wasn't very bright, deserted from the British Army in Canada and arrived in Fairfield. There he met and married a widow, Mrs. Elizabeth Gilmore, who owned a fifty-acre farm. They had an infant daughter, Mary Ann.

Rumors around town had it that he was seeing another widow with a bigger farm. Whatever the case, he decided to kill his wife and child.

On October 16, 1842, he lied to his wife that a friend across Fairfield Pond invited them for a visit. He rowed his wife and baby daughter across the pond in his log canoe. No one ever saw her or the infant alive again.

Eugene said Elizabeth had tried to wrap her shawl around Mary Ann, but fell in the water with the baby in her arms. But when the bodies were discovered, the shawl was missing.

The next night a neighbor dreamt she found the shawl partially buried near the pond. When she awoke, she went to the spot she'd dreamed of and found the shawl.

Then Eugene came up with another story: A strong wind had rocked the canoe so violently his wife and daughter fell overboard, and he fell in trying to save them. When he realized the distance to shore he grabbed the oars and swam to solid ground. His changing story and his failure to rescue his wife and baby aroused the coroner's suspicion. Eugene died five years later in prison, a raving madman.

Fairfield Pond is also known as Dream Pond.

3. MARIPOSA MUSEUM, PETERBOROUGH, NEW HAMPSHIRE

Peterborough's Baptist Church at 26 Main Street was a little unusual: The first floor was configured as residential rental space, so rental income would help support the working-class congregation.

In 1881, an Irish couple, Patrick and Eileen Walsh, lived in a rear apartment of the church with their three small children. Patrick, a peddler, was broke and needed a job. Eileen, a widow, had an eighteen-year-old son from her first marriage and worked in a factory.

Patrick drank up Eileen's earnings. People who knew him said his drinking made him crazy and he couldn't get work. He also abused Eileen. Neighbors described her as pleasant, peaceable, and intelligent for someone in her station in life.

In January 1881, Patrick decided he needed fifty dollars so he could leave Eileen. She wouldn't give it to him. He left to raise the money but failed, and then he returned home. In front of her children, Eileen put on her hat and shawl. Patrick said, "Where are you going?" He then grabbed her by the throat, threw her on the bed, and cut her throat with a razor. Then he cut his own.

Eileen and Patrick staggered into the kitchen, got up and went outside, where they fell in the snow. She lived just long enough to recognize one of her sons. Patrick lived a few minutes longer. In the final moments of his life, he raised himself on his hands and knees with a desperate effort. Then he crawled to her in the snow and kissed her several times.

The local newspaper reported everyone who knew him believed he wouldn't have committed the crime if he had found a job. The church is now the Mariposa Museum.

4. WOOD ISLAND, BIDDEFORD POOL, MAINE

Fred Milliken, a thirty-five-year-old game warden, lived with his wife and three stepchildren in a modest house on tiny Wood Island. He also owned an old chicken coop that he rented to Howard Hobbs and William Moses, two fishermen about twenty-four years old.

On Sunday, May 31, 1896, the two fishermen went on a drunken spree in Old Orchard Beach. They spent the night and then got drunk again on their way home. When their boat pulled into the island landing, Milliken and his young son were working nearby. Milliken said, "Howard, I want to see you a minute." But the two fishermen kept on walking.

They went into the hennery and Hobbs picked up a rifle. Then the two went to see Milliken. Milliken asked if the gun was loaded, and Hobbs said no. "I'll see whether it is or not," Milliken said, and started toward Hobbs. Hobbs fired, hitting him in the abdomen.

Fred Milliken lived another forty-five minutes.

Howard Hobbs left, then returned to learn Fred Milliken had died. He went to the hennery, lay down on his bed, held the barrel of his rifle six inches from his head, and pulled the trigger with his toe.

The *Biddeford Daily Journal* reported on June 2, 1896:

SHOT ANOTHER, THEN HIMSELF
Murder and Suicide at Wood Island Yesterday.
Repeating Rifle the Weapon.
Howard Hobbs killed Frederick W. Milliken.
Bullet in his own Brain.
Liquor Mainly Responsible For the Tragedy.

5. 141 MAIN STREET, DEEP RIVER, CONNECTICUT

At the end of the nineteenth century, Deep River, Connecticut, had acquired great wealth from the ivory trade. The town's factories churned out combs and piano keys from ivory shipped up the Connecticut River.

The Deep River Savings Bank was believed to have more than one million dollars in deposits, and bankers got a tip about a planned robbery. So they hired a night watchman, a local man named Harry Tyler.

Sure enough, on the night of December 13, 1899, four men approached the bank at 141 Main Street. One, described as having a long black moustache, tried to jimmy open the window. Tyler fired at the robber with his shotgun, hitting him in the face. The other three fled, leaving their accomplice to die in Deep River.

No one knew the man's identity, so the town buried him in Fountain Hill Cemetery near the railroad tracks. He was buried in a grave under a stone inscribed with the letters XYZ.

The townspeople claimed a woman in black walked from the railroad station to the XYZ marker every December for forty years. She always left a small flower and she never said a word. Or maybe she left a bouquet. Or maybe she came in summer. No one ever knew who he or she was.

The story goes to show that a good story can outlive the facts. Two months after the robbery, the local newspaper reported the Pinkerton Detective Agency identified XYZ as known criminal Frank Howard, also known as P.E. King. The American Bankers Association had hired the detectives, which is how the bank knew it was likely to be robbed. The detectives never arrested the accomplices for lack of evidence.

A different bank building now stands on the Deep River Savings Bank site, but inside you can see a display case with the gun, shell casing, and some photos.

6. 79 GAINSBOROUGH STREET, BOSTON, MASSACHUSETTS

For nearly two years in the early 1960s, a serial killer known as the Boston Strangler spread terror through Boston and surrounding cities. Starting in 1962, he strangled thirteen single women and raped nearly all of them. Police found no signs of forced entry at any of the crime scenes. That convinced them the victims either knew their killer or he had persuaded them he was making a delivery or doing some maintenance.

The first victim, fifty-six-year-old Anna Slesers, lived at 79 Gainsborough Street in the Fenway neighborhood. She'd been strangled with her bathrobe belt and sexually assaulted with some kind of object. Twelve more women between the ages of nineteen and eighty-five died in a similar manner—in nearby Cambridge, Lynn, and Lawrence.

Not until his fourth victim did police believe that one man killed all those women. They began to notice he tied bows around their necks with the stocking or belt he'd strangled them with.

In October 1964, police picked up Albert DeSalvo, a petty thief and Army veteran. They charged him with raping a young woman who identified him in a photo.

While in prison, DeSalvo confessed he was the Boston Strangler. His police confession included details of the crime scenes that hadn't been made public. In 1967 he received a sentence of life in prison. Seven years later, he was found stabbed to death in his cell.

Some people thought DeSalvo didn't do it. Others still think several people committed the Strangler murders, and that DeSalvo just confessed because he needed attention. In 2013, a test of DNA from semen found at the 1964 murder scene of Mary Sullivan showed it matched DeSalvo's DNA.

SOURCES AND
FURTHER READING

How the States Got Their Names

Megan Gambino, "John Smith Coined the Term New England on This 1616 Map," *Smithsonian* magazine, Nov. 24, 2014.

"John Mason," *Dictionary of Canadian Biography, www.biographi.ca/en/bio/mason _john_1E.html.*

Origin of Maine's Name, Maine State Library, *web.archive.org/web/20061124144408/ http://www.maine.gov/msl/services/reference/meorigin.htm.*

"How the New England State Names Came To Be," New England Historical Society; *newenglandhistoricalsociety.com/new-england-state-names-came/.*

Edward Field, *The Antinomians and Aquidneck, State of Rhode Island and Providence Plantations at the End of the Century: A History, Illustrated with Maps, Facsimiles of Old Plates and Paintings and Photographs of Ancient Landmarks, Volume 1*, 1902.

Joseph-Andre Senecal, "Vermont: Samuel de Champlain and the Naming of Vermont," *vermonthistory.org/journal/77/VHS770203_119-128.pdf.*

Towns with Unique Names

Christopher Lenney, *Sightseeking: Clues to the Landscape History of New England.*

Sandy Nestor, *Indian Placenames in America.*

Silas R. Coburn, *History of Dracut, Massachusetts, Called By The Indians Augumtoocooke And Before Incorporation, The Wildernesse North Of The Merrimac. First Permanent Settlement In 1669 And Incorporated As A Town.*

Paul T. Helman, *Historical Gazetteer of the United States*, p. 701, *epdf.pub/historical-gazet teer-of-the-united-states.html (Henniker).*

Patricia A. Mehrtens, Town Historian, Burrillvillehistory.net, "James Burrill" (Burrillville).

"A Brief History of St. Johnsbury," St. Johnsbury Athenaeum, *stjathenaeum.org /a-brief-history-of-st-johnsbury.*

Places Named Out of Spite

Blandford, Federal Writers Project, *The WPA Guide to Massachusetts: The Bay State.*

Emerson W. Baker, *Formerly Machegonne, Dartmouth, York, Stogummor, Casco and Falmouth: Portland as a Contested Frontier in the Seventeenth Century.*

"Jackson, N.H., Gets a New Name," New England Historical Society, *newenglandhis toricalsociety.com/jackson-n-h-gets-new-name/.*

Elisha Reynolds Potter, *The Early History of Narragansett: With an Appendix of Original Documents, Many of which are Now for the First Time Published, Volume 3.*

"Town of Westbrook" by James A. Pratt, from *The History of Middlesex County, 1635–1885*

"Six Places Renamed Out of Spite," New England Historical Society, *newenglandhistori calsociety.com/six-places-renamed-for-spite/; Annual Report of the American Sunday-School Union*, American Sunday School Union, 1914; Philip R. Jordan, "Timeless Treasure," *Vermont Magazine*, March/April 2015 (Adamant).

Places with French Names

"Town beginnings…", Orange Historical Society, Orange, CT, orangehistory.org.

Rev. J. H. Hincks, "Washington County (Vermont)," *A History of New England: Containing Historical and Descriptive Sketches of the Counties, Cities and Principal Towns of the Six New England States, Including, in Its List of Contributors, More Than Sixty Literary Men and Women, Representing Every County in New England, Volume 2, 1881*, ed R. H. Howard, Henry E Crocker (Barre).

Ron Petersen, "The Origins of the Town of Orleans," *historicorleans.org.*

"Calais," Maine, An Encyclopedia, *maineanencyclopedia.com/Calais.*

National Park Service, NRHP Inventory-Nomination Form, "Lafayette Village."

"About Fremont," Town of Fremont, New Hampshire, fremont.nh.gov.

Towns Named Warren

Statewide Preservation Report, B-W-1, Rhode Island Historical Preservation Commission (Warren, RI).

Austin Jacobs Coolidge, John Brainard Mansfield, *A History and Description of New England, General and Local* (Warren, NH; Maine, VT).

"Warren," *Connecticuthistory.org, connecticuthistory.org/towns-page/warren/;* Rick Green, "Village Center on the Block," *Hartford Courant*, July 7, 2006.

Olney I. Darling, *History of Warren Massachusetts.*

INDIAN TRAILS THAT ARE NOW SCENIC BYWAYS

Chester B. Price, *Historic Indian Trails of New Hampshire*; New England Trails: Overview, New England Greenway Vision Plan, umass.edu/greenway.

"Old King's Highway Historic District," Massachusetts Cultural Resource Information System, *mhc-macris.net/Details.aspx?MhcId=BRN.M.*

"Old Connecticut Path," alltrails.org; John Adams, Charles Francis Adams, *The Works of John Adams, Second President of the United States: Diary, with passages from an autobiography. Notes of debates in the Continental Congress, in 1775 and 1776. Autobiography*; Dennis A. Connole, *The Indians of the Nipmuck Country in Southern New England, 1630-1750: An Historical Geography.*

"The Ancient Dominions of Maine, Pathways and Canoe Routes of Native Americans," Davistown Museum, *davistownmuseum.org/TDMNativeTrails.html.*

Thaddeus Piotrowski, ed., *The Indian Heritage of New Hampshire and Northern New England.*

Eric Jaffe, *The King's Best Highway: The Lost History of the Boston Post Road, the Route That Made America.*

"Vermont 22A," *myscenicdrive.com.*

CANALS THAT CHANGED NEW ENGLAND

Don Brian, "A canal runs through it," Manchester Oblique, *manchesteroblique.blogspot.com,* Feb. 25, 2012.

National Park Service, NRHP Nomination Form, "Amoskeag Mfg. Co. Housing."

Richard DeLuca, "New England's Grand Ambition: The Farmington Canal," *ConnecticutHistory.org,* July 13, 2019.

National Park Service, NRHP Nomination Form, "Songo Lock."

National Park Service, *Lowell National Historical Park Handbook.*

Richard E. Greenwood, "The Blackstone Canal: A Brief Overview of Its Historical Significance," *WorcesterHistory.org.*

"Pine Street Barge Canal Breakwater Site," Lake Champlain Maritime Museum, lcmm.org; "Pine Street Barge Canal," Lake Champlain Basin Project, lcbp.org.

STAGECOACH STOPS YOU CAN STILL VISIT

"Inn History at a Glance," Longfellow's Wayside Inn, *wayside.org*; "Roads and Travel in New England 1790-1840," *teachushistory.org;* Alice Morse Earle, *Stage-coach and Tavern Days.*

Richard DeLuca, "Early Turnpikes Provided Solution to Lack of Reliable Roads," ConnecticutHistory.org, Sept. 19, 2012, and "Boston Post Road Carved out Three Travel Routes through State," *ConnecticutHistory.org,* Nov. 26, 2015; "History," RivertonInn.com.

"A History of Maine Roads 1600–1970," Maine Department of Transportation, State Highway Commission, *digitalmaine.com;* "About Us," CoachStopInn.com.

George Barstow, *The History of New Hampshire, from its Discovery, in 1614, to the Passage of the Toleration Act, in 1819;* "Dining That's Rich In History," *coachstopnh.com.*

"History of The Old Stagecoach Inn," oldstagecoach.com; Allan S. Everest, "Early Roads and Taverns of the Champlain Valley," *Vermont History: The Proceedings of the Vermont Historical Society*, Autumn 1969.

National Park System, NHPR, Nomination Form, "Wyoming Village Historic District"; Stagecoach House, *stagecoachhouse.com/.*

Stops on the Underground Railroad

Cherry A. Banks and James A. Banks, *March Toward Freedom: A History of Black Americans*; Russell DeSimone, "Narrative of an Ashaway Teenager's Role in the Underground Railroad Rediscovered," *smallstatebighistory.com/narrative-of-an -ashaway-teenagers-role-in-the-underground-railroad-rediscovered/.*

"Nathan & Polly Johnson," New Bedford Whaling, National Park Service, *nps.gov/nebe /learn/historyculture/nathanpollyjohnson.htm.*

"Austin F. Williams House and Carriagehouse," Aboard the Underground Railroad, National Park Service, *nps.gov/places/austin-f-williams-carriagehouse-and-house.htm.*

National Park Service, National Historic Landmark Nomination, "Rokeby."

Michelle Arnosky Sherburne, *Slavery & the Underground Railroad in New Hampshire.*

"Abyssinian Meeting House," Aboard the Underground Railroad, National Park Service, *nps.gov/nr/travel/underground/absmeethouse.html;* Candace Kanes, "Blacks in Maine," Maine History Online, *mainememory.net;* National Park Service, NRHP Continuation Sheet, "Abyssinian Meeting House"; H. H. Price, Gerald E. Talbot, *Maine's Visible Black History: The First Chronicle of its People.*

Historic Train Rides

"About the Train," The Essex Steam Train & Riverboat, *essexsteamtrain.com/.*

Robert Farson, *Cape Cod Railroads*; "History of the Cape Cod Central Railroad," *capetrain.com.*

"A History of the Vermont Rail System, Passenger Service, Green Mountain Railroad," *rails-vt.com.*

"A Trip Through Time," *trains.ri.com.*

"Winnipesaukee Scenic Railroad," *hoborr.com*.

"History of the Downeast Scenic Railroad," *DowneastScenicRail.org*.

MILITARY ROUTES

"The Highway of History - Mohawk Trail," *mohawktrail.com*; National Park Service, NRHP Inventory-Nomination Form, "Mohawk Trail."

"History," The Crown Point Road Association, *crownpointroad.org*.

Simon Goodell Griffin, Frank H. Whitcomb, Octavius Applegate, Jr., *A History of the Town of Keene from 1732, When the Township Was Granted by Massachusetts, to 1874, When It Became a City*.

Caleb Haskell, *Caleb Haskell's Diary, May 5, 1775-May 30, 1776*, ed. by Lothrop Withington; "Arnold Expedition Historical Society," *ArnoldsMarch.com*;

"Danbury Raid and the Forgotten General," *ctamericanrevolution.com*;

"Route To Victory," Washington-Rochambeau Revolutionary Route, National Park Service, *nps.gov/waro/index.htm*.

Holly Ramer, "Fishermen Beat Pilgrims to New World," *Associated Press*, Dec. 8, 1996; St. Croix Island, the Lost French Colony of Maine, New England Historical Society, *.newenglandhistoricalsociety.com/st-croix-island-lost-french-colony-maine/*; New England's Real First Thanksgiving—Maine Style, New England Historical Society *newenglandhistoricalsociety.com/new-englands-first-thanksgiving-maine-style/*.

OLDEST CONTINUOUSLY OPERATIONAL RESTAURANTS

National Park Service, NRHP Inventory-Nomination Form, "White Horse Tavern."

"About Us," *GriswoldInn.com*.

"History of the Inn," *HancockInn.com*.

National Park Service, NRHP Inventory-Nomination Form, "Dorset Village Historic District"; "Our History," *DorsetInn.com*.

National Park Service, National Historic Landmark Inventory-Nomination Form, "Union Oyster House."

National Park Service, NRHP Registration Form, "Biddeford Main Street Historic District"; "History," Palace Diner, *PalaceDinerME.com*.

THE OLDEST HOUSES

National Park Service, National Historic Landmark Nomination, "Whitfield, Henry, House."

"The House Built for the Family of Jonathan & Grace Fairebanks," FairbanksHouse.org; "Fairbanks House, Massachusetts," Survey of Historic Sites and Buildings, Explorers and Settlers, National Park Service, *nps.gov/parkhistory/online_books/explorers /sitec25.htm.*

National Park Service, NRHP Inventory Nomination From, "Historic Resources of North Kingstown, R.I."; "Stephen Northup Family," *northupfamily.com.*

"Jackson House," HistoricNewEngland.org, *historicnewengland.org/property/jackson -house/;* National Park Service, NHRP Inventory-Nomination Form, "The Richard Jackson House."

Rachel Forrest, "Rocker restores historic Kittery, Maine home," *seacoastonline.com,* Feb. 27, 200; National Park Service, NRHP Inventory-Nomination Form, "Bray House."

Jane Griswold Radocchia, "Passing by: Defoe-Mooar-Wright House," *Bennington Banner,* March 9, 2015, Keith Whitcomb Jr., "Historic Pownal house to be renovated," *Bennington Banner,* May 1, 2009.

General Stores

"The Old Country Store and Museum," *nhcountrystore.com.*

Roberta Barboza, "Historic Davoll's General Store in Dartmouth is coming back to life," *South Coast Today,* Aug. 16, 2017; Jonathan Carvalho, "With 200 years of Dartmouth history behind it, Davoll's General Store for sale," *South Coast Today,* Aug. 10, 2014.

"Our History," *brownandhopkins.com.*

Eric D. Lehman, *Connecticut Town Greens: History of the State's Common Centers*; Ryan Flynn, "Historic Colebrook Store to re-open in coming months," *The Register Citizen,* Oct. 27, 2014.

"About The Dorset Union Store," dorsetunionstore.com; National Park Service, NRHP Inventory-Nomination Form, "Dorset Village Historic District."

Jenna Lookner, "Historic Hope General Store seeks next owners," *PenBay Pilot,* May 4, 2018.

Colonial Homes Photographed by Wallace Nutting

"Six Colonial Homes By Wallace Nutting," New England Historical Society, *neweng landhistoricalsociety.com/six-colonial-homes-by-wallace-nutting/;* Thomas Andrew Denenberg, *Wallace Nutting and the Invention of Old America.*

"Arnold House (1693), Historic New England, *historicnewengland.org/property /arnold-house/.*

Wallace Nutting, *Vermont Beautiful.*
"The Wadsworth–Longfellow House," Maine Historical Society, *mainehistory.org.*
"History of the Webb House, 1752-1913," Webb-Deane-Stevens Museum, *webb-deane -stevens.org.*
 National Park Service, NRHP Inventory-Nomination Form, "Wentworth-Gardner House."
"Hazen-Spiller House," Massachusetts Cultural Resource Information System, *mhc-macris.net/Details.aspx?MhcId=HVR.275.*

Historic Vessels

William Avery Baker, "Vessel Types of Colonial Massachusetts, 1977," Colonial Society of Massachusetts, *colonialsociety.org.*
"Flashback Photo: Old Ironsides Rescued From the Scrap Heap," New England Historical Society, *newenglandhistoricalsociety.com/flashback-photo-old-ironsides-rescued -scrap-heap/;* Old Ironsides Earns Her Nickname, New England Historical Society, *newenglandhistoricalsociety.com/old-ironsides-earns-nickname/.*
"Charles W. Morgan," mysticseaport.org; Derek Thompson, "The Spectacular Rise and Fall of U.S. Whaling: An Innovation Story," *The Atlantic,* Feb. 22, 2012.
National Park Service, Maritime Heritage of the United State NHL Theme Study— Large vessels, "Lewis R. French (Schooner)."
National Park Service, NRHP Inventory-Nomination Form, "Ticonderoga"; "Steamboat Ticonderoga," Shelburne Museum, *shelburnemuseum.org.*
"12 US 17 Weatherly, 1962 America's Cup Winner," *AmericasCupCharters.com.*
"What is a gundalow?" Gundalow.org.

Covered Bridges

"Covered Bridge Trivia," National Society for the Preservation of Covered Bridges, *coveredbridgesociety.org/cb-faq.html.*
"West Cornwall Covered Bridge: An Icon of New England Craftsmanship," May 5, 2016, *ConnecticutHistory.org.*
National Park Service, NRHP Inventory-Nomination Form, "Artists Bridge."
National Park Service, NRHP Registration Form, "Burkeville Bridge."
"Honeymoon Bridge, Jackson, New Hampshire," *NH.gov/nhdhr/bridges/p97.html; New Hampshire Covered Bridges,* by Richard Marshall.
"Mt. Orne Bridge, Lancaster, New Hampshire and Lunenburg, Vermont," *NH.gov /nhdhr/bridges/p97.html.*
William S. Caswell, *Connecticut and Rhode Island Covered Bridges;* Benjamin D. and June R. Evans, *New England's Covered Bridges.*

Revolutionary War Battlefields

"When Paul Revere Rode to New Hampshire," New England Historical Society, *newenglandhistoricalsociety.com/paul-revere-rode-new-hampshire/*; "Military History of Fort Constitution (Fort William and Mary)," NHStateParks.org.

"Minute Man," National Park Service; "Lexington Battle Green," TourLexington.us.

"Hubbardton Battlefield," State Historic Sites, Agency of Commerce and Community Development, *historicsites.vermont.gov/hubbardton-battlefield*.

"The Penobscot Expedition, America's Forgotten Military Disaster," New England Historical Society, *newenglandhistoricalsociety.com/penobscot-expedition -americas-forgotten-military-disaster/*.

Site of the Battle of Rhode Island, The Historical Marker Database; National Park Service, NRHP Inventory-Nomination Form, "Battle of Rhode Island Historic District."

National Park Service, NRHP Inventory-Nomination Form, "Fort Griswold."

Revolutionary-Era Taverns

National Park Service, NRHP Inventory-Nomination Form, "Peleg Arnold Tavern."

"Timothy Keeler, Resident from 1769 to 1818," Keeler Tavern Museum, *keelertavernmuseum.org*.

"The Old Constitution House," State Historic Sites, Agency of Commerce and Community Development, *historicsites.vermont.gov/constitution-house*.

"Vermont: The Land of Green Mountains," Vermont Bureau of Publicity, Office of Secretary of State, 1913, The Old Constitution House, 15 North Main Street, Windsor, Windsor County, VT PHOTOS FROM SURVEY HABS VT-35, Library of Congress.

"Wyman Tavern," Historical Society of Cheshire County, *hsccnh.org/plan-a-visit /historical-society-of-cheshire-county-group-visits/our-buildings/wyman-tavern/*.

"Burnham Tavern History," Burnham Tavern.com; National Park Service, NRHP Inventory-Nomination Form, "The Burnham Tavern."

"The Warren Tavern in Charlestown, Massachusetts, National Trust for Historic Preservation," SavingPlaces.org, *savingplaces.org/stories/historic-bars-warren -tavern-charlestown-massachusetts#.XaTSE0ZKiyI*.

Revolutionary War Forts

John Thurber, "Fort Halifax," Maine Historical Society, MaineMemory.net, *maine memory.net/bin/Features?t=fp&feat=8&supst=Exhibits*.

"Fort Washington," CambridgeHistory.net; "FRIENDS OF FORT WASHINGTON-
    Preservation for the 21st Century," *FriendsofFortWashington.org*; "History of Fort
    Washington, 1775-1815," *NorthAmericanForts.com.*
National Park Service, NRHP Inventory-Nomination Form, "Fort Nathan Hale."
National Park Service, NRHP Inventory-Nomination Form, "Conanicut Battery."
"Mount Independence State Historic Site," *VermontVacation.com.*

LOYALIST HOUSES

The true story of Putnam Cottage, FreePages.*Rootsweb.com*; "Historic Putnam
    Cottage c.1690 Known as Knapp's Tavern during the American Revolution,"
    putnamcottage.org.
National Park Service, NRHP Inventory-Nomination Form, "Lucas-Johnston House."
Hoke P. Kimball, Bruce Henson, *Governor's Houses and State Houses of British Colonial
    America, 1607-1783: An Historical, Architectural and Archaeological Survey.*
"Isaac Royall House, Massachusetts," Colonials and Patriots, Survey of Historic Sites
    and Buildings, National Park Service; The Royalls, *RoyallHouse.org.*
Everett Schermerhorn Stackpole, *Old Kittery and Her Families*; National Park Service,
    NRHP Inventory-Nomination Form, "William Pepperrell House."
"A Short History of The Deming House," *DemingHouse.com.*

GRAVESITES OF REVOLUTIONARY WAR HEROINES

Elizabeth Correia, "Hannah Bunce Watson: One of America's First Female Publishers,"
    ConnecticutHistory.org, Jan. 26, 2016.
"The Love Letters of Lucy and Henry Knox," New England Historical Society,
    newenglandhistoricalsociety.com/love-letters-lucy-henry-knox/; "Lucy Knox, Wife
    Of Revolutionary War Patriot Henry Knox," WomenHistoryBlog.com, *women
    historyblog.com/2009/04/lucy-flucker-knox.html.*
Rebecca Beatrice Brooks, "Deborah Sampson: Woman Warrior of the American Revo-
    lution," *historyofmassachusetts.org*, Dec. 29, 2011; "Deborah Sampson Gannett,"
    findagrave.com; "Deborah Sampson: Massachusetts' Revolutionary Woman
    Warrior," New England Historical Society, *newenglandhistoricalsociety.com
    /deborah-sampson-massachusetts-revolutionary-woman-warrior/.*
"Elizabeth Page Stark," findagrave.com; Fred W. Lamb, "Anecdotes of General and
    Molly Stark," *Collections, Manchester Historic Association, 1897.*
"How the Daughters of Liberty Fought for Independence," New England Histori-
    cal Society, *newenglandhistoricalsociety.com/daughters-liberty-fought-independence/*;
    "What We Are Doing. Reminiscences of the Daughters of Liberty," *Daughters of*

the American Revolution Magazine, Volume 5, 1894.Kate Van Winkle Keller, *Dance and Its Music in America, 1528–1789*.

A.H. Copeland, *History of Salisbury, Vermont*.

PLACES WHERE REVOLUTIONARY HEROES LIVED

"Adams," National Park Service, Adams National Historical Park, *nps.gov/adam/index.htm*.

Frances Phipps, "Coventry Honors Nathan Hale," *New York Times*, July 2, 1978.

National Park Service, NRHP Inventory-Nomination Form, "John Stark House."

"History of the Homestead," *NathanaelGreeneHomestead.org*.

David J. Blow, "Ethan Allen's Burlington Home 1787-1789," *Chittenden County Historical Society Bulletin*, April 1978.

"Henry Knox: Six Surprising Facts About the Father of American Artillery," New England Historical Society, *newenglandhistoricalsociety.com/henry-knox-six-surprising-facts-father-american-artillery/; KnoxMuseum.org.*

NEW ENGLAND'S OLDEST BUSINESSES

Kirk Johnson, "350-Year-Old Farm Survives the Odds," *New York Times*, March 13, 1989; "Field View Farm," *ctvisit.com/listings/field-view-farm*.

"History of the Seaside Inn—Since 1660 (At Least)," "Seaside Inn," *kennebunkbeachmaine.com*.

William T. O'Hara, "Family Business - The World's Oldest Family Companies," *Family Business, griequity.com/resources/industryandissues/familybusiness/oldestinworld.html*.

Sacha Pfeiffer, "Emery Farm preserves the land, and a way of life," *Boston Globe*, Sept. 5, 2007; Emery Farm, *emeryfarm.com*.

National Park Service, National Register of Historic Places, Inventory-Nomination Form, "White Horse Tavern."

Tom Woodman, "Park Perspectives: Chillin' on the ferry," *Adirondack Explorer*, July 1, 2013.

SIX PRODUCTS AND WHERE THEY WERE MADE

Garry Apgar, ed., *A Mickey Mouse Reader*.

"Behind Factory Doors: The History of Bates Heritage Bedspread," batesmillstore.com, Aug. 11, 2015, *batesmillstore.com/blogs/news/40477057-behind-factory-doors-the-history-of-bates-heritage-bedspread;* "The Bates Bedspread, America's Favorite

Counterpane," New England Historical Society, *newenglandhistoricalsociety.com /bates-bedspread-of-maine-americas-favorite-counterpane/*.

Philip Orbanes, *The Game Makers: The Story of Parker Brothers from Tiddledy Winks to Trivial Pursuit*.

Lynn Downey, *Levi Strauss & Co*.

L. Francis Herreshoff, *Capt. Nat Herreshoff, the Wizard of Bristol: The Life and Achievements of Nathanael Greene Herreshoff, Together with an Account of Some of the Yachts He Designed*.

Dan Swainbank, "St. Johnsbury's Fairbanks Scales, Weighing the World," *Vermont Magazine*, March/April 2019.

Places Where Iconic Foods Were Born

"Town History: The Early History of Londonderry," Londonderry Historical Society, *londonderryhistory.org/history/*.

John F. Mariani, *Encyclopedia of American Food and Drink*; "The Maine Ship Captain Who Invented the Modern Donut," New England Historical Society, *newengland historicalsociety.com/maine-ship-captain-invented-modern-donut/*.

Anthony V. Riccio, *The Italian American Experience in New Haven: Images and Oral Histories (SUNY series in Italian/American Culture)*.

U.S. Rep. Michael Capuano, "New England Confectionery Company," Local Legacies, The American Folklife Center, The Library of Congress, *memory.loc.gov/diglib /legacies/loc.afc.afc-legacies.200003102/*.

Erin DeJesus, "Digging Up the History of Clams Casino, a New England Classic," eater. com, Jan. 29, 2015, *eater.com/2015/1/29/7928997/relive-the-fuzzy-history-of-clams -casino-a-new-england-classic*.

"Owned by Farm Families," Cabot Cheese Co-op cabotcheese.coop, *cabotcheese.coop /about*.

Landmark Signs

"Original Installation Of The Weirs Beach Sign," *weirsbeach.com/reasons-to-visit /atmosphere/weirs-beach-sign/weirs-beach-sign-bw/*.

"New Britain, Connecticut: Super Cow - Dairy Mascot," *roadsideamerica.com/tip/33135*; "Who is Guida's Dairy?," *supercow.com/company/history*.

"The Big Blue Bug: A Local Icon," *bigbluebug.com/the-big-blue-bug*.

"The World Traveler Signpost of Lynchville," *The Maine Thing Quarterly*, *visitmaine.com /things-to-do/lighthouses-sightseeing/the-world-traveler-signpost-of-lynchville*.

Derek Carson, "Big chair for sale," *Brattleboro Reformer*, Feb. 23, 2018.

Downtown Department Stores

"When Downtown Department Stores Spelled Christmas," New England Historical Society, *newenglandhistoricalsociety.com/downtown-department-stores-meant-christmas/;* Department Store Museum Blog, *thedepartmentstoremuseum.org.*

National Park Service, NRHP Inventory-Nomination Form, "Department Store Historic District."

Chamber of Commerce Journal of Maine, Volume 19, 1906.

Robert Hendrickson, *The Grand Emporiums: The Illustrated History of America's Great Department Stores.*

Janice Brown, "John B. Varick Co.—New England's Largest Hardware Business in 1915," New Hampshire's History Blog, Feb. 16, 2015, *cowhampshire.com.*

"URI Shepard Building," Shopping: Old & New, downtownprovidence.com; Amelia Golcheski, Shepard Company Building, Rhode Tour, *rhodetour.org/items/show/204.*

National Park Service, NRHP Registration Form, "Burlington Montgomery Ward Building."

The First Shopping Malls

"Four New England Shopping Malls: Landmarks of Changing Times," New England Historical Society, *newenglandhistoricalsociety.com/four-new-england-shopping-malls-landmarks-changing-times/.*

Dan D'Ambrosio, "At 100, Tony Pomerleau attributes success to seizing the right moment," *Burlington Free Press*, Sept. 22, 2017.

"Pine Tree Shopping Center," zayre88, Discount stores from Woolworth to Walmart, *sites.google.com/site/zayre88/pine-tree-shopping-center.*

Jennifer R. Copley, "John Winthrop and the "City upon a Hill," History Now, the Gilder Lehrman Institute of American History, gilderlehrman.org; "A Model of Christian Charity," World Heritage Encyclopedia, self.gutenberg.org, *self.gutenberg.org/articles/eng/a_model_of_christian_charity.*

Oldest Courthouses

Juliet Haines Mofford, *"The Devil Made Me Do It!" Crime and Punishment in Early New England; William B. Stoebuck*, "Reception of English Common Law in the American Colonies," Scholarship Repository, William & Mary Law School, *scholarship.law.wm.edu.*

"Plymouth, 1749 Court House and Museum," seeplymouth.com; *Jon C. Blue, The Case of the Piglet's Paternity, Trials from the New Haven Colony, 1639–1663.*

"Pownalborough Court House," Lincoln County Historical Association, *lincolncounty history.org*; "John Adams in Maine: 'The Sharpest Thorn on which I ever set my foot'," New England Historical Society; *newenglandhistoricalsociety.com /john-adams-maine-sharpest-thorn-ever-set-foot/.*

National Park Service, NRHP Inventory-Nomination Form, "Old Grafton County Courthouse."

National Park Service, NRHP Inventory-Nomination Form, "Kent County Court House."

National Park Service, NRHP Inventory-Nomination Form, "New London County Courthouse (now State Courthouse)."

"Newfane Village Center Tour," Historical Society of Windham County, *historical societyofwindhamcounty.org.*

Historic One-Room Schoolhouses

Jess Webb, "Nation's Oldest Schoolhouse Turns 285," *Portsmouth, Rhode Island Patch*, Oct. 6, 2010.

National Park Service, NRHP Inventory-Nomination Form, "Old Schoolhouse, York."

National Park Service, NRHP Inventory-Nomination Form, "District #5 School, Shrewsbury."

"Eureka Schoolhouse," State Historic Sites, Agency of Commerce and Community Development, *historicsites.vermont.gov/eureka-schoolhouse.*

"Gaylordsville Schoolhouse," *gaylordsville.org.*

Michael Morton, "Red Brick School not the oldest," *Milford Daily News*, Sept. 21, 2007; Madison Kramer, "One-Room School Houses Still in Operation in NH," *New Hampshire Magazine*, August 9, 2013.

Oldest Public High Schools

"History of Boston Latin School," *archive.org* from *bls.org*; "Notable Alumni," bls.org.

"A Brief History of HPHS," *law.hartfordschools.org.*

"History," Pinkerton Academy, *pinkertonacademy.org.*

"Classical High School," *providenceschools.org.*

Lewis Cass Aldrich, Frank R. Holmes, *History of Windsor County, Vermont.*

"What was it like having Stephen King as your high school English teacher?" *quora.com /What-was-it-like-having-Stephen-King-as-your-high-school-English-teacher;* "History of Hampden Academy," Hampden Academy, *ha.rsu22.us/about/history -of-hampden-academy/.*

HISTORIC POST OFFICES

Historian United States Postal Service, "First U.S. Post Offices: Research Challenges and Sources of Information," *aboutusps.com*, September 2019.

Gordon Harris, "The Ipswich Post Offices," Historic Ipswich on the Massachusetts North Shore, *historicipswich.org*.

Maggie B. Cassidy, "Hinsdale, N.H.: It's the oldest continuously operating Post Office in the nation," *Brattleboro Reformer*, Aug. 3, 2016.

"East Windsor Hill Post Office (1757)," Historic Buildings of Connecticut, *historic buildingsct.com/east-windsor-hill-post-office-1757/*.

National Park Service, NRHP Nomination, "Grafton Post Office."

"Castine: 2nd Oldest Post Office," Postal Facts, *facts.usps.com/map/*.

"First Automated Post Office in the U.S. Issue," *postalmuseum.si.edu/collections/object -spotlight/first-automated-po.html*.

OLDEST PUBLIC LIBRARIES

"History," Redwood Library, *redwoodlibrary.org*.

"Our History," Scoville Memorial Library, *scovillelibrary.org*.

"History," Peterborough Town Library, *peterboroughtownlibrary.org*.

"Welcome to Maine's Oldest Municipal Library," Witherle Memorial Library, *witherle.lib.me.us*.

"History," Sturgis Library, *sturgislibrary.org*.

National Park Service, NRHP Nomination, "Peabody Library."

OLDEST HOSPITALS

"History of Tufts Medical Center," Tufts Medical Center, *tuftsmedicalcenter.org*.

"History and Heritage," Yale New Haven Hospital, *ynhh.org*.

National Park Service, NRHP Inventory-Nomination Form, "Butler Hospital."

"History," Maine Medical Association, *mainemed.org*.

Sarah L. Dopp, "Our History: The Legacy of Mary Fletcher," UVM Medical Center Blog, Oct. 9, 2014, *medcenterblog.uvmhealth.org/community/history-legacy -mary-fletcher/*.

National Park Service, NRHP Registration Form, "Portsmouth Cottage Hospital."

PLACES WHERE WORKERS WERE KILLED

Sidney Perley, *Historic Storms of New England*.

Robert Pike, *Tall Trees, Tough Men*.

"The Amoskeag Mill Disaster of 1891," New England Historical Society, *newengland historicalsociety.com/1891-amoskeag-mill-disaster/*.

Scott Molloy, *Trolley Wars: Streetcar Workers on the Line*.

"Chronological Summary of Events in the State During the Year Just Closed," *St. Albans Daily Messenger*, Dec. 31, 1903; Wendy Richardson, "The Curse of Our Trade": Occupational Disease in a Vermont Granite Town," *Vermont History: The Proceedings of the Vermont Historical Society*, Winter 1992.

Milton Bracker, "3 Dead, 6 Missing in Munition Blasts, 38 Others Hurt in Explosions in Plants in Bridgeport and Staten Island," *New York Times*, March 29, 1942, "DEATH TOLL MOUNTS IN MUNITION BLASTS; Reaches Five at Staten Island Plant—Bridgeport Missing Now Put at Seven EXPLOSION LAID TO NAIL Remington Arms Co. Convinced a Primer Was Struck in Closing a Packing Case," *New York Times*, March 30, 1942; "Six Places Workers Were Killed in New England," New England Historical Society, *newenglandhistoricalsociety.com /six-places-workers-killed-new-england/*.

IRISH LANDMARKS

Michael J. O'Brien, "Isles of Shoals, Irish Mariners In New England," *The Journal of the American Irish Historical Society, Volume 17*.

"Irish Canal Workers Burial Site," Connecticut Irish-American Heritage Trail, *ctirish heritage.org/website/publish/inventory/inventoryDetail.php?Irish-Canal-Workers -Burial-Site-142*.

"Champlain, the Irish Lake," New England Historical Society, *newenglandhistorical society.com/champlain-the-irish-lake/*.

"The Murder of Amasa Sprague," New England Historical Society, *newenglandhistorical society.com/murder-amasa-sprague/*.

"The Portland Rum Riot Ends a Teetotaler's Career," New England Historical Society, *newenglandhistoricalsociety.com/portland-rum-riot-1855-ends-teetotalers-career/*.

Scott Molloy, *Irish Titan, Irish Toilers: Joseph Banigan and Nineteenth-century New England Labor*; "Main Street Historic District, Millville, Mass.," Massachusetts Cultural Resource Information System, *mhc-macris.net/Details.aspx?MhcId=MLV.J*.

New Deal Projects

"The CCC in Acadia National Park," Maine Folklife Center, The University of Maine, *umaine.edu/folklife/what-we-do/exhibits/ccc-in-acadia-national-park/*.

"Cape Cod Canal History," US Army Corps of Engineers, New England District; *nae.usace.army.mil/Missions/Recreation/Cape-Cod-Canal/History/*.

The 1937 Terminal, New Hampshire Aviation Historical Society; *nhahs.org/about/43 -museum/history/51-the-1937-terminal*.

Dan Barry, "Through years of change, Pawtucket, R.I., always had McCoy Stadium," *New York Times*, Feb. 24, 2015.

Frederick W. Stetson, "The Civilian Conservation Corps in Vermont," *Vermont History: Proceedings of the Vermont Historical Society*, Winter 1978.

"Post Office Mural—Torrington CT," The Living New Deal, *livingnewdeal.org/projects /post-office-mural-torrington-ct/*.

Little Italys

"Little Italy in New England: Some Lost, Some Thriving," New England Historical Society, *newenglandhistoricalsociety.com/little-italy-new-england-lost-thriving/*.

"How the Italian Immigrants Came to New England," New England Historical Society, *newenglandhistoricalsociety.com/how-the-italian-immigrants-came-to-new-england/*.

"Little Italy: Boston's North End," Italian Aware, *italianaware.com/BostonNorthEnd.html*.

"Coin-O-Matic," Rhode Tour, *rhodetour.org/items/show/151*.

J. Dennis Robinson, "Urban Renewal Evicts Little Italy," *seacoastnh.com/Places-and -Events/Historic-Tours/urban-renewal-evicts-little-italy/*.

"Little Italy," Vermont Italian Cultural Association, *vermontitalianclub.org/little-italy -burlington-vermont.html*.

Poorhouses

Michael Westerfield, "The History of Connecticut Poor Houses," *connecticutpoorhouses .info/index.html*; National Park Service, NRHP Inventory-Nomination Form, "Middletown Almshouse."

Nick McCavitt, "A Poor House with a rich history," *Falmouth, Mass., Patch*, June 13, 2011.

Emily Burnham, "Bangor's former Poor Farm spills its secrets," *Bangor Daily News*, Nov. 25, 2017.

"Dexter Asylum Records," Rhode Island Historical Society Manuscripts Division, *rihs. org/mssinv/MSS067.htm*; "Dexter Donation," City of Providence, *providenceri.gov /dexter-donation/*.

"The Sheldon Poor Farm 1833 to 1978," Sheldon Historical Society, *sheldonvthistorical .org/Poor%20Farm.html*.

National Park Service, NRHP Inventory-Nomination Form, "Strafford County Farm."

LITTLE CANADAS

Henry Epp, Angela Evanci and Mitch Wertlieb, "How There Came To Be A 'Little Canada' in Winooski," Vermont Public Radio, May 17, 2018; Michael A. Bellesiles, Betsy Beattie, "Migrants and Millworkers: The French Canadian Population of Burlington and Colchester, 1860-1870," *Vermont History: The Proceedings of the Vermont Historical Society*, Spring 1992.

"The 40 Angels of St. Ann, the Sistine Chapel of Woonsocket," New England Historical Society, *newenglandhistoricalsociety.com/the-40-angels-st-ann-the-sistine-chapel-of -woonsocket/*; National Park Service, NRHP, "Historic Resources of Woonsocket, Rhode Island: Partial Inventory, Historic and Architectural Resources."

National Park Service, Registration Form, "North Grosvenordale Mill Historic District."

"Le Patrimoine franco-américa, Franco-American Heritage in New Hampshire, A Photo Essay," by Gary Samson, Originally published in *1999 Smithsonian Folklife Festival Program Book*.

Mark Paul Richard, "This Is Not a Catholic Nation": The Ku Klux Klan Confronts Franco-Americans in Maine," *The New England Quarterly*, June 2009.

Lowell History Chronology, Lowell Historical Society, *lowellhistoricalsociety.org/time line/*; "The Little Canadas of New England," New England Historical Society, *newenglandhistoricalsociety.com/the-little-canadas-of-new-england/*; "Little Canada, Lowell, MA," National Archives, *archive.org/details/umllittlecanada*.

GHOST TOWNS

"Exactly How New England's Indian Population Was Decimated," New England Historical Society, *newenglandhistoricalsociety.com/exactly-new-englands-indian -population-decimated/*; "The Maypole That Infuriated the Puritans," New England Historical Society, *newenglandhistoricalsociety.com/maypole-infuriated-puritans/*.

"Hanton City," *ghosttowns.com/states/ri/hantoncity.html*; "Scenic Drives Around Rhode Island," *Providence Monthly*, providenceonline.com, Sept. 5, 2014, *providenceonline .com/stories/scenic-drives-around-rhode-island-maps,13180?*.

"Monomoy," *Harper's New Monthly Magazine*, Volume 28, edited by Henry Mills Alden, 1864, Monomoy Point, MA, *lighthousefriends.com*.

Hans DePold, town historian, "Gay City or Factory Hollow," Bolton Historical Society, Bolton, Conn., Feb. 2014; *boltoncthistory.org/gaycity_factoryhollow.html.*

Paula Tracy, "Exploring ghost towns in White Mountains," WMUR.com, May 28, 2014; "Zealand and Zealand Valley Railroad," *whitemountainhistory.org/Zealand.html;* "NH Timber Baron Takes the Money and Runs," New England Historical Society, *newenglandhistoricalsociety.com/new-hampshire-timber-baron-takes-money-runs/.*

D.L. Soucy, "The Territory of Perkins Maine," *Maine History News,* March 21, 2012, *touringmaineshistory.wordpress.com/2012/03/21/the-territory-of-perkins-maine/.*

Scott Meacham, "All that remains of Lewiston, Vermont," Nov. 23, 2004, *dartmo.com /lewiston/.*

ABANDONED PLACES

Joann Greco, "The Psychology of Ruin Porn," Jan. 6, 2012, City Lab, *citylab.com/design /2012/01/psychology-ruin-porn/886/.*

Ed Brouder, WPOP Home, *wdrcobg.com/,* John Ramsey, *Images of America, Hartford Radio.*

"The Ghost Locomotives of the Great Maine Wilderness," New England Historical Society, *newenglandhistoricalsociety.com/ghost-locomotives-maine-wilderness/.*

Old Franklin Park Zoo Bear Pens, Atlas Obscura; *atlasobscura.com/places/old-franklin -park-zoo-bear-pens.*

New Hill Village historical marker, authors' personal knowledge.

National Park Service, NRHP Nomination Form, "Historic Resources of Pawtucket, Rhode Island"; Jonathan Belcher, "Changes to Transit Service in the MBTA district, 1964-2019," *get-bus.co.il/changes-to-transit-service-in-the-mbta-district -1964-2018.pdf;* Edward J. Ozog, "The Pawtucket-Central Falls Station," sites. google.com/site/pawtucketcentralfalls/.

Natalie Clunan, "The Story Behind This Abandoned Road To Nowhere In Vermont Is Truly Fascinating," Only In Your State, Vermont, Dec. 29, 2018, *onlyinyourstate .com/vermont/interstate-189-vt/.*

MYSTERIOUS STONE STRUCTURES

Paul Tudor Angel, *The Mysterious Megaliths of New England,* The Ensign Message, ensignmessage.com, https://ensignmessage.com/articles/the-mysterious -megaliths-of-new-england/.

"Gungywamp," Denison Pequotsepos Nature Center, https://dpnc.org/gungywamp -structures/.

"Hirundo Stone Structures," Hirundo Wildlife Refuge, http://lacdor.blogspot.com/2011 /06/hirundo-stone-structures.html.

Kathleen Burge, "Chamber of mystery," *Boston Globe*, July 12, 2012; "Upton, Massachusetts Stone Chamber," Stone Structures of Northeastern United States, stonestructures.org, http://www.stonestructures.org/html/upton-chamber.html.

Edward Gilbert, *History of Salem, New Hampshire*, Pamela Selbert, "America's Stonehenge," *Chicago Tribune*, Dec. 10, 2000; "America's Stonehenge," stonehengeusa.com.

National Park Service, NRHP Inventory-Nomination Form, "Queen's Fort."

Benjamin Lord, "Lost Histories: The Story of New England's Stone Chambers," *Northern Woodlands*, Winter 2013; Benjamin Lord, Lost Histories: The Story of New England's Stone Chambers, Northern Woodlands, Winter 2013, northernwoodlands.org; Giovanna Neudorfer, "Vermont's Stone Chambers: Their Myth and Their History," *Vermont History, Proceedings of the Vermont Historical Society*, Spring 1979.

Strange Rocks

Owen Rogers, "Discovered Dinosaur Tracks Re-Route Highway and Lead to State Park," Aug. 23, 2019, *connecticuthistory.org*.

The "Mystery Stone," New Hampshire Historical Society.

Devil's Footprint: J.W. Ocker, The New England Grimpendium.

New England Historical Society, The Mystery of Dighton Rock.

Chris Church, Man claims he carved rune stone markings in '64, The Independent, June 28, 2014.

Joseph Citro, *The Vermont Monster Guide*.

Homes of Nutty Millionaires

Peter Lindert, Jeffrey Williamson, "Unequal gains: American growth and inequality since 1700," VOX, CEPR Policy Portal, June 16, 2016, voxeu.org.

"Timothy Dexter, the Ridiculous Millionaire Who Sold Coals to Newcastle," New England Historical Society, *newenglandhistoricalsociety.com/timothy-dexter-ridiculous-millionaire-sold-coals-newcastle/*.

Emily E. Gifford, "Holmes at Home: The Life of William Gillette," Feb. 27, 2019, *connecticuthistory.org/holmes-at-home-the-life-of-william-gillette/*.

Spinzia, Raymond E. "In Her Wake: The Story of Alva Smith Vanderbilt Belmont," *The Long Island Historical Journal* 6 (Fall 1993):96-105; "History," Belcourt, belcourt.com.

"Castle History," Searles Castle, *searlescastle.com*; "The Many Mansions of Edward Searles," New England Historical Society, *newenglandhistoricalsociety.com/many-mansions-edward-searles/*.

"Another Look at Hetty Green, The Witch of Wall Street," New England Historical Society, *newenglandhistoricalsociety.com/another-look-hetty-green-witch-wall-street/*; "Hetty Green (1834-1916)," Virtual Vermont, *virtualvermont.com/history/hgreen .html.*

Dan and Leslie Landrigan, *Bar Harbor Babylon: Murder, Mayhem and Misbehavior on Mount Desert Island.*

HAUNTED HOUSES

J.W. Ocker, *The New England Grimpendium*; "New Hampshire Legend: Ocean-Born Mary," New England Historical Society, *newenglandhistoricalsociety.com/ocean-born -mary-new-hampshire-legend/.*

National Park Service, NRHP Inventory-Nomination Form, "Beckett's Castle"; Madeline Bilils, "There's a Haunted Castle for Sale in Cape Elizabeth," *Boston Magazine*, Oct. 19, 2017.

Paul Dale Roberts, Deanna Jaxine Stinson, *HPI: Stranger Things.*

National Park Service, National Historic Landmark Nomination, "The Breakers," Arthur T. Vanderbilt, *Fortune's Children: The Fall of the House of Vanderbilt;* Julie Tremaine and Tony Pacitti, "14 Things That Go Bump in RI," *Providence Monthly*, Sept. 13, 2017.

Ray Bendici, "Seaside Sanatorium, Waterford, Damned Connecticut," April 2017, *damnedct.com/seaside-sanatorium-waterford*; Rick Rojas, "In Ruins by the Shore, Some See Connecticut's 'Crown Jewel'," *New York Times*, Sept. 19, 2017.

Joe Durwin, "Ubiquitous Ghosts of Southern Vermont College," These Mysterious Hills, June 5, 2006, *mysterious-hills.blogspot.com/2006/06/ubiquitous-ghosts-of -southern-vermont.html.*

PRESIDENTIAL RETREATS

John Adams, "1771. Tuesday. June 4th," *Diary of John Adams, volume 2*, Adams Papers Digital Edition, Massachusetts Historical Society, *nerfc.org/publications/ adams-papers/index.php/volume/DJA02/pageid/DJA02p23;* "John Adams Has A Spa Day in 1771—At Connecticut's Fashionable Stafford Springs," New England Historical Society, *newenglandhistoricalsociety.com/john-adams-has-a-spa-day -in-1771-at-connecticuts-fashionable-stafford-springs/.*

Dan and Leslie Landrigan, *Bar Harbor Babylon: Murder, Mayhem and Misbehavior on Mount Desert Island.*

Wilson, Hugh M. Wade, Stephen Powell Tracy, Dwight C. Wood, *A Brief History of Cornish, 1763-1974.*

Coolidge, National Park Service, Calvin Coolidge Homestead District, President Calvin Coolidge State Historic Site.

Peter Hannaford, *Presidential Retreats: Where the Presidents Went and Why They Went There*; Jean Edward Smith, *Eisenhower in War and Peace*.

Kennedy The Presidents (Kennedy Compound), National Park Service. *nps.gov/park history/online_books/presidents/site30.htm*.

THE *GREEN BOOK* GUIDES AFRICAN AMERICANS TO SAFETY

"The Green Book," New York Public Library Digital Collections, *digitalcollections .nypl.org/collections/the-green-book#/?tab=about*; The Green Book Guides African-Americans to Safety in New England (and Elsewhere), New England Historical Society, *newenglandhistoricalsociety.com/the-green-book-guides-african-americans-to -safety-in-new-england-and-elsewhere/*.

National Park Service, NRHP Nomination-Inventory Form, "Downtown Providence Historic District"; Michelle San Miguel, "Numerous sites in Rhode Island appear in historic 'Green Book,'" NBC 10 News, Feb. 21, 2019.

Jessica Harris, "The alternative Martha's Vineyard that you won't read about in the press," America Al-Jazeera, Aug. 8, 2014, *america.aljazeera.com*; "Shearer Cottage's History on Martha's Vineyard," Shearer Cottage, *shearercottage.com*.

National Park Service, NRHP Registration Form, "Cummings' Guest House."

"Our History," The Center for Family Justice: From the beginning . . ., *centerforfamily justice.org/about-us/history/*.

Sarah Yahm, "Before the Civil Rights Act, Vermont's 'Tourist Homes' Welcomed Black Travelers," *Seven Days*, Feb. 22, 2017, *sevendaysvt.com/vermont/before-the-civil -rights-act-tourist-homes-welcomed-black-travelers/Content?oid=4164681*.

Twin Lake Village, twinlakevillage.com.

GORGEOUS CHURCHES BY RALPH ADAMS CRAM

Douglass Shand-Tucci, *Boston Bohemia, 1881-1900: Ralph Adams Cram: Life and Architecture (Volume 1)*.

National Park Service, NRHP Registration Form, "Emmanuel Church."

"St. James Episcopal Church," History of St. James, *stjameswoodstock.org*.

Six Churches (All Gorgeous) Designed by Ralph Adams Cram, New England Historical Society, *newenglandhistoricalsociety.com/6-churches-gorgeous-designed -ralph-adams-cram/*.

"All Souls Congregational Church," Bangor Historic Register, *Maine, An Encyclopedia*, *maineanencyclopedia.com/bangor-historic-register/*.

National Park Service, NRHP Inventory-Nomination Form, "All Saints' Church."

Island Escapes

Maine Bureau of Parks and Lands, Coastal Island Registry, *maine.gov*; Geographic Names Information System, U.S. Geological Survey.

Increase Mather, *Remarkable Providences Illustrative of the Earlier Days of American Colonization*.

Doris Licameli, *Rowing To The Rescue: The Story of Ida Lewis, Famous Lighthouse Heroine*.

"Reddy the Blacksmith and His New York Bowery Boys Invade Connecticut," New England Historical Society, *newenglandhistoricalsociety.com/reddy-the-blacksmith -and-his-new-york-bowery-boys-invade-connecticut/*.

William H. Caldwell, "The Guernsey Cattle - Introduction to America," *The Guernsey*. 1941.

Edward Dean Sullivan, *The Snatch Racket*, "Charles Lindbergh Hides Out in Maine, New England Historical Society, *newenglandhistoricalsociety.com/charles-lindbergh -hides-out-in-maine/*.

"Neshobe," *The Vermont Encyclopedia*, edited by John J. Duffy, Samuel B. Hand, Ralph H. Orth.; Harpo Marx, *Harpo Speaks!*; Samuel Hopkins Adams, *Alexander Woollcott: His Life and His World*.

Cemeteries

Epitaphs Tell Tales in New England's Graveyards, New England Historical Society, *newenglandhistoricalsociety.com/epitaphs-tell-tales-new-englands-graveyards/*.

Eugene Joseph Vincent Huiginn, *The Graves of Myles Standish and Other Pilgrims;* Patrick Browne, "Opening the Grave of Myles Standish . . . Thrice," Historical Digression, *historicaldigression.com/2014/05/10/digging-up-myles-standish-thrice/*.

Glenn A. Knoblock, *Portsmouth Cemeteries*.

National Park Service, NRHP Inventory-Nomination Form, "Historic Resources of East Providence, Rhode Island: Partial Inventory, Historic and Architectural Resources."

Mount Hope, Bangor in Focus, Mount Hope Cemetery, *bangorinfo.com/Focus/focus _mount_hope_cemetery.html*.

Andrew Nemethy, "Beyond the Grave," *Seven Days*, Aug. 17, 2011.

Wildlife Sanctuaries

"Landscape History of Central New England," Harvard Forest, *harvardforest.fas.harvard
.edu/diorama-series/landscape-history-central-new-england*.

"Helen Woodruff Smith Bird Sanctuary, Meriden Bird Club," Connecticut River Joint
Commission, *crjc.org/heritage/N09-12.htm*.

National Park Service, National Historic Landmark Nomination, "Birdcraft Sanctuary."

Julie Dobrow, *After Emily: Two Remarkable Women and the Legacy of America's Greatest
Poet*; Hog Island Audubon Camp, *hogisland.audubon.org/*.

"September 9, 1922, Massachusetts Audubon Society Makes First Land Purchase,"
*massmoments.org/moment-details/massachusetts-audubon-society-makes-first-land
-purchase.html*.

National Park Service, NRHP Registration Form, "Smith-Gardiner-Norman Farm
Historic District."

"Marsh-Billings-Rockefeller," National Park Service, National Historical Park Vermont,
nps.gov/mabi/index.htm; George Perkins Marsh, *Man and Nature*.

Places Where a Hanging Took Place

Juliet Haines Mofford, *"The Devil Made Me Do It!" Crime and Punishment in Early New
England*; Ted Robert Gurr, "Historical Trends in Violent Crime: A Critical Review
of the Evidence," *Crime and Justice*, Vol. 3, 1981, The University of Chicago Press
Journals.

Arianna MacNeill, "Proctor's Ledge in Salem confirmed as witch execution site," *Salem
News*, Jan. 11, 2016.

J. Dennis Robinson, "Ruth Blay Hanged Here in 1768," *seacoastnh.com/History/History
-Matters/ruth-blay-hanged-here-in-1768/*.

Gregg Flemming, *At the Point of a Cutlass*, "The Day Rhode Island Hanged 26 Pirates,"
New England Historical Society, *newenglandhistoricalsociety.com/the-day-rhode-island
-hanged-26-pirates/*.

*"A Most Unusual Criminal Execution in New London," connecticuthistory.org, December 20,
2017, connecticuthistory.org/a-most-unusual-criminal-execution-in-new-london-2/.*

*George Augustus Wheeler, History of Castine, Penobscot, and Brooksville, Maine: Including
the Ancient Settlement of Pentagöet; Lines made on Ebenezer Ball, who was executed
at Castine, October 31st, for the murder of Mr. John Tileston Downes. Two poems. One
written the day before his execution, and the other written the day he was executed. 1811.
Pdf. https://www.loc.gov/item/rbpe.02601100/.*

Don Wickman, "The Wayward Bones of David Redding," *Rutland Herald*, Oct. 27, 2006.

PROHIBITION-ERA SPEAKEASIES YOU CAN STILL VISIT

"Six Prohibition Speakeasies You Can Still Visit," New England Historical Society, *newenglandhistoricalsociety.com/6-prohibition-speakeasies-you-can-still-visit/*.

SCANDALOUS LOVE NESTS

Jon C. Blue, *The Case of the Piglet's Paternity, Trials from the New Haven Colony, 1639–1663*; "Thomas Kemble, the Kissing Puritan," *New England Historical Society*; "Mary Latham Marries an Older Man—And Regrets It," *New England Historical Society*, Juliet Haines Mofford, *"The Devil Made Me Do It!" Crime and Punishment in Early New England*.

Peg A. Lamphier, *Kate Chase and William Sprague: Politics and Gender in a Civil War Marriage*, By Peg A. Lamphier; "Rhode Island's Sprague-Conkling Affair (or the 1879 Episode at Narragansett)," New England Historical Society, *newenglandhistoricalsociety.com/rhode-islands-sprague-conkling-affair-1879-episode-at-narragansett/*.

Polly Longsworth, *Austin and Mabel: The Amherst Affair and Love Letters of Austin Dickinson and Mabel Loomis Todd*.

Stanley Olson, *Elinor Wylie: A Life Apart: A Biography*.

Adam Clayton Powell, Jr., *Adam by Adam: The Autobiography of Adam Clayton Powell, Jr.*

Anne Edwards, *Katharine Hepburn, A Remarkable Woman*; Joe Wojtas, "Hepburn in Fenwick: 'She Was Just One of Us'," *The New York Times*, July 6, 2003.

George Kelly, "50 Shades of Grace, The Impact of "Peyton Place" on New Hampshire 60 Years Later," *New Hampshire Magazine*, March 1, 2013.

ARMED ROBBERY

Juliet Haines Mofford, *"The Devil Made Me Do It!" Crime and Punishment in Early New England*; Ted Robert Gurr, "Historical Trends in Violent Crime: A Critical Review of the Evidence," *Crime and Justice*, Vol. 3, 1981, The University of Chicago Press Journals.

Frederic James Wood, *The Turnpikes of New England and Evolution of the Same Through England, Virginia, and Maryland*, 1919; Northern Rail Trail, New Hampshire, My TrailLink, *traillink.com*; Janice Brown, "New Hampshire's Last Highwaymen," *New Hampshire's History Blog, cowhampshireblog.com*, citing *New Hampshire Patriot and State Gazette*, August 20, 1821 and "Robber Caught," *Portsmouth Journal of Literature and Politics*, August 25, 1821.

Virginia Shultz-Charette and Verna Gilson, "Winsted Bank Robbery," *Winsted and Winchester*; Peter C. Vermilyea, Warren E. Weber, *Wicked Litchfield County*;

Research Department, Federal Reserve Bank of Minneapolis, "Early State Banks in the United States: How Many Were There and When Did They Exist," December 2005.

National Park Service, "NRHP nomination for St. Albans Historic District"; "St. Albans Raid: The Northernmost Land Action of the Civil War," St Albans Raid Commemoration Committee, *stalbansraid.com/history/the-raid/*.

Paul Campbell, John Glancy, and George Pearson, *Providence Police Department* (Shootout at HoJos).

"Dexter Savings Bank," *Rhodes' Journal of Banking ...: A Practical Banker's Magazine*, Volume 14; J. North Conway, *King of Heists: The Sensational Bank Robbery of 1878 That Shocked America*.

Joseph James O'Keefe, *Brinks Robbery The Men Who Robbed Brink's: The Inside Story of One of the Most Famous Holdups in the History of Crime*.

CORRUPTION, RAILROAD STYLE

Paul Mills, "Did Gould bribe the premier?" *Lewiston Sun Journal*, Jan. 27, 2008.

Jerome L. Sternstein, "Corruption in the Gilded Age Senate: Nelson W. Aldrich and the Sugar Trust," *Capitol Studies: A Journal of the Capital and Congress* (Spring 1978); "Rhode Island: A State For Sale, What Senator Aldrich Represents—A Business Man's Government Founded Upon the Corruption of the Peoples Themselves," by Lincoln Steffens, February 1905, *McClure's Magazine*.

Philip E. Johnson, *The Hampden Railroad-The Greatest Railroad that Never Ran*; "Mellen, Former New Haven Man, To Face Trial," *The Tribune-Republican*, Scranton, PA, June 30, 1914.

Journals of the Honorable Senate and House of Representatives of the State of New Hampshire, 1887.

Robert B. Shaw, *The Great Schuyler Stock Fraud*; Sidney Withington, *The Strange Case of Robert Schuyler*; National Park Service, NRHP Inventory-Nomination Form, "Movable Railroad Bridges on the Northeast Corridor in Connecticut Thematic Resource."

PLACES WHERE PEOPLE WERE MURDERED

Juliet Haines Mofford, *"The Devil Made Me Do It!" Crime and Punishment in Early New England*; Ted Robert Gurr, "Historical Trends in Violent Crime: A Critical Review of the Evidence," *Crime and Justice*, Vol. 3, 1981, The University of Chicago Press Journals.

Karen R. Ellsworth, "Jackson Was Murdered And Carter Was Hanged For It—But That Is All We're Sure About," *smallstatebighistory.com*.

"Fairfield Pond Murder," Vermont Homicides 1821 to 1846, Criminal Justice Research Center, The Ohio State University.

"Patrick Walsh Murder," New Hampshire Homicides 1881-1890 Criminal Justice Research Center, The Ohio State University.

"Maine haunts to visit if you dare," *Portland Press Herald*, Oct. 28, 2010, "Murder and Suicide," Wood Island Lighthouse, *woodislandlighthouse.org*.

John Guy LaPlante, "The Burglar XYZ," *ValleyNewsNow,* Aug. 13, 2011.

Ginger Adams Otis, "DNA confirms Albert DeSalvo's link to 'Boston Strangler' killing of Mary Sullivan: authorities," *New York Daily News*, July 19, 2013; Hayley Glatter, "Throwback Thursday: The First Victim of the Boston Strangler Is Found," *Boston Magazine*, June 14, 2018.

INDEX

NEW HAMPSHIRE

RHODE ISLAND

VERMONT

CPSIA information can be obtained
at www.ICGtesting.com
Printed in the USA
BVHW092224030222
627290BV00003B/7